# THIRSTY CITY

# THIRSTY CITY

## Politics, Greed, and the
## Making of Atlanta's Water Crisis

### SKYE BORDEN

Published by State University of New York Press, Albany

For information, contact State University of New York Press, Albany, NY
www.sunypress.edu

Production by Ryan Morris
Marketing by Fran Keneston

**Library of Congress Cataloging-in-Publication Data**

Borden, Skye, 1984-
    Thirsty city : politics, greed, and the making of Atlanta's water crisis / Skye Borden.
        pages cm
    Includes bibliographical references and index.
    ISBN 978-1-4384-5278-4 (paperback : alk. paper)
    ISBN 978-1-4384-5279-1 (hardcover : alk. paper)  1. Water supply—Management—Geor-
gia—Atlanta. 2. Water consumption—Georgia—Atlanta. 3. Water resources development—
Georgia—Atlanta. 4. Atlanta (Ga.)—Economic conditions. 5. Atlanta (Ga.)—Politics and
government. 6. Atlanta (Ga.)—Environmental conditions. I. Title.
    TD225.A82B67 2014
    363.6'109758231—dc23

                                        2013038325

10   9   8   7   6   5   4   3   2   1

*This book is dedicated to Alan Panebaker, who loved the water.*

# CONTENTS

# ACKNOWLEDGMENTS

This book would not have been possible without the help of so many people. First and foremost, thank you to my husband, James Walter, for loving, supporting, and encouraging me throughout law school and beyond it. And thank you to my wonderfully talented mother, for her kind advice and keen editing eye, and to the rest of my family for believing in me.

I would never have written this book, or even become interested in water law, if it weren't for the mentorship and teaching of Professor John Echeverria. Thank you, John, for sharing your knowledge with me and for slogging through the first rough drafts of this book. I'd also like to thank the long line of inspiring teachers who led me to find my academic passion, particularly Gene Johnson, Cheryl McKiearnan, and Jon Isham.

Thank you to the librarians at Vermont Law School, especially Christine Ryan and Michelle LaRose, for remaining patient despite my constant interlibrary loan requests and legal research questions. Thank you, as well, to the Auburn University in Montgomery Special Collections Department, the Emory University library staff, and the staff at the Atlanta History Center for curating the historical resources that assisted my research.

Finally, thank you to my editor Michael Rinella, his assistant Rafael Chaiken, Senior Production Editor Ryan Morris, copyeditor Dana Foote, and everyone else at State University of New York Press for their willingness to work with an unpublished author, their interest in the book, and their guidance throughout the entire publishing process.

# PROLOGUE

In its most narrow sense, this book tells the story of Atlanta's water supply, but in many ways it also tells the story of every major city's water supply. Some exceptional circumstances do exist in Atlanta's history, of course. Not many American cities have ever been burned to the ground by enemy troops, and very few urban areas have experienced as much racial tension, suburban sprawl, or rapid growth as the Atlanta metro region. Yet, despite these outlying events, so many of Atlanta's experiences are reflective of trends shared among the majority of our nation's largest urban centers.

At every major water law epoch since the city's inception, Atlanta has contributed in some fundamental way to the nation's dialogue. After the Civil War, when America engaged in a cleanliness campaign to sanitize urban areas, Atlanta's blighted slums registered some of the highest mortality rates in the nation. During the New Deal, when the federal government created programs aimed at bringing running water to all American citizens, two Atlanta neighborhoods became the first test sites for America's slum clearance program. As America waded into the twentieth century's big dam era, Atlanta moved to the front of the line to receive pork barrel spending. When industrial and municipal pollution threatened America's waterways, legislators took a tour of Atlanta's pollution along the Chattahoochee before writing the groundbreaking Clean Water Act. As the nation grew increasingly urbanized and suburbanized, Atlanta experienced the fastest growth in the world and suffered from one of the nation's worst cases of suburban sprawl.

Unfortunately for Atlanta today, it continues to be at the epicenter of many of America's current water woes. Like so many others in an era of resource scarcity, Atlanta is embroiled in a multistate water conflict. Alabama,

Georgia, and Florida have been fighting over water in the Apalachicola-Chattahoochee-Flint River basin for the past two decades with no end in sight. The legal battle impacts at least 60 percent of the city's water resources and it has brought uncertainty and scarcity to the region's water supply.

Like hundreds of other American cities, Atlanta also struggles with century-old water infrastructure. Its drinking water pipes are crumbling with age, and the city's outdated sewers constantly spew a cocktail of raw sewage and toxic pollutants into Atlanta's rivers and streams. The city currently faces crippling federal fines and ballooning municipal expenditures as it attempts to upgrade its neglected water system.

To fix its infrastructure problem, Atlanta is spending billions of dollars that it can scarcely afford. In the upcoming years, it will probably spend at least a billion dollars more to construct a water supply sufficient for its growing population. For now, however, Atlanta remains perched on a tightrope between water scarcity and infrastructural calamity, delicately balancing between two equally unpalatable fates. Another drought, another lawsuit, another deadline the EPA refuses to extend—anything could knock the fragile city off its course.

Atlanta is certainly in the midst of a water crisis, and this book is about that, too. The history of Atlanta's water supply is inherently also the history of its crisis, for the city's current water problems have been a century in the making and entirely its own doing. Every day, the city confronts the shortcomings of its past miscalculations and indiscretions. Current lawsuits comb through phrases written seventy years ago, and today's construction crews unearth sewer lines that were last seen during the Roosevelt administration. The city is haunted by the ghosts of its past.

This book starts at the very beginning of Atlanta's water story. Chapter 1 describes the city's unlikely origins and offers its unusual topography as a partial explanation for the city's current fate. Chapter 2 describes the city's quest to draw water from the Chattahoochee River and its development of the water infrastructure that remains in use today. Chapter 3 tells of Atlanta's legacy of racial inequality and its effects on the city's health during Reconstruction and beyond. Chapter 4 describes Atlanta's quest for a Chattahoochee dam and the city's ill-fated attempt to avoid paying for it. Chapter 5 details the river's deplorable condition following Atlanta's urban growth. Chapter 6 describes the city's suburbanization and its lingering effects on water quality and water consumption. Chapter 7 analyzes the corruption and graft that contributed to the city's infrastructural deficiencies. Chapters 8 and

9 fit the pieces of the puzzle together and explain how the cumulative weight of Atlanta's past actions created the city's current problems.

In explaining the origins of Atlanta's crisis, I also hope to provide some insight into the ways in which the city should develop in the future. If its current leaders act with courage and foresight, I believe that Atlanta can avoid recreating the mistakes of its past. For that reason, I conclude with a description of the way in which the city is resolving its current problems. In doing so, I also offer a glimpse into the future problems that may be caused by the city today.

# 1

# LIFE BEFORE THE CHATTAHOOCHEE

Atlanta is, in many ways, an accidental city. It began as just a surveying footnote, and then it grew in a place where no one assumed a city could be. The land around Atlanta was a vast wilderness until 1838, when a major rail line sliced through the region's dense woods. The future city center began as a small clearing at the end of this line, a junction place where trains filled with coastal plantation cotton met Midwestern wheat-belt freight.

A decade before, Georgia governor William Schley had hired an engineer named Stephen Harriman Long to survey the northern part of the state for a railroad line to connect Georgia's plantation communities to the Tennessee River. Long immediately packed his bags and headed into the heart of Cherokee country, but he couldn't have picked a worse time to survey. His trip was timed after the Indian Removal Act but before the Trail of Tears, and the entire region was roiling with tension between the white settlers, the federal government, and the local Cherokee tribes. Aside from the rough crew of prospectors that still panned for gold in the hills around Dahlonega, few white people chose to travel through the wilderness of the Georgia piedmont.[1]

Long himself didn't rough it in the wilderness for a lengthy time. Instead, he hired three principal assistants to lead separate survey brigades, and then he rode back home for a few months to "take care of his affairs." Each of his brigades consisted of a principal assistant, three surveyors, two chainmen to take measurements, two axmen to clear routes for the surveys, one commissary to bring food to the crew, one cook, and one active lad to run errands for the others.[2] These men did the bulk of the surveying work and then reported the results to Long.

In Long's official reports to the state legislature in 1837, there is no mention of the city-building capacity of the railroad's terminal point. In fact, there is no mention of the terminal point at all.[3] Neither Long nor the state legislature seemed to care what happened at the end of the tracks. The state's only directive was that the terminal point needed to be the "most eligible for the running of branch roads" to Athens, Madison, Milledgeville, Forsyth, and Columbus.[4] The final law specified that the official route would connect Chattanooga, then called Rossville, to Montgomery's ferry on the Chattahoochee, but it left the line's terminal point to be determined at a later date.[5]

Sometime in the fall of 1837, a crew of surveyors led by Albert Brisbane measured the slope, elevation, and soil quality of a site seven miles from the Chattahoochee River. Their measurements indicated that rail lines could be brought into the area from all sides. Without any fanfare, the crew drove a stake in the ground to mark it as the rail line's terminal point, Mile Marker Zero.[6]

In retrospect, this mundane surveying act of hammering a stake into the ground is the starting point of the city of Atlanta, the time when the city was first tied to a fixed geographic location. Everything that Atlanta is today—the Buckhead mansions, the skyscraper skyline, the bypasses of Spaghetti Junction—can all be traced back to this one stake in the ground.

In the summer of 1838, a crew of state workers descended upon the wilderness around Mile Marker Zero and began to cut down trees to clear the line. By 1845, fifty-two miles of rail had been graded and the track had been laid. The next year, access railroads from the cotton-producing town reached the end of the line. Four years later, in 1851, the first train ran from the Chattahoochee to Chattanooga, Tennessee, and the Western and Atlantic Railroad was complete.[7]

During the same time, the rail line's terminal point underwent its own transformation. Although originally referred to only as "Terminus" on engineering maps, the city incorporated as Marthasville in 1843. In 1845, after rail men complained that its name was too long to print on tickets, the town was renamed Atlanta, the feminine version of the mythical city Atlantis.

In light of how much the city has grown, it is amazing to think about just how arbitrarily the city was located and created. The fact that so much has grown up from one tiny little surveying stake might seem less absurd if the stake were marking a beneficial geophysical characteristic, like fertile soil or a salt lick or a mountain spring. That a massive city with millions of people could be founded upon soil whose only distinguishing characteristic was an even, low grade slope is a testament to just how divorced from the natural world our human development had become.

Americans now build cities in the desert, drive cars through mountain-top tunnels, and build encampments on the South Pole, but at the time of Atlanta's creation, most of our nation's development still arose from some kind of relationship to the physical landscape. Military posts developed in naturally defensible areas, agrarian communities thrived in places with rich soils and ample sunlight, and cities formed along major waterways. Atlanta defied this convention, and, like any other entity at the forefront of a movement, the city encountered serious obstacles and setbacks as a result of its precociousness.

The land around Mile Marker Zero was dense with sourwood, goose-berry, and chinquapin shrubs underneath a canopy of scrubby oaks and pines.[8] Around the site, there were only a few tiny streams. To the west and north, three of the Chattahoochee's tributaries—Peachtree Creek, Utoy Creek, and Nancy's Creek—flowed down from nearby ridges.[9] To the east, the headwaters of the South River formed and flowed to the Ocmulgee River and the Atlantic Ocean.[10] To the south, the Flint River began as just a trickle and then flowed through 350 miles of forest and plantation farmland before joining with the Chattahoochee River at the shared border among Georgia, Alabama, and the territory of Florida.

Today, the Chattahoochee River is an urban stream. It traverses through the rapidly expanding suburb of Dunwoody and across the city's unofficial barrier between suburbia and the inner city, "the Perimeter" of Interstate 285. It flows by industrial parks and high-rise condominiums, and under-neath interstate overpasses and neighborhood thoroughfares. In aerial pic-tures of the city, a long tendril of hazy gray asphalt extends out from the Perimeter on either side of the river's banks.

The Chattahoochee, however, was not always so inextricably intertwined with Atlanta's urban landscape. The statistical metropolitan area of today's Atlanta encompasses over eight thousand square miles. Over the past 170 years, the city has grown beyond the Chattahoochee River, spreading west to the Tallapoosa River and north to the Coosa. It grew past the South River to cover the majority of the Ocmulgee basin and much of the Oconee basin beyond it. The city's homes, businesses, and stores have spread out into the countryside and blanketed millions of acres of forestland in urban devel-opment. Atlantans now drink water from the streams, rivers, and lakes of fifteen different counties and six major watersheds.[11]

In the 1850s, however, the city limits extended to an area less than one half of 0.01 of a percent of Atlanta's present statistical boundary. Atlanta's original incorporation line circled a one-mile radius from the center of town at Peachtree and Marietta streets to a northern boundary at the present-day Ivan Allen Jr. Boulevard and a southern boundary around the Georgia State Capital. The farthest reaches of the city were still a full six miles removed from the Chattahoochee, and the distance between the two was blanketed by a thick, impermeable forest.

By today's standards, six miles is a trifling distance to travel and a minor infrastructural hurdle to overcome. Even in the crushing Atlanta traffic, I could drive the seven miles on Interstate 20 from the city center to the Chattahoochee in a half an hour or less. By now, the city of Atlanta has also laid down over 2,400 miles of water mains, which could cover the distance between the capital and the Chattahoochee four hundred times over. In fact, if stretched in a line, the city's pipes could extend across the country and tap into Portland, Oregon's water supply on the Columbia River.

At the time the city was founded, though, seven miles was a substantial distance. Even on the relatively even ground beside the train tracks, the trip to the riverbank and back would take about five hours on foot. Horseback riders could take a road to the ferry and back in about a half a day, but few ever made the trip unless they planned to travel. The city also didn't have any water mains, let alone thousands of miles of them.

Without modern water infrastructure or access to rapid transportation, Atlanta was unable to draw from the Chattahoochee's relatively abundant supply of water. Instead, the city found itself in the unusual position of supporting a substantial population without a reliable water source.

Atlanta's lack of a navigable waterway was a serious economic obstacle. At that time in the nineteenth century, railroad transportation was still an upstart industry. The old, established trading routes were on America's inland waterways, and many businesses used barges and steamboats exclusively to transport freight. Without an inland port, Atlanta would miss out on a lot of these commercial opportunities. And, in the absence of waterborne competition, the railroads also had a habit of price-gouging landlocked cities on freight rates.

In addition to transportation concerns, Atlanta's lack of water made the city more vulnerable to widespread fires. In the era before electricity, households and businesses used fireplaces, wood-burning stoves, and gas lamps for heating, cooking, and light. Accidents occurred regularly, and house fires were commonplace. Firefighters in cities along large waterways could draw water directly from a river to fight large-scale blazes, but none of Atlanta's streams were large enough to combat a significant fire event.

It was incredibly rare for a city to develop away from a large body of water. Throughout the nineteenth century, only two American cities—Indianapolis and Denver—were able to grow to more than 100,000 residents without a navigable waterway. Both cities were anomalies: Indianapolis was created based on the false assumption that the White River would become navigable, and Denver was part of the Colorado gold rush boom. It seemed unfathomable to many that Atlanta would defy the odds and become the nation's third landlocked city.

At first, very few people believed that Atlanta would become a city of any size or importance. Stephen Harriman Long infamously wrote that the site was suitable only for a "tavern, a blacksmith's shop, a general store, and nothing else."[12] Richard Peters, the future Atlanta streetcar magnate, wrote to a friend, "The place can never be much of a trading *city*, yet may be of some importance in a *small way*."[13] Land sales were also initially sluggish. The first land auction in 1842 drew only a handful of spectators, and by the end of three years, only three out of seventeen parcels had been sold.[14]

A handful of early settlers, however, remained irrationally optimistic. In the first few years of railroad development, the settlers cleared five acres for a public square and this became the center of town.[15] The town's few residents also began to develop infrastructure to support the depot's scheduled train traffic. When the president of the Georgia Railroad stepped off the train for the first time, he almost fell into an open well that was being dug at the depot.[16] Upon completion of the railroad in 1845, most of the remaining plots of land were purchased, and as many as two hundred people moved to the area.[17]

In terms of water infrastructure, antebellum Atlanta was like any other small city at the time. There was no municipal water supply or central reservoir for drinking water. Instead, early inhabitants hauled water in buckets from the nearby streams and creeks for drinking, cooking, and washing.[18] To avoid the daily trips to the streams, some families built barrels next to their homes to collect rain, and many wealthier residents built cisterns or spring pumps.[19]

Before long, the settlement began to struggle in the absence of an abundant, centralized water supply. Denver and Indianapolis may have not had *navigable* rivers in town, but at least the cities had rivers large enough to meet the drinking water and fire protection needs of an urban populace. Atlanta's tiny streams were barely able to provide enough water for cooking and drinking, with little left over for firefighting or any other use. As Atlanta began to slowly transform into a mercantile center, it became clear that major waterworks would be necessary to sustain the town's growth.

Although there had been grumblings about the water supply before, the town's first fire turned the area's limited water availability into a *cause célèbre*. One night in 1850, a robber set fire to two prominent businesses, including a large cotton warehouse, on opposite sides of town. While the undetected man cleaned out the railroad depot's money drawer, the rest of the town hastily formed a "bucket brigade" to put out the flames. Although the structures were saved, the warehouse lost much of its inventory.[20] After the flames had died down, the townspeople began to agitate for an official fire department, complete with a reliable water supply.

Before the town could get any municipal services, however, its government would need a major overhaul. At the time, Atlanta was a divided town. Many of the earliest inhabitants and visitors were old miners from Georgia's short-lived 1828 gold rush. Others were hardscrabble pioneers and wanderers, or out of work rail men who stuck around after the Western and Atlantic construction had ended. They were a rough crowd, and their presence single-handedly supported the thriving bars and brothels that sprung up in the shantytown on Murrel's Row. Under the influence of these first rowdy residents, Atlanta's municipal government had more of a Wild West approach to law and order. Peacekeepers tended to look the other way, and every man had to fend for himself.

On the other side of the tracks from Murrel's Row, however, a number of legitimate businesses had formed and were operating out of the area around the depot. By 1850, the town had enough business to support a handful of hotels, a courthouse, churches, and a small commercial district styled after New Orleans's downtown. As the town developed its own limited cultural attractions, more businessmen began to move their families to Atlanta as well. This new and growing commercial class needed a stable government to foster economic growth and wanted the town to take a more active role in fire protection and public safety.

The two sides of Atlanta—its underbelly and its commercial district—were practically at war. After the fire, Atlanta's merchants formed their own political party, aptly named the Moral Party, and advocated for a liquor tax to pay for firemen, wells, and other infrastructural projects. The liquor tax outraged the old-timers on Murrel's Row, who formed their own Rowdy Party to run against the Morals. The next mayoral race was turbulent. Moral Party candidate John Norcross distributed fruits and candies to families during the day, and Rowdy Party candidate L. C. Simpson passed out free liquor in the bars at night.[21]

When Norcross won by a narrow margin, the Rowdies refused to concede quietly. A few weeks after the election, when a Rowdy man was convicted of assault, he brandished a knife and lunged at Norcross from across the courtroom. The new mayor also received death threats in the mail. In a particularly creative display of aggression, an enterprising group of Rowdies bought a cannon in nearby Decatur and dragged it in front of Norcross's general store one night. They didn't have any proper ammunition, but they packed the weapon with dirt and rocks from the road and repeatedly fired large sprays of debris onto the store's front. When Norcross came to open his store in the morning, its front was plastered in dirt, and the culprits had nailed a note to the porch warning that they'd buy real cannonballs the next time.[22]

If the Rowdies truly believed they could frighten John Norcross, they didn't know the man very well. Norcross was a stern, no-nonsense Puritan from Orono, Maine, who had left the Down East wilderness to strike it rich. After a series of unsuccessful business ventures in North Carolina and Cuba, he had come to Marthasville and finally succeeded in running a lucrative general store and sawmill business. He was determined to hold onto his long-sought fortune, and the Rowdies' threats only strengthened his resolve to promote law and order in the town.[23]

Amid the post-election mayhem, Norcross began to enact meaningful reforms. He collected taxes and enforced ordinances against cockfighting and prostitution.[24] During his first year in office, he and the six new councilmen also embarked on a number of infrastructural projects, including the creation of the town's first public watering holes. Although larger wells were initially planned, the town-funded crews dug three different five-by-five-foot wells at the street corners of Mitchell and Whitehall, Hunter and Whitehall, and Marietta and Peachtree streets. Each well was covered by a wooden plank and accompanied by a small wooden cistern. The crews also dug a larger fifteen-by-fifteen-foot reservoir behind the Holland House at the corner of Alabama and Whitehall streets.

The wells were a slight improvement over the town's bucket brigade, but they didn't provide much more than a symbolic protection from fire. Each well was supposed to protect an entire block of development, and yet with ten cubic feet of storage, the wells were only the size of a modern bathtub.

The reservoir was slightly larger, but it still didn't provide enough water to stop even a moderately sized house fire. All four sites were also concentrated in a four-block stretch of road, and many of the town's residences were too far away for the wells to be of any use.

After the wells and reservoir were constructed, fire continued to be a daily concern for Atlanta's residents. In his antebellum diary, Atlanta merchant Sam Richards constantly wrote that he worried about losing his store in a blaze. In the span of three years, his diary mentions at least eight different fires near the downtown business district. Every time the fire alarm rang, Richards would scan the sky to pinpoint the location of the blaze. One night, on December 9, 1863, Richards wrote: "I heard the alarm bell ringing and upon looking out of the window discovered a fire exactly in the direction of our store. I hastily dressed and ran down to the scene of action fully prepared to find our store in flames."[25] Although Richards didn't lose his store that night, his worst fears were realized less than a year later, when General William Tecumseh Sherman and his Union soldiers burned the entire commercial district to the ground.

In the years before Sherman's Atlanta campaign, when the threat of civil war had loomed over national politics but not yet exploded into armed conflict, the city had grown into a regional mercantile and shipping center. The Western and Atlantic became Georgia's predominate transportation network, and merchants like Richards had profited from the town's easy rail access. Along with the moderate growth, Atlantans had begun to develop the unchecked ambition and bravado that remains characteristic of the city today, and they believed themselves to be the best suited for the capital of the new Confederacy.

Although the town lost its initial capital bid to nearby Montgomery, Alabama, Atlanta was nevertheless able to profit substantially during the earliest stages of conflict. During the first years of battle, Atlanta's population doubled with rural refugees who had fled their homes to receive food and clothing at the impromptu aid distribution center near the railroad junction in town.[26] Atlanta's businessmen also profited from the war by manufacturing Confederate goods. The town made percussion caps, canteens, bullets, and other munitions, and then transported them on rail to embattled Confederate areas.[27]

Because it was located at a pivotal railroad junction, Atlanta soon became, in the words of one historian, the "operational center of the Confederate universe."[28] The town's booming wartime business caught the attention of

Union generals, who began to view its destruction as a key strategic goal. In the summer of 1864, Sherman began his famous assault on the town. "We have been fighting Atlanta all the time in the past," said Sherman, referring to the town's manufactures. "Since they have been doing so much to destroy us, and our Government, we have to destroy them."[29]

On August 24, after weeks of skirmishes on the edge of town, Sherman's artillery came within range of Atlanta's business district. The town's residents huddled in basements and bomb shelters, hoping to avoid the cannon fire.[30] A shell set fire to a cotton warehouse early in the morning, and firemen used all the cisterns' water in an attempt to contain the blaze.[31] The town had just resupplied the cisterns when, four days later, enemy shells set fire to another two buildings on Alabama Street, and the firemen once again drained the town's supply. With no water left and mortar shells falling every day, Atlanta's remaining cotton warehouses were like giant piles of kindling, ready to ignite the entire commercial district.

On September 2, Sherman took control over the town and ordered all remaining civilians to leave. Union soldiers occupied the remaining buildings for more than two months until November 14, when Sherman directed his chief engineer, Colonel O. M. Poe, to burn Atlanta to the ground.[32] Poe leveled the Georgia Train Depot with a battering ram and then set the entire commercial district on fire.[33]

While Sherman watched from a hill with his military band playing, his army set fire to more than three thousand buildings across the town.[34] From his vantage point, Sherman later recalled, he could see Atlanta "smouldering in ruins, the black smoke rising high in air, and hanging like a pall over the ruined city."[35] The town's cisterns, which the departing Union soldiers had drained of water and filled with waste and dead animals, sat impotent and unused on the burning street corners.

When Atlantans returned to their homes, they arrived to a commercial district that had been reduced to twisted metal, broken bricks, and charred wood. Although some homes on the fringe of town remained intact, most of Atlanta's structures were not salvageable. "It was indeed a prospect to discourage all but the most determined," wrote historian Franklin Garrett. "Yet hope springs eternal, and with . . . visions of a greater city, coupled with the immediate necessity of earning a living, the returning citizens doffed their coats, rolled up their sleeves and went to work."[36]

Atlanta recovered at a shockingly fast pace, considering the municipal government had only $1.64 in reserves at the start of 1865.[37] With the help

of private enterprise and federal reconstruction efforts, Atlanta's businessmen and townspeople cleared the rubble, rebuilt roads, and managed to
return nearly to a sense of normalcy by the end of the decade.

Chicago reporter Sidney Andrews described Atlanta's postwar construction boom:

> From all this ruin and devastation a new city is springing up with
> marvelous rapidity. The narrow and irregular and numerous streets
> are alive from morning till night with drays and carts and hand-
> barrows and wagons, with hauling teams and shouting men, with
> loads of lumber and hundreds of packed boxes, with mortar-makers
> and hod-carriers, with carpenters and masons, with rubbish remov-
> ers and house-builders, with a never-ending throng of pushing and
> crowding and scrambling and eager and excited and enterprising
> men, all bent on building and trading and swift fortune-making.[38]

As the plantation economies in Savannah and Macon slumped after the war,
Atlanta's rapid development soon earned the town a reputation as the best
place for business in the state.[39] The town rebranded itself as the "Gate City
of Georgia" and enticed bankers, manufacturers, and wholesale distributors
to relocate there.

Although Atlanta was undoubtedly on an upward projection after the
war, its lack of available water continued to be a stumbling block. With the
depredations of widespread fire freshly cemented in the town's collective
consciousness, Atlanta's citizens called for the town to develop a large, func-
tional reservoir that could provide enough water to fight large-scale fires in
the commercial district. In the morass of Atlanta's post–Civil War politics,
however, the municipal government seemed virtually incapable of embarking
on any significant public works projects. If it were not for the efforts of one
man, Anthony Murphy, the town would have likely gone another few decades
without a reliable water supply.

Anthony Murphy was the son of Irish peasants. He was tall and lanky,
with a shaggy mop of bright red hair and a plump, curled mustache that
perched above his lips like two commas lying against one another. He'd
immigrated to America at the age of nine and had worked as a machinist for
most of his young adult life. Before the start of the Civil War, he left the hard
labor of the Trenton, New Jersey, machine shops for a slightly better position
with the Western and Atlantic Railroad. He worked hard and was promoted
to woodshop foreman.

In 1862, Murphy became an accidental Civil War hero after he helped to stop a group of Union soldiers from hijacking a train.[40] The story received a great amount of press—the *Southern Confederacy* newspaper called it the "most thrilling railroad adventure that ever occurred on the American continent"[41]—and it turned Murphy into a local celebrity overnight.

After the war, he capitalized on his heroic reputation and ran a successful campaign for the Atlanta City Council. At the railroad, Murphy had overseen the fire crews, and he believed more than anyone else that Atlanta needed a newer, bigger water supply to fight fires. Once elected, he immediately began to research the town's options for a new water source.

In October of 1866, Murphy unveiled his research results in an open report to the town council. He observed that the town's existing cisterns rarely, if ever, had a sufficient supply of water for fighting fires. The town's mules and horses drank them dry for most of the day, and the pumps could barely produce enough water to replenish the cisterns at night. Murphy proposed to supplement the existing supply with a large, million-gallon reservoir on the westernmost side of the town limits.[42]

Murphy wasn't the only one to notice the inadequacy of Atlanta's water supply. Reconstruction-era businesses in Atlanta were getting gouged by fire insurance companies. Without a substantial reservoir, Atlanta's insurance rates were high enough to discourage new businesses from moving there. Competitor cities referenced their rates in comparison to Atlanta's in a bid to lure businesses away from the growing town.[43] Murphy's commission estimated that the insurance savings and water rate revenue alone would offset the cost of a large reservoir project in town.[44]

Although Murphy's plan was popular with Atlanta residents, it took a while to gain traction with the city council. Murphy's compatriots also wanted a larger water supply, but they wanted someone else to pay for it. Most of the council belonged to the Democratic Party, which at the time wished to privatize most governmental functions. Atlanta's Democrats were firmly resistant to any large governmental expenditures and any projects that would raise taxes on the city's struggling residents.

At first, it seemed like the Democrats were in luck. A month after Murphy's proposal, and again in 1869, private water companies came forward with bids to create a for-profit reservoir and water supply. The first group, the Atlanta Canal and Waterworks Company, received a charter to build a canal from the Chattahoochee River into town, but it disbanded without starting the project. The second group, the similarly titled Atlanta Canal and Water

Company, proposed to build a reservoir on Utoy Creek, but confusion during contract negotiations led to litigation, and the company withdrew its offer.

After the second private water deal imploded, some Democratic councilmen began to relinquish their former zeal for privately run enterprise, and Murphy finally pieced together enough council votes to force a referendum on whether the city should create its own water works system.[45] The measure passed by an overwhelming majority public vote.[46]

Despite the public support, progress on the waterworks project was slowed by political infighting. Democrats refused to attend city council meetings whenever the waterworks were being discussed.[47] One Democratic resident also brought a constitutional challenge to the project, claiming that the waterworks' authorizing legislation violated his due process rights. The state supreme court later dismissed his claim, but the litigation succeeded in delaying construction even further.

In 1873, the nation dipped into a recession after the railroad industry faltered and many banks failed.[48] City governments across the country slashed expenditures in anticipation of decreased tax revenue. Atlanta was particularly hard hit because its commerce was still intimately tied to the railroads. The city's budget plummeted from $64 million in 1874 to a mere $6 million by 1880.[49] Nearly all municipal services, including water, sewerage, and sanitation, received little to no funding for ten years.[50]

Luckily for the city's Board of Water Commissioners, the city's waterworks were not entirely dependent on municipal expenditures.[51] The board was financed by user fees and a $300,000 municipal bond that had been issued at the time the board was created.[52] Thanks to the existing bond, Atlanta's waterworks contractors were able to break ground at the beginning of 1874, just as the banking panic was causing other governmental functions to falter and shut down.

That year, 109 convicts from the Georgia State Prison began the long, laborious task of constructing a dam and digging a reservoir by hand.[53] Although Murphy's original plans had called for a different location, Atlanta's new reservoir was on the headwaters of the South River at Poole's Creek, where Lakewood Park is now located. The convict crew built a fifty-one-foot-tall dam that stretched 350 feet across the creek and held back a pool of water twenty-five feet deep at its lowest point. A separate crew also built a tower beside the reservoir that housed a water pump and a boiler to create steam power.[54] At the same time, another crew was hard at work digging trenches and burying water pipes alongside Atlanta's main streets. They laid eight miles of cast-iron pipe throughout the business district and spaced seventy-five hydrants at even intervals alongside the roads.[55]

When the pipes were finally connected to the pump and it was time to test the system, a crowd of people gathered at each hydrant, anxious to see the first drop of water flow from the city's pipes. They listened intently as the water pushed air out of the pipes, but soon the crowd began to grow impatient. "One elderly gentleman on Hunter Street, after listening profoundly for some time, gave his opinion that the whole thing was going to end in air," wrote an *Atlanta Constitution* editor. "There burst forth, something under a dozen gallons of thick yellow water, ruining said citizen's shirt . . . filling his pockets, and putting more mud in his ear than he can dig out in a fortnight."[56]

The first tests were a success, and on September 11, 1875, the entire town gathered to celebrate the official opening of the municipal waterworks. The event was the biggest of the decade, and probably the biggest since the town had been formed. Representatives from the neighboring cities of Columbus, Macon, and Chattanooga were in attendance, as were all of Atlanta's political figures and bureaucrats. Hundreds of rural homesteaders from the surrounding countryside also came into town for the big show. People packed onto the downtown streets, and the town police force struggled to push the crowd back to the sidewalks and away from the hydrants. Other spectators jockeyed for a good vantage point from the windows of the downtown buildings.[57]

The reservoir's main function—that of fire prevention—was on full display during the celebration. Atlanta had invited a number of different fire departments to participate in the town's celebratory hydrant tests. Around 2 p.m. that day, the firemen assembled in town, each one wearing the distinct uniform of their department. They gathered on Pryor Street while a big band played at the steps of a nearby hotel. The crews dispersed to six different hydrants, attached their long hoses to the hydrants' end, and waited for a signal. Then, all at once, the men turned on their hydrants and shot water over 150 feet into the air. A cool gust of wind blew the sprays onto the crowd, and everyone cheered as they ducked under awnings and ran down the street.

The crews conducted similar celebratory tests at hydrants along Peachtree and Marietta streets. Twice, the power of the water overwhelmed the firemen, and their grip slipped from the hoses. Both times, the streams shot directly on a few unlucky spectators and drenched them in an instant.

Later in the afternoon, one crew ran a complete reenactment of a staged firefight. The group waited in their firehouse until an alarm bell sounded, and then they ran their hose car to a hydrant at the corner of Whitehall and

Garret streets, where they doused imaginary flames in buildings at the street corner. Other departments held a race down Decatur Street to see who could first spray the landmark Kimball House. By the end of the day, every nook and cranny of Atlanta's business district was dripping in reservoir water.

As the sun began to set, the town's dignitaries crowded into the municipal engineer's office to drink champagne and toast to Atlanta's success. "The meeting was entirely informal," wrote the *Atlanta Constitution*, "and there were no set speeches, but plenty of good stories."[58] It seemed to the men as though they had just bested the town's greatest foe. With a large reservoir and new hydrants, they were sure that they'd never see their town burned to the ground again.

But, even as the men celebrated, a new threat lurked underneath the surface of the town's sparkling reservoir. It was invisible to the human eye but every bit as devastating and deadly as a widespread fire. It would poison the town's residents and spark an outrage, and the response to its widespread depredations would forever shape Atlanta's urban infrastructural landscape. The threat was bacteria, and before long, every person in the town would learn its name.

# 2

# TAPPING THE 'HOOCH

In early December of 1899, Atlanta merchant Arthur Beall walked home from his dry goods store after a long day at work. His forehead felt slightly warm to the touch, and he was chilled by the cold night air. Later that night, Arthur developed a piercing headache, and he worried that he might have caught a virus from one of the many customers who filed in and out of his shop that day. A week later, a young and baby-faced attorney named William Wade packed his bags into a carriage and began the week-long trip from Atlanta to his home in Quitman, Georgia. The drive tired him more than it had in times past, and by nightfall, he felt nauseated and had no appetite for the boarding-house dinner that was offered to him.

In just three weeks, both Arthur and William were dead. While in Atlanta, both men had ingested a bacterium named *Salmonella typhi*. A colony of bacteria had multiplied exponentially in their small intestines until it grew large enough to burst through the intestinal wall. From there, the bacteria colonized their blood streams and their vital organs, multiplying in the bodies until either their bowels burst or their hearts became too inflamed to function. It was a horrible death, and yet it was one that occurred all too often in all different corners of the city, from the cramped tenement boarding rooms of Buttermilk Bottom to the palatial master bedrooms of Peachtree Street mansions. Arthur and William, along with at least a hundred others that year, were victims of Atlanta's typhoid epidemic.[1]

In the last quarter of the nineteenth century, Atlanta had grown from an outpost into a city. Its population ballooned from 21,000 in 1870 to 90,000 in 1900. By the turn of the century, Atlanta was the forty-third largest city in America, and in the Deep South, only Memphis and New Orleans were larger. The glut of new residents presented unanticipated problems for Atlanta's urban planners, and the city's accompanying status as a regional urban center also raised expectations for the quality of municipal services offered by the government.

As the city grew, Atlanta's residents became increasingly unwilling to draw their household water from nearby streams. Some lived too far away from the waterways; others were too engaged in the city's bustling commercial activity to take the time. Many were also concerned about the stream water's quality and taste. Businesses and households alike began to draw more of their drinking water from the city's firefighting cisterns, and the vessels naturally transitioned into multipurpose water supplies.

At the same time, however, modern urban sanitation and development was still very much an evolving science. Although a handful of cities had more than a million residents by the mid-1800s, the vast majority of the world's population—at least 90 percent—still lived in rural areas.[2] Of those few urbanized spaces, only a handful of European cities had been significant population centers for a hundred years or more. Every other city, including every American urban center, was relatively new to the game, and many made typical rookie mistakes during their first formative years of urban development.

As towns like Atlanta began to become urbanized, there weren't many successful examples of good public infrastructural development to emulate. At the time, all of the world's largest cities still struggled with mountains of improperly disposed sewage, poor-quality drinking water, inadequate firefighting and fire prevention, ineffective waste collection and disposal, and insufficient health and medical services. A city like Atlanta could only hope to learn from others' mistakes, while also trying to anticipate and avoid future mistakes of its own.

The shortcomings in nineteenth-century urban development were particularly glaring for drinking water and wastewater infrastructure. Only recently had scientists discovered and isolated bacteria cells, and the linkage between bacteria and disease was still poorly understood. Many urban planners and health officials still rejected the new bacterial science and stubbornly held onto the belief that miasmas, or bad smells, caused diseases like dysentery and cholera.

During this time period, almost every major city seemed to have its own water-related catastrophe. In London during the "Great Stink" of 1858, the smell of sewage in the Thames became so strong that the House of Commons had to soak the building's curtains in chloride of lime to prevent its members from passing out. In New York, the city's waste management program dumped the trash from its three million residents directly into the ocean, where the tides promptly deposited it back onto Long Island and New Jersey shores. While the urban myth that 90,000 Chicago residents died of cholera in 1885 is untrue, hundreds of Chicagoans did die of waterborne disease outbreaks from contaminated drinking water every year. And in New Orleans during the last half of the 1800s, more than forty thousand people died of yellow fever from mosquitos that bred in the stagnant water surrounding the city.

As these examples illustrate, the consequences of poor urban development were much more serious than the mere political fallout that is generally experienced by today's municipal planners. Nineteenth-century American cities were constantly poised on the brink of an epidemic or a natural disaster, and one poor decision could cost hundreds or thousands of lives.

After the Civil War, as Atlanta's population doubled and then tripled, city leaders began to fear that Atlanta was poised for disaster, too. The city was drowning in its own filth, literally covered in the human waste of nearly a hundred thousand residents. All it took was one contagious person and one poorly drained outhouse or latrine, and the entire city could fall ill at once.

Atlanta's sanitation problems had begun as soon as the city's first water mains connected to homes. Almost immediately after the reservoir was complete, running water became one of Atlanta's most influential real estate status symbols. New businesses and houses in upper-income neighborhoods were built with running water, and many older structures were also retrofitted with plumbing. As Atlanta grew and renovated, real estate listings like this 1876 advertisement became increasingly common: "For Rent: one-half of a desirable boarding house running through the block and fronting on two of the main streets in the city, *furnished with water from the reservoir* and other conveniences" (emphasis added).[3] By the late 1880s, there were nearly three thousand flush toilets scattered across the city with another thousand being added each year. The city's nine thousand privies were still the norm, but for Atlanta's wealthy upper class, the era of flush toilets had begun.[4]

Atlanta's first toilets were similar to today's fixtures with one glaring exception: the city's original toilets' plumbing didn't connect to a sewer system. Atlanta, in fact, didn't even have a sewer system. Throughout the entire waterworks planning process, it apparently never occurred to the waterworks commission that the water pumped into the city might eventually need to be pumped out again. Without a cohesive sewage plan, Atlanta's homeowners laid pipe underground to the edge of their property, at which point the privately owned plumbing pipes dumped raw sewage and wastewater directly onto the ground.

Before the reservoir and the rise of the flush toilet, Atlanta had a few ditches that had, by default, served as impromptu sewers. The largest one originated behind the Kimball House and ran along Lloyd Street, which is now known as Central Avenue.[5] The ditch was formed by the banks of a spring at the South River's headwaters, and residents had begun dumping outhouse waste there after the Civil War. The ditch was a smelly eyesore, but the spring water was able to partially dilute the outhouse waste and carry it downstream and away from residences. The other ditches around town operated in the same crude fashion: residents dumped their outhouse waste into a small streambed and waited for rain to wash it away.

Many of the city's nicest homes were along the Lloyd Street ditch. When these houses converted to flush toilets, the residents built underground plumbing through their backyards that dumped waste directly into the streambed. The plumbing kept their estate grounds tidy, but it wreaked havoc on the ditch. The wastewater from the new toilets overwhelmed the ditch's limited capacity and its banks brimmed with liquid raw sewage. By 1880, just five years after the first water mains connected to homes, the city had to line the Lloyd Street ditch with rocks and cover it to prevent constant overflows. Other neighborhoods followed suit, and many of the city center's ditches were soon converted to crude sewer drains.

The sewers themselves, however, were mere conveyances. Instead of addressing Atlanta's new liquid sewage problem, they merely moved the problem from one neighborhood to another. The sewer outlets dumped waste directly onto homes and businesses outside the city's narrow "Sanitation District," and conditions at these outlets worsened as the sewer lines expanded and more flush toilets were added to homes around town. Furthermore, even in their limited capacity as conveyances, the sewers were subpar: the rocky lining constantly snagged trash and caused blockages and overflows onto the street.[6] Sewage also seeped into the city's groundwater through cracks in the rocky lining.[7]

Between the accidental overflows and the intentional sewer outfalls, Atlanta suddenly became a much wetter place than it had ever been before. The city's new mains pumped water into faucets and toilets, but there was no corresponding infrastructure to effectively pump the used water back out again. Instead, the wastewater collected in puddles on the street, causing conditions that could only be described as a state of perpetual flooding.

By the early 1880s, the streets were so saturated with sewage that even the city's main thoroughfares contained large, impassable stretches of sludge. An 1881 *Daily Constitution* feature on Atlanta's roads described Broad Street after a rain: "This macadamized thoroughfare was half a leg deep in mud, and the black loblolly left by the thawed snow made the street look like the sluggish waters of a filthy canal."[8] The article continued its coverage with the story of a dapper businessman who had avoided soiling his outfit by paying a stranger to pick him up and carry him across the muck at the corner of Pryor and Hunter streets.

The muck was a nuisance. It soiled suits, for sure, but it also hindered commerce and damaged Atlanta's reputation. Wagons and buggies became mired in street sludge, which slowed transportation to and from the business center. Atlanta's sewage-ridden streets also conflicted sharply with the powerful, up-and-coming image that city leaders so desperately wished to promote. In a follow-up piece to its first road sludge article, the *Constitution* chastised the municipal government for lagging behind other cities in sewage infrastructural development. "Just now the condition of the streets is a severe reflection upon our vaunted progress and prosperity," wrote the editors. "Even poor, debt-ridden Savannah has an efficient street corps constantly employed upon her thoroughfares."[9]

In fairness to the city, Atlanta did have its own street corps, although the relative efficiency of the group was definitely questionable. Since 1878, the city had employed the labor of fifteen or so chain-gang members to rake up muck from the road and cart it away from the business district.[10] The street-cart men were all debtors to the city, and most had been unable to pay criminal fines levied upon them. These street-cart men and the city's equally unreliable "night soil cart" men, who carried away outhouse waste, formed the seedy cadre of Atlanta's first waste disposal effort.

Cart-men had actually been employed with great success in other parts of America and Europe. The practice first originated in London in the 1700s when a group of entrepreneurial men began to charge fees for shoveling outhouse waste into wheelbarrows and carting it to farms on the other side of the Thames.[11] London's system, and others like it, worked because it created a win-win situation for both the exporting urban community and the importing rural one: London got to rid itself of excess sewage, and the surrounding agrarian communities got free compost.

Atlanta's cart system sought to mimic this practice, but city leaders only adopted half of the cycle. The city ordinance never designated a place to dispose the waste, and the municipal government never entered into agreements with farmers to convert the waste into usable compost.[12] The ordinance merely specified that the waste should be dumped "outside the sanitation district."[13] In the absence of any further clarification, the poorly trained and unsupervised cart carriers began to take shortcuts by dumping their carts in vacant lots within the city. After a decade, there were dozens of impromptu dumping spots around town, each with several feet of decaying refuse covering the ground.[14] One spot was adjacent to the city's main reservoir. Cart carriers also dumped dead horses, hogs, cows, and offal there.[15] Visibly dirty runoff from the site flowed directly into the reservoir whenever it rained.

Runoff from the cart dumps, however, was the least of Atlanta's water quality concerns. The city's new sewage drains effectively conveyed wastewater downstream and into every major water body within the city limits, including the branches of the South River that fed into Atlanta's new reservoir. In total, a thousand homes had been built within the South River watershed by the late 1880s, and almost every one discharged its sewage into the reservoir, either directly through wastewater pipes or indirectly through outhouse runoff.[16]

In response to the flooding and muck, the city began to pave its main thoroughfares beginning in 1881.[17] The paved streets were much more convenient and clean than the muddy roads they replaced. However, the newly paved roads were outfitted with sidewalk gutters that drained directly into the city's existing sewers, and so the street filth simply compounded the amount of wastewater and sewage that was already being flushed from the sewer lines into the city's streams.

Between the runoff from the paved streets and the covered sewers, Atlanta's waterways and its reservoir became increasingly polluted. The city's water supply was a persistent and looming threat. Fecal matter, household cleaners, industrial wastes, decaying animals—all the bacteria and chemicals and diseases associated with nineteenth-century urban life—flowed into the reservoir unabated. For the first time, many in the community began to worry about the safety of the city's water supply.

In the face of Atlanta's obvious governmental inaction, a couple of ambitious businessmen attempted to create private alternatives to Atlanta's municipal waterworks. The first major water proposal came from the Atlanta and Grand Western Canal Company, a group that had previously received a state charter to build a transportation canal from the Chattahoochee to the Ocmulgee River.[18] The canal company was the brainchild of Colonel B.W.

Frobel, an ambitious West Point graduate and Confederate war hero who had unsuccessfully sought political office in Georgia after the war.[19]

Frobel offered to build a large canal that stretched from the Chattahoochee through Atlanta.[20] The proposal was designed to address both of Atlanta's most pressing water issues at once: the northern part of the canal would bring clean water to new city reservoirs, and the southern part would carry away the city's sewage.[21] Once completed, city's new canal-fed reservoirs would be twenty-five times larger than Atlanta's existing reservoir.[22]

Frobel's offer came with one catch. In exchange for building the canal, the city of Atlanta had to agree to transfer its entire municipal water supply system to the canal company, including all of its water rights and the right to charge residents a fee for municipal water use.[23] Thus, Frobel's plan was a very early water privatization venture, an idea that would reemerge repeatedly in the course of Atlanta's history.

The city was unwilling to relinquish control over its relatively new public waterworks system and it declined the proposal. Although the city council voted in favor of the plan, the city's waterworks commission opposed it, and the Board of Aldermen rejected it in the spring of 1884.[24] Frobel was unwilling to dig the canal without Atlanta's water rights, and his company withdrew its proposal.[25]

A new engineer with a new plan emerged to take Frobel's place. Colonel John W. Baum was a Yankee from Oswego County, New York. He was a rotund man, weighing 232 pounds despite his small 5'9"-frame. He also had a peculiar way of dressing: at a time when most men of his pedigree were eschewing working clothes in favor of sleek modern sportswear and business shoes, Baum dressed as if perpetually on the front lines. He wore billowing pant legs tucked year-round into a thick pair of winter boots that rose above his knees.[26]

Baum came to Atlanta after building hundreds of wells in other cities, and he was confident that he could build a well in Atlanta that would provide a lasting solution to the city's water crisis. Colonel Baum proposed to supply water from an artesian well in the center of the city at the corner of Peachtree and Marietta streets.[27]

Although he promised that the well would meet all of Atlanta's water needs, city leaders were skeptical and first refused to grant funding for the project. Once Frobel's canal was scrapped, however, the council was desperate enough to explore Colonel Baum's plan and agreed to expend ten thousand dollars to launch the project.[28]

The well was an instant failure. Before construction began, a local geolo-
gist found trace levels of salt in the water, which indicated that the city's
sewage was seeping into the well.[29] At the time, Colonel Baum insisted that
the well tapped into artesian water beneath the city's bedrock and below the
contaminated surface water. Because salt was merely an indicator of sewage
and not conclusive proof, the city begrudgingly permitted construction to
continue.

Once the well was fully operational, the quantity of water also fell short
of the colonel's promise. At the height of its use, the water produced by the
well met less than 2 percent of the city's demand.[30]

In the end, Baum's glistening "artesian well" turned out to be little more
than a puddle of surface water drainage. Three years after the well was dug,
testing established beyond a doubt that sewage-ridden rainwater from the
city streets ran directly into the well.[31] Instead of solving the city's contamination issues, Baum's well seemed to merely exacerbate them. Concerned about
the risk of typhoid and disenchanted with Colonel Baum, the city council cut
off the well from the water supply, just four years after the project began.

By the time Colonel Baum's well was shut off in 1888, Atlanta was desperate for a new water source. Two of the reservoir's three feeder streams had
truly egregious levels of contamination. In 1890, the city's Board of Health
became so concerned with the reservoir's filthy state that it ordered Atlanta's
waterworks commission to completely drain and scour the reservoir's only
settling tank. In just one night, thousands of gallons—an amount roughly
equal to the flow of the Chattahoochee, by one account—were released from
the tank into the gorge below the reservoir, and then city workers scrubbed,
dried, and swept the tank's sides before allowing the tank to fill again by
morning.

When problems persisted, the city was forced to cut off the two offending streams. Todd Branch, which supplied half of the city's water until the
late 1880s, had dense development throughout its watershed and drained the
sewage of thousands of people into the reservoir.[32] A continuous stream
of sewage actually ran down the hillside and intersected the stream, and the
sheer quantity of it was enough to discolor the water for a quarter of a mile.[33]
After another tense meeting with the Board of Health, the city ordered its
chain-gang to reroute Todd Branch around the reservoir and away from the
municipal water supply. Harden Branch, the smallest of the reservoir's three
feeder streams, was cut off soon thereafter when a massive refinery fire contaminated its water with cottonseed oil.[34]

After the Harden and Todd branches were separated from the water supply, Atlanta quickly realized that it had another problem entirely. With the South River providing the reservoir's only supply of water, the city's demand exceeded capacity and water levels dropped precipitously.[35] The city's growing demand for water had reached three million gallons a day, but without Todd Branch, the reservoir's remaining feeder streams only replenished 800,000 gallons a day during dry weather.[36] Many worried that if there were a prolonged drought the city's withdrawals could easily deplete the reservoir and leave it completely dry.

Even under relatively normal weather conditions, Atlanta's reservoir would drop to dangerously low levels. During the summer of 1891, the city's water pressure served as a constant, aching reminder of the city's perilous state. Each morning, water pressure would start off relatively strong because the reservoir had filled with water over night, but as the day progressed and residents and businesses used water for their daily activities, the flow of faucets would slow to a trickle.[37]

The city was clearly on the brink of a major water shortage, and yet by 1891, the mayor and the waterworks commission had still not come up with a definitive plan to solve Atlanta's problem. Or, perhaps more accurately, the mayor and waterworks commission had arrived at *many* plans but had not yet settled upon one.

Since 1885, two factions from within the city government had been engaged in a philosophical stand-off with each other about the future of Atlanta's water supply. On one side was George Hillyer, Atlanta's twenty-ninth mayor, who argued that Atlanta should select an unpopulated watershed in the mountains, purchase and preserve it in its entirety, and then bring the clean water to Atlanta via canal or aqueduct. On the other side was John Thomas Glenn, Atlanta's thirty-first mayor, who pushed for Atlanta to draw its water from a nearby point along the Chattahoochee.

At the heart of the debate was whether or not running water purified itself of bacteria and toxins. A handful of large communities, like Gainesville and Smyrna, discharged their sewage into the Chattahoochee River. The Marietta Paper Mill disposed of its waste into a Chattahoochee tributary above Atlanta's proposed waterworks site, and a number of carpetbaggers had plans to build heavy industries along the river as well.[38]

Chattahoochee advocates argued that the river's rushing water would break down the pollutants before reaching the city. In his final report endorsing the Chattahoochee as a water source, Mayor Glenn's consulting engineer

Rudolph Herring wrote of this principle: "The creeks contain large quantities of decaying vegetable matter in an unoxidized form, while the large rivers, from the abundant aeration given to the water, have had an opportunity of ridding themselves of such matter."[39] We now know that this assertion is only somewhat true. Exposure to air from rushing water can speed up the breakdown of some harmful organic materials, but the effect is not nearly as pronounced as Herring believed it to be.

George Hillyer, on the other hand, was skeptical of Herring's water-cleansing theory. During his term as mayor, Hillyer had taken a tour of Northeastern cities' municipal waterworks. On that trip, he had seen many municipal water sources compromised by pollution from upstream communities, and his personal experience led him to believe that even large rivers were unable to cleanse themselves from pollution. Hillyer worried that the Chattahoochee, like the Northeast rivers he had toured, would eventually become unsafe to drink once the watershed became more populated. In his mind, the only safe water supply was one that was completely removed from human development.

Hillyer's proposed watershed preservation plan had some supporters among the waterworks commission members, but no one could agree on which watershed to preserve. Hillyer believed that the Peachtree watershed would work the best, while another member named J. C. Hendrix advocated for the Soque River to be preserved, and another named A. J. McBride pushed for the Amicalola River.[40]

Even though no one could agree on a watershed, public support seemed in favor of Hillyer's "mountain water" preservation plans. Before the Buford Dam forever changed the Chattahoochee into a cool, fast-running trout stream in the 1950s, the river was slow flowing, shallow, and very silty. Downstream Columbus, Georgia, reported that the Chattahoochee's water was so discolored that it would stain clothes a deep reddish brown if used for washing.[41] It was also unpleasant to drink. In a brilliant act of political theater, Hillyer took samples from the mountain streams as well as the Chattahoochee and then left them all on his desk for the public to inspect. The Chattahoochee sample was noticeably discolored and after a few weeks, it even began to grow mold.[42] Many Atlantans had a visceral reaction to the Chattahoochee water, and few initially wanted it as the city's water source.

Eventually, however, the city's sense of urgency overrode its qualms about the river water. In 1891, around the same time that residents' faucets started slowing to a trickle every afternoon, Hillyer and his anti-Chattahoochee supporters were still debating which watershed to preserve. They had completed studies on each of the potential watersheds, and all led to the same basic conclusion: preserving a mountain watershed would provide cleaner water than the Chattahoochee, but it would also provide less of it and at a much greater expense. The great water debate spilled onto the *Atlanta Constitution*'s op-ed pages, which were regularly filled with arguments for and against each source. Doctors wrote about pollutants in the Chattahoochee, businessmen wrote about the paltry water supply from the mountains, other residents wrote about the projects' relative costs.[43]

Just when the debate between the pro-Chattahoochee and anti-Chattahoochee factions had broken into a fever pitch, an unanticipated proposal from a private company forced the city's hand. In May 1891, the Chattahoochee Water and Power Company publicly proposed to take over the city's waterworks and build a new canal from the Chattahoochee River. The company offered to pay for the required infrastructure, but in return it asked for a steep fee: 3.5 cents for every thousand gallons pumped.[44]

With public unrest about the city's water at an all-time high, the city council knew that it needed to either accept the company's proposal or start in earnest to implement an alternative municipal scheme. Because Atlanta didn't have enough money to begin work on any of the mountain watershed preservation plans, George Hillyer and his supporters finally relented and agreed to support Mayor Glenn's plans. On the same day the city council rejected the company's offer, it unanimously adopted the following resolution: "Resolved, That the city of Atlanta build its own waterworks and that the supply be drawn from the Chattahoochee River."[45]

The city broke ground in the winter of 1892, with a hundred men on crew.[46] One pumping station was constructed on the east bank of the Chattahoochee River near Bolton, Georgia, and another was built on Peachtree Creek closer to the center of town.[47] One large water main connected the first station to the second pump, which then carried the water to a new filtering reservoir on Hemphill Avenue.[48] Workers dynamited bedrock for the first section of pipe from the Chattahoochee and dug trenches for the rest of the way.[49] Massive sections of cast-iron pipe were bolted together and then caulked with molten lead to make the connections watertight.[50] The lines were underground for most of their length, except for a small stretch where they had to be suspended above the city's heavily used train tracks.[51]

On Hemphill Avenue, the city built a new two-story red brick building to house the waterworks' turbines, filters, and administrative offices.[52] The building, named Hemphill Station, pumped water from the settling reservoir to city water mains. At full capacity, the new station could pump ten million gallons each day.[53] Water mains from Hemphill Station ran underground from Hemphill Avenue to Luckie Street. The mains then traveled down Luckie to its intersection with Peachtree Street, where they connected to the few existing underground water mains from the city's original reservoir.[54]

The new fifty-acre reservoir adjacent to the Hemphill Station could hold up to two hundred million gallons of water.[55] On one end, a submerged tower connected the Chattahoochee Station pipes to the reservoir and regulated the reservoir levels with a system of valves.[56] On the opposite side, a similar tower regulated flow into the Hemphill pumping station.[57]

Borrowing from late-Victorian industrial styles, the architects surrounded the station and reservoir with open green space for the public.[58] The new grounds were described by one gushing reporter as "the most beautiful, delightful and entrancing place in the country for the weary and languid."[59] The area's original forest was cleared and replaced with a manicured stand of oak trees and gently sloping grassy lawns.[60] A three-quarter-mile drive encircled the reservoir for the city's growing number of buggy driving enthusiasts.[61]

On June 28, 1893, a large crowd of city politicians and citizens gathered to watch as the pumps began gushing Chattahoochee water into the reservoir.[62] Three weeks later, after the reservoir had filled, Chattahoochee water flowed through Atlanta's water mains and into homes across the city.[63]

Today, more than one hundred years later, the Hemphill pumping station continues to bring Chattahoochee water to the city. The city has expanded the pump station house many times, and the station's filtering mechanisms have been replaced by more advanced water purifying technology. The city has also expanded the reservoir's capacity many times and added another reservoir next to the original one. The original station house was listed on the National Register of Historic Properties in 1978.[64]

The grounds around the reservoir are no longer a rural respite for the weary; urban development swallowed the surrounding land many decades ago. The property is now partially encircled by a tangled cluster of railroad tracks and the remaining sides border expensive restaurants in the gentrifying neighborhood of Berkeley Park in Midtown West. Once open to the public, the reservoir grounds are also now completely blocked off. Homeland Security erected a tall fence around the reservoir to protect the city's water from a terrorist attack.

Considering how much has changed above the surface, the city's underground infrastructure has changed shockingly little in the past one hundred years. Atlanta has added billions of dollars of wastewater and drinking water infrastructure to numerous sites on along the Chattahoochee, but the Hemphill Station and the downtown pipes remain largely the same. The same cast-iron pipes take water from the station house to the mains in town. The pipes still travel down Luckie Street to Peachtree, where the lines meet with the city's first cast-iron pipes underneath a city block that now holds the Atlanta Aquarium and the Centennial Olympic Park.

Today, Atlanta metro's water withdrawals are just shy of nine hundred million gallons a day; in another twenty years, the city's daily needs are projected to top 1.1 billion gallons.[65] Considering the staggering amount of water that Atlantans now consume, it's almost impossible to imagine the city relying exclusively on any of the mountain streams proposed by George Hillyer or his supporters so many years ago.

It's also equally difficult to imagine Hillyer's proposed stream, Peachtree Creek, with a completely preserved watershed. The formerly pristine stream has now been completely consumed by suburbia. Its watershed boundary extends north from downtown to Home Park and Pine Hills, then northeast to Chamblee and Doraville, and then completes the loop through Clarkston, Scottsdale, Decatur, Edgewood, and back to downtown. The watershed's population density of 3,800 people per square mile makes it one of the most urbanized watersheds in the state of Georgia.[66]

What would Atlanta look like if the land around Midtown, Druid Hills, Edgewood, and Decatur had all been carved out and preserved in its natural state? And what would Atlanta be like if it hadn't tapped the Chattahoochee more than a hundred years ago?

Many articles, papers, and books have been written about Atlanta's impact on the Chattahoochee River, but few stop to think about the river's impact upon Atlanta. Today, the city's monumental weight and force have created a nearly unstoppable momentum toward expansion and growth, but a hundred years ago, the difference between one water source and another could have been the single decision that projected Atlanta forward as a booming economic center or forever confined it to a state of relative obscurity.

Without the Chattahoochee, Atlanta could not possibly have become the city that it is now. If Atlanta had chosen to preserve Peachtree Creek watershed instead of drawing water from the Chattahoochee River, the city would have found itself under a mountain of debt and with an available water supply less than half of the Chattahoochee's size.[67] With high water rates to pay for the project, and a limited supply of water to offer, Atlanta would have had difficulty attracting large industries and businesses to the city in the early twentieth century.

Even if Atlanta had attracted businesses under Hillyer's plan, where would residents have lived? Peachtree Creek's preserved watershed boundary would have created a permanent wilderness in the exact area of the city that was most amenable to high-income development: high and dry land. With a city ringed by preserved land and low-lying sewer drains, developers may have abstained from working on large projects in the Atlanta area. Perhaps Atlanta wouldn't have grown as large or wouldn't have suffered from as much suburban sprawl. Or perhaps the developers would have pushed the city government to reverse its decision and Atlanta's development would have continued along the exact same path it took to get to where it is today.

Atlanta was undoubtedly shaped by Mayor Glenn's decision to draw water from the Chattahoochee but how or to what extent is anyone's guess. Every city today is a layered tapestry of urban planning decisions, both past and present. Each city block is shaped by a myriad of ideas and plans. Someone decided to lay down a railroad line, while someone else made a plan for sewers, and another surveyed for a road; someone bulldozed a housing project, and another mapped an interstate overpass.

To what extent any individual decision has shaped the landscape is difficult to discern. As far as the city's water infrastructure is concerned, all that we can truly know is this: in 1891 in Atlanta, someone sited a water pipe along the Chattahoochee and the city continued to grow.

# 3

# WATER TO THE PEOPLE

By the turn of the twentieth century, Atlanta had become one of the Deep South's premier business locations. Over five hundred companies shipped goods through distribution centers in Atlanta, and the city also became the region's central place of business for insurance providers, financial institutions, and communications networks like Southern Bell Telephone and Western Union.[1] There was money to be had in Atlanta, and many of the city's leading businessmen turned their modest incomes into vast fortunes during this time.

Atlanta's newfound wealth, however, existed alongside profound poverty. Atlanta in the 1900s consisted of two distinct worlds: one for the entrepreneurial white middle class and another for the multitudes of poor rural immigrants that packed into the city's urban slums.

In today's urban centers, municipal services are often great equalizers. In modern Atlanta, the ritziest Buckhead mansion and the grungiest public housing units use the same drinking water supply and wastewater systems, and trash is collected just as often from curbsides inside the Perimeter as for those outside. At the start of the 1900s, however, Atlanta's city services were not universal and instead served to exacerbate inequalities rather than alleviating them.

After the city first laid water mains downtown, Atlanta expanded the pipes beyond the commercial district. By the turn of the century, all of the city's finest neighborhoods had water connections in each home. Atlanta's mansions had kitchen and bathroom faucets, flush toilets, and bathtubs that drew water from the city's municipal supply. The city also began to replace the open sewer trenches with buried sewer lines that transported wastewater from each of the finer homes. Atlanta's rich would never again have to come in contact with their waste; everything washed neatly down a drain.

Like today's granite countertops and Sub-Zero refrigerators, Atlanta's up-and-coming middle class coveted running water, and they eagerly purchased overpriced lots wherever the city dug new water mains. Developers like Richard Peters and George Adair paid the city to bring water and sewer lines to their properties and then sold the rural lots in parcels to upper- and middle-class buyers.[2] Billed as clean safe-havens from the overgrown and dangerous downtown, nearly forty different garden home communities sprung up on the northern outskirts of the city around new water mains during the first part of the twentieth century.[3] In Inman Park, the "gem of all suburbs," many of the city's wealthiest citizens built massive mansions along newly paved streets. Every home lot had underground gas, water, and sewer connections.[4] In addition to running water, the residents also had access to a large grassy park with a pond and natural spring for their aesthetic enjoyment.[5] The city maintained all the park's water features free of charge.

In 1904, banker John Murphy and his wife moved into their new home at the corner of Peachtree and 14th streets, just a few miles north of Inman Park. The house, which Mr. Murphy named Hillcrest, was the embodiment of Atlanta's newfound commercial success—and also the embodiment of its excesses. Hillcrest's long, sloping lawn led visitors up to a wraparound front porch supported by massive, hand-carved Corinthian columns. The double front doors opened to an entryway with red velvet–paneled walls and a sweeping, three-story mahogany staircase. Oversized Tiffany glass chandeliers hung from the gilded ceilings and thick Italian silk curtains were draped against the walls.[6]

Hillcrest was just a block away from the city's newest real estate acquisition, Piedmont Park. The 185-acre field had been used by a private company as the site for Atlanta's famous 1895 Cotton States and International Exposition. In May of 1904, around the same time the Murphy home was completed, the city purchased the entire park and began to maintain its grounds, walking trails, and buildings.[7]

Although the clean, bucolic landscape around Piedmont Park seemed like a completely alternate universe, Hillcrest was just a short trolley ride from the commercial district downtown. John Murphy could catch the Number 10 trolley in front of his house and ride it three miles down Peachtree to his office in the Atlanta National Bank on Alabama Street.[8] He would have been in good company. Each morning, and again during the evening commute, the Number 10 Peachtree–Whitehall line and its adjacent line, the Number 9

Piedmont–Courtland, were packed with Atlanta's most successful merchants and professionals.

If they had chosen to look outside the trolley windows, the businessmen on the Number 10 would have confronted the stark inequalities among Atlanta's residents on a daily basis. In the span of a single mile, the streetcar tracks left the smoothly paved avenues of Atlanta's elite suburbs and dropped down into an abyss of poverty and filth named Buttermilk Bottom.

Buttermilk Bottom was one of many slum neighborhoods scattered across the city. Like all the others, it was wedged into a low-lying, swampy area in between the glittering wealth of the suburbs and the modern street lights and tall buildings of downtown. In all the slums, Atlanta's poor festered and rotted in horrific living conditions on par with the worst modern-day slums in Brazil and India. The Buttermilk Bottom neighborhood, and others like it, were composed of a maze of tightly packed shanties made from found objects and salvaged building materials. Dotted among the makeshift shacks were a few decrepit multistory tenement houses, which were packed to the brim with Atlanta's poor.

In the 1900s, it was in the slums that most of Atlanta's new population came to live—not in the sprawling new mansions of Ansley Park but in the crowded shanties of Buttermilk Bottom, Darktown, and Beaver Slide. The ranks of slum residents grew every day. They streamed in from the countryside on trains, wagons, and often on foot. They came to the city with big dreams and a desperate desire to escape the agricultural depression that had gripped the countryside.[9] For many of Georgia's rural black men and women, Atlanta also presented safety in numbers and an opportunity to escape the rural lynch mobs.

None of the slum houses had running water or interior bathrooms. In the absence of modern toilets, Atlanta's recent slum immigrants resorted to the rural sanitation habits that they had practiced in the countryside: they dug a pit and built an outhouse over it. But, as residents were made painfully aware, rural outhouses were not suitable in an urban environment. The presence of outhouses increased in pace with the rising population density in the slums, and by 1908 in Beaver Slide, a single block of homes had forty-five different outhouses in it servicing up to seventy-five people.[10] With so many packed into a small space, at least a few of the outhouses were bound to be overflowing, leaking, or otherwise malfunctioning at any given time.

At the same time, slum residents were also reliant upon crude wells for drinking water. Piedmont Park residences, downtown businesses, and other structures in the "sanitation district" had direct connections to the city's new water supply, but the water mains stopped short of Atlanta's poorest neighborhoods. By 1908, city health officials estimated that 50,000 people— roughly half the city's entire population—lived without running water.[11] In the absence of in-house taps, Atlanta's poor had to either travel to a downtown public water spigot or to collect rain and surface water from wells within the neighborhood. Out of convenience, many chose the latter. The wells, however, were often located alongside the outhouses and were rife with bacterial contamination.

Even basic city sanitation services were woefully inadequate in the slums. For the entire Beaver Slide area, with its 10,000 outhouses, the city employed only fifteen night soil carts to dispose of outhouse waste.[12] Under ideal conditions, the cart service could clean an outhouse once every two weeks, but conditions were rarely ideal.[13] These neighborhoods had few, if any, traversable streets, and most houses were accessible only through winding pathways that splintered from the main road arteries. Every slum around town was located in a pocket of low elevation, and the dirt-covered side alleys would become swamped with mud during every rain. Whenever this happened, cart service would stop for weeks or even months.

Even when dry weather permitted ingress and egress, the cart carriers often slacked off and avoided work. A prominent Methodist pastor reported on the indifference of the cart carriers to the *Atlanta Constitution*: "They are only on the job when the 'man higher up' is on the job. . . . I have seen boys driving the sanitary wagons get busy only when they thought an inspector was coming. And what chance has an inspector to enforce the law . . . when there is only one inspector to a huge section?"[14] Between the rainy weather and the slothful cart carriers, Atlanta's slum outhouses constantly overflowed with filth.

The abject poverty of the slum residents also added to the area's sanitation problems. Few residents could afford to buy a watertight catchment basin for their outhouses, so they continued to use handmade wooden basins that rotted and leaked. No one could afford window screens to keep out disease-carrying houseflies, and no one could afford to buy a trash can, so the residents also eschewed the city's curbside garbage pickup and opted instead to toss garbage in dispersed dumping grounds around the neighborhood.

One such dumping ground was on Elm Street between West Fair and Parson Street, where Clark Atlanta University's University Park now stands. Offal, bones, food scraps, feces, and other waste were piled in a ditch directly adjacent to homes.[15] Children played next to puddles of green scum, and washerwomen hung garments on the edge of the dump's sludge. Every spring, and throughout the summer and into fall, the entire neighborhood would swarm with flies.[16]

As if the slum's garbage wasn't enough, residents also had to contend with the sewage from others. The covered sewers from upland neighborhoods, like Ansley Park, all drained into natural streams and waterways around town. If the low-lying slums were lucky, the sewage outfall discharges would merely flow through their neighborhood streams and past the shacks. If there was a heavy rain or an obstruction in the creek bed, the streams would back up and overflow, flooding entire neighborhoods in liquid raw sewage.

Unsurprisingly, disease ravaged the slums. Hookworm, roundworm, influenza, diphtheria, and tuberculosis raced through the poor neighborhoods. Typhoid was particularly prevalent. Local doctor Homer Nash later recalled, "Those were the days when typhoid fever was rampant, every which way."[17]

There was very little that poor residents could do to treat themselves if they became ill. No one could afford proper medical care, and those who were fortunate enough to have a job couldn't afford to lose a day's pay to seek treatment. Medical facilities were also limited; in all of Atlanta, there was not a single medical center willing to treat a black person with a communicable disease.

In 1905, widely publicized census data confirmed what everyone in Atlanta already knew: the city was in the midst of a public health crisis. Atlanta's death rate was an embarrassing 150 percent above the average rate reported by the 338 other American cities that participated in the U.S. Census.[18] That year, an estimated eighteen hundred people in the city died from preventable, communicable disease.[19] This accounted for the majority of deaths in Atlanta. More people died from communicable disease than from natural causes, violence, accidents, heart disease, and cancer combined.[20]

The 1905 census data was actually the first time that Atlanta's health had been objectively ranked against other American cities. Before then, and in the absence of accurate statistical comparisons, Atlanta's city leaders had combatted rumors of disease with denials and shameless propaganda. For example, in response to a true rumor of a citywide typhoid epidemic in 1893, the *Atlanta Constitution*'s editor L. L. Knight wrote a fiery missive that described Atlanta as a disease-free haven. He wrote, "To look for a better atmosphere or a more salubrious climate, is like searching for the end of the rainbow, or trying to overtake the horizon."[21] To further quell rumors of disease from going public, the city council also enacted harsh criminal penalties for anyone caught spreading "false" news about epidemics within the city limits.[22] Under the 1897 ordinance, the punishment for spreading disease rumors that could "damage the status of the city" was sixty days of hard labor on the public chain gang.[23]

When the 1905 census exposed Atlanta's poor track record of disease prevention, the city's propaganda machine spun in its tracks, uncertain of who or what to blame. In its coverage of the census returns, the *Atlanta Constitution* finally admitted that the city had serious sanitation concerns, but it also played homage to some of the city's more harmful racial stereotypes. The article quoted Atlanta Board of Health president Dr. Bernard Wolff, who explained the city's high mortality this way: "What appears to be an abnormal death rate in Atlanta can, to an extent, be explained by the fact that 40 percent of our population is composed of negroes, with their notoriously unhygienic and unsanitary modes of living, and their established susceptibility to disease." In the same article, another doctor also emphasized the "tendency of the negro to avoid medical treatment whenever possible," and another reiterated the idea of "negro susceptibility" and "unhygienic methods of life."[24]

Still others, however, called for the city to improve garbage, sewer, and drinking water services for all residents. In Georgia, the 1903 state legislature created a Department of Public Health to study and prevent the spread of infectious disease in the state.[25] It was authorized to "investigate and report upon the water supply, sewerage, disposal of excreta, or ventilation" of any public place.[26] Atlanta, too, revived its own citywide Board of Health around the same time.[27] Both local and state health officials publicly pressured Atlanta to expand and improve its water and sewer systems to prevent disease.[28]

Unfortunately, any hopes for honest sanitation reform in Atlanta were dashed during the state's unusually negrophobic gubernatorial campaign of 1905. In a shameless bid for votes, candidates Hoke Smith and Clark Howell raced across Georgia, giving stump speeches that fomented white anger and fear toward the state's black population. In the city, Atlanta's white politicians followed suit, leading campaigns against "black vice" that relied heavily upon stereotypes of black men as sexual predators, violent criminals, and drunken self-abusers.[29] After an alleged attack on a white woman, racial tensions in Atlanta clashed in the three-night rampage of violence, arson, and looting now referred to as the Atlanta Race Riot of 1906.

In the months and years following the riot, the drumbeat of racism overtook the honest cries for sanitation reform, and race-oriented pseudoscience received as much attention as modern epidemiology. Dr. Charles W. Stiles, a renowned zoologist and public health reformer, claimed that the nation's urban hookworm epidemic was brought from Africa by slaves.[30] According to Stiles, white people became sick because they were exposed to African diseases, and black people were sickened by European diseases.[31] Segregation of the races, he said, was the only long-lasting cure for disease.

This belief appears to have been adopted by Atlanta city councilman Claude Ashley, who first proposed that the city enact residential segregation laws. In a letter to the newspaper, Ashley wrote that segregated housing was "for the betterment of the health" of the city.[32] The ordinance, Ashley claimed, would "wipe away the little huts occupied by both white and black and eradicate the breeding places of tuberculosis, smallpox, typhoid and other diseases."[33] He estimated that segregation would reduce the city's incidence of disease by at least 50 percent. This pseudoscientific racism dominated the city's discourse for another year until 1914, when a well-publicized incident forced the city's leaders to confront the damaging shortcomings of Atlanta's sanitation and health services.

Although many continued to choose race-baiting over honest science, one well-publicized 1915 incident began to redirect the public conversation toward sanitation reform. C. G. Lambert, one of Atlanta's most prominent businessmen, owned a lovely home on 14th Avenue, just one block away from the Murphys' Hillcrest estate and two blocks from Piedmont Park. One January morning, Lambert's live-in cook Suzie contracted a highly contagious, highly deadly form of diphtheria.

When Lambert and his physician engaged in a frenzied hospital search to relocate Suzie, the two stumbled upon a reality that, surprisingly, none of the city's white male leaders had ever noted before. There was not a single place in town that could treat a contagious black person. Suzie sat in an ambulance for nearly a day while the two men searched for a hospital, doctor's office, or nurse that could treat her. After hours of pleading, Atlanta's white hospital reluctantly accepted Suzie in the storage basement of their contagious disease center. The basement had no windows and no heat, but it was better than being left to die in the street.

While Suzie slowly recovered, the *Atlanta Constitution* ran a story detailing the incident. White Atlanta's initial reaction to this story was not one of sympathy for Suzie but of fear for themselves. Every white family who employed a black servant, the *Atlanta Constitution* claimed, was vulnerable to diseases from "the vast reservoir of the Black Peril in Atlanta."[34] Breathless accounts of the "immaculate" white household, struck by disease from an "ignorant, untended negro" were printed and reprinted in Atlanta's newspapers.[35] "The lives of white people are in danger," warned a local physician, "Every sick negro is a menace."[36]

Although couched in racism and fear-mongering, there was some truth to their concerns. It was pure fantasy to believe that 50,000 poor, mostly black, residents could live in abject squalor without impacting or infecting others. Social contact between classes and ethnicities was rare, but business arrangements frequently caused the two worlds to collide. Many of Atlanta's slum residents were employed in the city's service industry as shop boys, washerwomen, delivery men, shoe shiners, waiters, butlers, and even nurse-maids. These men and women were exposed to horrible, unsanitary conditions in their homes at night and then went to work every morning handling the food, clothing, and children of the privileged upper class.

After the incident with Suzie, many black leaders used the wave of publicity to advocate for better health and sanitation services for black neighborhoods and slum houses. Some, like W. E. B. Du Bois, were rightly indignant. He wrote,

> The Atlanta rich have wrung city taxes out of poor black and poor whites and then squandered wealth to lay mile upon mile of beautiful boulevard through silent and empty forests with mile upon mile of nine inch water mains and sewers of the latest design, which here and there rise grudgingly the spreading castles of the Suddenly Rich; but in the city's heart . . . the children sicken and die because there is no city water.[37]

Others, however, were more tempered in their response. In the wake of Atlanta's race riot and amid continuing racial tension, some of Atlanta's black leaders seemed concerned that calls for equality, or even charity, would fall on deaf ears. Sounds of alarm, on the other hand, were likely to be heard.

In a risky tactical move, some leaders played into white Atlanta's racial stereotypes. In a piece advocating for sanitation improvements in the slums, Pastor E. L. Carter wrote, "I'm pleading as much for the white man as I am for the negro. The reservoir of disease in our race menaces your race."[38] Methodist minister E. H. Oliver struck a similar tone while advocating for a black hospital and fines for slum-housing owners: "The thing to remember is that the white man, who rules the city and the south, for that matter, suffers most from the negro's disregard of sanitation. So I ask not for philanthropy, but that the white man conserve his own interest."[39] By playing into the white population's existing fears and stereotypes, Atlanta's black leaders hoped to rally white, middle-class support for substantial, long-lasting sanitation improvements in the slums.

At first, the fear tactics seemed to work. Immediately after Suzie's illness made headlines, the city established a small, makeshift hospital for black residents with contagious disease.[40] The "black man as menace" storyline, however, was a double-edged sword. Although it brought about some sanitation improvements, it also had the unintended effect of further rallying support for residential segregation.

For the next twenty years, Atlanta city councilmen would attempt to enact some form of segregated zoning throughout the city. From 1913 to 1922, Atlanta's attempts at segregated zoning were struck down by the Georgia Supreme Court as arbitrary exercises of policing powers.[41] Undeterred, the 1928 state legislature passed a constitutional amendment permitting segregated zoning, and the Atlanta City Council tweaked the language of its zoning laws to obscure their intent.[42] One ordinance, for example, prevented anyone from moving onto a street in which "the majority of the residences . . . are occupied by those with whom said person is forbidden to marry."[43] This had the practical effect of banning black people from moving onto an all-white street because racial intermarriage was illegal in Georgia at the time.

Prior to 1910, Atlanta's black residents were scattered in many different all-black or mixed-race communities throughout the city. In the aftermath of the race riot, and in the midst of the city's various segregated zoning laws, black Atlanta began to slowly consolidate into two large neighborhood areas, one in between downtown and Atlanta University, and the other on the east side of town now known as the Old Fourth Ward.[44] Some middle-income black neighborhoods, like Auburn Avenue, had paved roads, running water and underground sewers, but many of the lower-income black neighborhoods on the east side remained without city services for a long time. By the end of the 1920s, four out of five black homes were still without running water, and only 7 percent of black homes had a bathtub.[45]

Unsurprisingly, Atlanta still hadn't made a dint in its astronomical death rate. The city ranked first among the nation in diphtheria deaths, and the local typhoid rate was twice the average of other large cities.[46]

Although the 1920s saw little change in Atlanta city hall's attitude toward sanitation inequality, a quiet water law revolution was taking place elsewhere. For the first time in American history, courts and legislatures across the

nation began to hold cities liable for sewage discharges into American waterways. This seemingly subtle shift would drastically change the way Atlanta
and other cities treated their sewage and drinking water systems, and it would
eventually bring relief to Atlanta's disease-ridden slums.

By 1920, all of America had a serious raw sewage problem. The homes
of almost fifty million Americans were linked to underground sewer systems,
but only 20 percent of these systems treated the waste before discharging it
into a waterway.[47] According to legal historian William Andreen, many of
America's rivers "had become little more than sewers carrying a noxious mix
of sewage and industrial pollutants."[48] The sorry state of the country's waterways, and the growing expense of municipal drinking water filtration, revived
a decades-old debate over whether cities should be obligated to treat sewage
before discharging it into rivers and streams.

This debate had begun in the 1890s, when scientists at the Lawrence
Experimental Station discovered a way to filter sewage using sand beds.
Aside from primitive "sewage farming" that used human waste as compost
for crops, this filtering technology was the first practice to rid sewage of
harmful contaminants before its disposal or discharge.[49] At the same time,
however, two important breakthroughs in water-filtering technologies for
municipal drinking water intake systems also occurred. The new filters and
sewage treatment systems presented a choice for American cities and health
reformers. When designing its infrastructure, a city could choose to disinfect
its drinking water, treat its sewage discharges, or do both.

In the absence of a coordinated national strategy, cities made self-inter-
ested infrastructural investments. Local voters wanted to be assured that
their water supply was clean and disease free, and on a local scale, there
was tremendous political momentum in favor of adopting filtering technologies. Conversely, there was very little local support for wastewater treatment
because it was expensive and primarily benefited downstream communities.
Because of this, water filters were quickly adopted while wastewater treatment continued to be relatively rare.[50]

This created a positive feedback cycle: the presence of sewage in American waterways forced cities to adopt water filters, which encouraged politicians to skimp on wastewater treatment expenditures, which in turn caused
more sewage and increased the need for drinking water filtering. By the 1920s,
however, the cycle of increased sewage in waterways and increased filtering
of drinking water began to spiral out of control, and many municipalities
reached the technological limits of their filtering capability.

To curb the rising costs of drinking water filtration, many states attempted to develop a coordinated strategy to control the amount of sewage that could be legally dumped into waterways. During the first quarter of the century, at least seventeen states enacted some form of water quality laws, although these were mostly aimed at criminalizing the unsanitary acts of private individuals.[51] Some states, however, also began to replace their permissive discretionary language with language imposing a firm duty on municipalities to provide proper sanitation to all citizens.[52]

Despite the language in the books, the statutes were weak and enforcement was tepid if not completely absent. At the same time that states began to enact pollution statutes, however, American courts also began to use common law nuisance principles to address the effects of municipal sewage discharges on downstream users. These common law efforts appeared to have much greater impact than the state laws. In the first third of the twentieth century, at least nineteen different state courts held that municipalities could be liable to downstream water users for damages from their sewage discharges.[53]

In anticipation of common law liability, Atlanta had already begun to treat some of the sewage in its existing underground sanitary sewers. In 1913 and 1914, Atlanta constructed three sewage treatment plants at existing outfall points on Proctor, Peachtree, and Intrenchment creeks.[54] Although primitive by today's standards, the plants were of the latest design at the time and even pioneered some cutting-edge filtering technologies.[55] All of the city's sewer lines were routed to one of the three facilities. Despite the new plants, the city continued to service the existing outhouses with night soil carts, and the cart dumping grounds constantly leached harmful contaminants into local streams and the Chattahoochee River.

If it weren't for two revolutionary Georgia Supreme Court cases in the 1920s, Atlanta might have waited another few decades before digging sewer lines in the slums. Before these cases, Georgia state courts had only ruled that sewer discharges directly onto another person's property were a nuisance.[56] To avoid liability under state common law, therefore, Atlanta only had to avoid directly dumping its sewage onto private property; runoff and discharges into waterways were fair game. In the 1926 case *Watkins v. Pepperton Cotton Mills*, however, the court extended its definition of nuisance to include sewage discharges into waterways that impacted downstream water users.[57] Two years later, in *Loughridge v. City of Dalton*, a farmer used that expanded interpretation of nuisance to successfully sue the city of Dalton, Georgia, for dumping sewage into a river the plaintiff used for irrigation. The *Loughridge* court ordered the city of Dalton to either pay damages to the farmer or to treat its sewage discharges.

These two cases, *Watkins* and *Loughridge*, set off shockwaves in municipal offices across the state. In the span of a few years, raw sewage discharges and night soil cart dumping grounds had transitioned from undesirable but accepted practices into glaring and costly legal liabilities.

Atlanta's city leaders were especially concerned. Although the city treated its sewer wastewater, runoff from night soil cart dumping grounds and from industrial sources was so great "that most of the waterways were offensive to sight and smell."[58] Officials in the downstream city of Columbus had been emboldened by the court rulings, and they also became more outspoken in their complaints over the Chattahoochee's water quality. "We have borne with the present conditions only in the hope that Atlanta would correct the matter without the necessity of taking the case to court," wrote one Columbus opinion editorial writer. "In the latter event there would be no question of a result in favor of Columbus."[59]

Atlanta officials seemed to agree. Atlanta mayor Isaac Ragsdale led the charge for expanded sewers in 1929 and urged the city to approve another bond to fund the work.[60] "Unless this is done," he warned the public, "the city is liable to become involved in serious legal trouble."[61] Before the stock market crashed in November, Ragsdale's municipal crews were able to extend over fifteen miles of new sewer lines in the city.[62]

The Depression crippled Atlanta's ability to finance sewer projects, and it also heightened the intensity of the city's urban slum problems. Although roughly half its population was unemployed by 1930, the city of Atlanta was still relatively prosperous in comparison to the blight-stricken countryside surrounding it.[63] Every day, an increasing number of rural refugees relocated to the city, and as the depression continued, the new residents also became increasingly destitute.

Like so many other cities during the depression, Atlanta looked to Roosevelt's New Deal agencies for aid. Atlanta and Fulton County requested funding for a sewer trunk line that would extend from the city to the rapidly growing Fulton suburbs to the north.[64] At first, Atlanta's request for assistance was denied.[65] Then, the short-lived Civil Works Administration gave the city a one-million-dollar grant, but Roosevelt dissolved the agency before Atlanta could begin construction.[66] For another two years, Atlanta appealed to other New Deal agencies, all of which refused to loan the city money.[67]

Atlanta's persistence finally paid off in 1935, when the Works Progress Administration agreed to partially fund the city's sewer lines. Atlanta voters approved a one-million-dollar bond for the project, and Fulton County set aside $400,000.[68] The local funds paid for a new water purification system for Atlanta's drinking water supply. In return, the federal government extended and enlarged the city's sewer lines and built new sewage treatment plants.[69]

Although the New Deal projects connected hundreds of homes to sewer lines and water mains, many of Atlanta's poorest black neighborhoods continued to suffer without plumbing or drinking water after the expansion. This time the oversight, however, seems to have stemmed from practical considerations rather than racial animus or political maneuvering. There was simply no efficient way to connect slum housing to plumbing. Slum housing blocks had no meaningful street design, and the ramshackle structures were often moved, expanded, or rebuilt. Designing a plumbing system to connect to an existing slum shack made about as much sense as building a connection line to a tent.

In the poorest neighborhoods, therefore, the federal Works Progress Administration constructed centralized cement privies in lieu of underground plumbing. In an oral history interview decades later, factory worker Ardell Henry remembered when a cement privy was installed in his neighborhood: "They used to build outside toilets. And, man, after they started building them things—they put a cement stool on them and all, and a thing that went like you used in a regular bathroom, the lid and all—and that was uptown. They thought they had something good."[70] In these areas, even small improvements were cause for celebration.

Some neighborhoods, however, were beyond repair. After decades without trash collection services, some of the city's creek beds were completely indistinguishable from the town's dump. The banks were lined with layers of household trash, rusted metal, broken furniture, and burnt appliances.[71] Aside the creeks were shacks built from moldy planks that slumped with age. Their walls contained holes where rainwater, wind, and rodents flowed freely between the creek bed garbage and the homes' interior rooms. These neighborhoods could not be helped by a single cement privy.

Increasingly, federal and local officials began to believe that the only way to improve these areas would be to start again from scratch. As the country gradually pulled itself out of the Depression, Roosevelt's New Deal agencies started to plan "slum clearance" projects across the country.[72] Two Atlanta slums were chosen by Public Works Administration head Harold Ickes as the first areas to be demolished and rebuilt under the new national program.[73] Atlanta nominated 279 shacks in Beaver Slide and Techwood for demolition.[74] Described as "a ragged panorama of . . . unpainted, weather-beaten frame houses, unpaved streets and barren yards," these areas were the poorest, most unsanitary neighborhoods in the city.[75] In the three years before being cleared, twenty-one babies had died there before reaching one year of age.[76] Another thirteen people had died from tuberculosis.[77] And four out of every five homes in the area lacked an inside bath or running water.[78]

On the sunny Saturday morning of September 19, 1934, Ickes ceremoniously dynamited the first Beaver Slide shack.[79] The already weak structural supports of the tenement house had been sawed in half, making dynamite demolition almost entirely unnecessary. The building could have been pushed over by a light breeze. "When Ickes thrust the plunger," recalled slum reformer Charles Palmer, "moldy planks flew sky-high, and only a hole in the ground remained."[80] Ickes demolished another shack in the Techwood neighborhood that same day.[81]

In a lofty speech following demolition, Ickes lauded the project as a "milestone in the social history of America."[82] But he also admonished the crowd:

> As a people we ought to be as deeply ashamed of our slums as we were about our child labor. Personally we have all rejoiced that we have not had to live in slums. We have hoped that the revolving wheel of fortune would never mean that our children would be forced by circumstances to eke out an existence in any such neighborhood. We have known that they are a disgrace to our civilization.[83]

From that day forward, Ickes promised, the federal government would launch a nationwide program to eradicate slums and insure that "every child born under the American flag shall have equal opportunity."[84]

Over the next year, the Public Works Administration built two of the nation's first housing projects in the place of the demolished shantytowns. In Beaver Slide, a black housing project called University Homes was constructed.[85] The demolished Techwood slum became an all-white housing project with the same name.[86]

Although many families' lives were improved because of the projects, the program failed to live up to Ickes's promise of creating "equal opportunity" for all Atlantans. The biggest problem was that the new buildings were nice—*too* nice. The apartments were spacious and had modern fixtures and amenities; the buildings even had outside pools for residents. Middle-class families jockeyed for units in the new structures, pushing out the more needy families whose homes had been demolished. At $7.30 a month, rent for Techwood and University was also more than any of the former neighborhood residents could afford.[87] Instead of moving into the new projects, the area's slum dwellers moved into nearby shantytowns and exacerbated existing overcrowding problems there. While the area surrounding the new housing projects slowly gentrified into a middle-class enclave, many of Atlanta's neighboring slums continued to decline.

Still, Atlanta politicians were able to point to the success of the housing project areas as a sign that the program was working as planned. Before the projects, the city council claimed, the cleared slums accounted for 69 percent of tuberculosis, 59 percent of arrests, and 72 percent of juvenile delinquency. As a result of reduction in these figures, the city council cited annual savings of $1,175,000 on police and health expenditures in the area of Techwood alone.[88] Of course, the city council neglected to mention that all of Techwood neighborhood's former residents had moved away to other slums.

After Techwood and University provided a superficial solution for Atlanta's slum crisis, the problem receded far into the background of the city's public dialogue. Atlanta continued to gradually add more public housing, but many pockets of the city still lacked basic sanitation.

The condition of these slums garnered little media attention until one summer day in 1947. That morning, *Atlanta Constitution* reporter Albert Riley decided to take a walk through Atlanta's slums—not the ones that had been gentrified by public housing projects but the ones that had remained unimproved and ignored. What he saw disgusted him. "Neither pictures nor words can bring the stink to your nostrils, nor show the crawling maggots or swarming flies," he wrote.[89] "It's a place where human beings exist in appalling disease-breeding, crime-breeding filth and squalor."[90]

The next morning, the paper received nonstop phone calls about the story.[91] Later in the week, letters started pouring into the newspaper's office.[92] Riley and his managing editor, Josh P. Skinner, seized upon the initial write-up's success and turned the story into a Pulitzer Prize–nominated series.[93] By the time Riley finished the last piece in his exposé, over forty of Atlanta's largest civic organizations had formed a coalition to solve Atlanta's slum problem.

The new coalition pushed the city council to find a legal solution to the area's sanitation woes. Atlanta already had health and building code regulations, but they were not being enforced in poor neighborhoods.[94] Under pressure from Atlanta's new reform coalition, the council agreed to create a supervisory board and add enforcement provisions to the existing laws.[95] The new sections also authorized the city to prosecute slum landlords for creating unsanitary living conditions on their rental properties.

The city council also formed a blue-ribbon Slum Clearance Committee.[96] The committee's initial inspection found that at least 32,000 housing units across the city were not meeting city health codes but were reparable.[97] Starting in January of 1948, the city planned to send fire and health inspectors to order the repairs necessary to bring each building that was out of compliance up to code.[98] In addition to the 32,000 salvageable properties, another six thousand units were found to be beyond repair.[99] These were all condemned and scheduled to be razed to the ground.[100] The city council recruited private building companies to submit plans to build safe housing in the cleared areas.[101]

Heeding the call to duty, as well as the lure of potential profits, the National Association of Home Builders joined with a local Atlanta group named the Citizens for Better Housing and began a five-year slum clearance program in the city.[102] Atlanta condemned buildings, which the Citizens for Better Housing then purchased. The group tore down the buildings, bulldozed the rubble into piles, and carted the waste to the dump. In just months, a neighborhood slum could be transformed into a clean, empty lot. In the place of the cleared slums, contractors erected new buildings with water and sewer connections in each apartment.

Today, the city's slum clearance program receives mixed reviews from historians. Many displaced slum residents were never relocated into new homes, and the program created an unknowable number of homeless people. The new housing was also often segregated, thus further solidifying existing informal racial boundaries throughout the city.[103] Despite these shortcomings, however, the city's slum clearance campaign did achieve an important milestone: by the 1950s, for the first time in Atlanta's history, every home in the city was hooked up to running water.

# 4

# TAMING THE FLOW

On March 1, 1950, Atlanta mayor William Berry Hartsfield squinted into the early morning sunlight as he walked from the doors of City Hall to a long, black sedan idling at the curb. On either side of the car's front, a flag hung limply. One bore the American stars and stripes and the other portrayed the state of Georgia's seal in a blue block adjacent to the unmistakable red, white, and blue cross of the Confederacy. Hartsfield climbed into the back seat, and his driver shut the door behind him before climbing into the car himself.

The car looped around a few blocks and then returned to an idle, this time toward the front of a nearly one-mile-long line of more than two hundred sedans. Some of the cars bore flags, others held thick bows from which loops of red, white, and blue bunting hung. After many noisy minutes of slamming car doors and curbside chatting, the first of the motorcade's police escorts edged slowly into the road and the long line of sedans followed.

The motorcade passed by many blocks of urban streetlights that were strung together with flags, ribbons, and streamers. Underneath the decorations, thousands of spectators screamed and waved. The crowds began to thin as Hartsfield's car wound through town and drove past the northern suburbs. By the time the parade turned onto the cracked and narrow rural road to Buford, Georgia, the only remaining onlookers were isolated farm families, watching and waving from front porches and lawn chairs.

On the hour-long drive out of town, Hartsfield would have had a rare moment to sit and reflect. There were certainly many worries to occupy the mayor's mind. Earlier in the year, the details of his plan to expand Atlanta's city limits had leaked to the press, and the news had been met with stiff opposition from citizens in Atlanta's unincorporated northern suburbs. Also, in less than a month, the U.S. Supreme Court was scheduled to rule on the constitutionality of Georgia's county unit voting system, a scheme that awarded a grossly disproportionate amount of voting power to rural residents at the expense of urban ones. Hartsfield had railed publicly against county unit voting, and in response to his position, he was still receiving threatening calls from Klansmen across the state.

Hartsfield's administration hadn't been all doom and gloom and racial tension; there had been bright spots, too. As his car lurched from the paved street to a slippery and rutted mud road, one of Hartsfield's crowning achievements came into view. It was a simple field, unremarkable except for the large grandstand built upon it and the black sedans in regalia circling its edge. This field was the key to one of Hartsfield's grandest dreams, and this day was the culmination of decades of media blitzes, backroom discussions, plaintive letters, and heavy-handed lobbying.

Around the grandstand gathered a veritable who's who of Georgia's political elite: U.S. Senators Richard B. Russell and Walter F. George, Representatives James C. Davis and John S. Wood, and Governor Herman Talmadge.[1] Hartsfield joined them, and he waited as five thousand spectators filled the field and overflowed onto the thick muck of the overused road.

Later that day, the politicians would give rousing speeches and the band would play soaring anthems, but the most emotional moment, the moment that everyone came to see, occurred when Hartsfield and six others lined up in the field with shovels. In choreographed synchronicity, the men dipped their spades into the ground and overturned the first few clods of dirt to officially begin construction of the Buford Dam.

The planned Buford Dam was a behemoth. When finished, it would stretch 1,639 feet across the Chattahoochee River.[2] Behind it, the pooled water would create a 37,000-acre reservoir with a 540-mile shoreline that zigzagged through the area's hilly terrain.[3] Construction would cost $42 million dollars and would last for the greater part of the decade.[4] Hartsfield believed that it was also the first step toward turning Atlanta into an inland sea port, and he knew that it would provide his city water security for decades to come.

The Buford Dam was a classic pork barrel project in an era of big plans, big dams, and big spending. On the same day that Hartsfield ceremoniously began construction in Buford, thousands of men were working on similar projects across the nation. In Idaho, crews neared completion on the Anderson Ranch Dam, which was at the time the highest earthfill dam in the world.[5]

In North Dakota, construction was underway on the Garrison Dam, which was just one link in chain of one hundred dams planned for the Missouri basin.[6] In the decade prior, many of the nation's largest dams had been built, including Washington's famed Grand Coulee dam on the Columbia River, as well as California's Shasta and Friant dams and Colorado's Green Mountain Dam.

In total, more than four thousand dams were constructed in the 1940s, and another twenty thousand were built in the twenty years after the Buford Dam's groundbreaking.[7] The dams were built by private individuals, public utilities, and state and local governments, but the king of dams—the group that built many of the largest dams in the nation—was the Army Corps of Engineers.

President Thomas Jefferson had established the Army Corps of Engineers in 1802.[8] Although it began solely as a military branch, the corps began to transition into internal civil works projects in 1824.[9] That year, Congress created a Board of Internal Improvements to study and expand upon the young nation's transportation network, and President James Monroe assigned two army engineers to the three-person board.[10] As part of the Internal Improvement Board, the corps was charged with improving the nation's water-based transportation network. As a result, the first fifty years of corps projects all revolved around linking navigable waterways to strategic commercial centers.

As the country expanded, so did the corps. By the end of the Civil War, the corps was working on projects across the entire length and breadth of the nation.[11] The corps opened harbors for steamships on the Great Lakes, built the Chesapeake and Ohio canals, and expanded previously unnavigable parts of the Mississippi, Missouri, and Ohio rivers.[12]

The corps was still an obscure, fledgling agency when it first worked on the Apalachicola-Chattahoochee-Flint River basin. In 1828 and 1831, the corps removed large obstructions to barge traffic from the river.[13] The corps returned again in 1874 to dredge a six-foot-deep, one-hundred-foot-wide navigation channel from Apalachicola, Florida, to Columbus, Georgia.[14]

Soon thereafter, the Army Corps expanded beyond navigation. Although it had previously dabbled in flood control issues, the corps was first officially authorized to work on flood control projects on the Sacramento and Mississippi rivers in 1917.[15] Later, the groundbreaking Flood Control Act of 1936 solidified the corps's position as the go-to agency for all major flood-related projects. The 1938 Flood Control Act again expanded the corps's authorized projects to include dams used for power generation.[16]

By the 1940s, the corps had become a massive bureaucracy with broad authority over the nation's infrastructure projects. It had the authority to build dams and dredge rivers, dig canals and reservoirs, produce and market hydroelectric power, and allocate surplus water for agricultural, domestic, and industrial uses.[17]

Although the corps is most well known today for its massive and controversial dam projects, the agency initially refused to build dams at all.[18] For its early flood control works, the corps repeatedly argued that dams and reservoirs were not feasible,[19] and it chose instead to build levees along the river banks to hold in floodwaters.[20] The corps stubbornly held onto its "levees-only" doctrine until 1927, when the Mississippi River broke through corps levees in 145 places in what continues to be the largest flood disaster in United States history.[21] Millions of acres of land were flooded, over seven hundred thousand people lost their homes, and over $300 million worth of property was destroyed.[22]

A critical backlash against the corps and its levees-only system followed. Other state-funded projects had built reservoirs for flood control,[23] and many across the nation were critical of the corps's refusal to build similar structures along the Mississippi.[24] Some even called for the Army Corps to withdraw from all public works projects entirely.[25]

In an official report on the floods, President Hoover wrote, "The levee system needs to be revised . . . and above all we must [build] some other safety devices."[26] One of his primary suggestions was for the Army Corps to build multipurpose reservoirs for flood control and power generation. Over the next several decades, the corps did just that: from 1930 to 1970, the Army Corps built two hundred dams and reservoirs and proposed another two hundred for future construction.[27] By the time Mayor Hartsfield began to scheme about public works on the Chattahoochee, the corps was building hydroelectric dams all across the nation, including many in the Apalachicola-Chattahoochee-Flint (ACF) River basin.

By many accounts, the northern Chattahoochee was an ideal site for a dam project. A large dam above the city would release water at regular intervals, maintaining a steady flow of water below. This would ensure a reliable supply of water year-round for Atlanta's municipal needs and alleviate some of the flooding problems that had hindered the city's industrial and residential growth. The area also needed an additional electrical supply source to generate power for the thousands of north Georgia homes that had been tied to the power grid after the implementation of Roosevelt's New Deal Rural Electrification Act. The dam could also help efforts to expand navigation from the Gulf of Mexico to Atlanta.

Over the course of the first half of the twentieth century, corps officials produced extensive reports on the feasibility of large water projects in
the ACF basin.[28] At the same time, Congress began to consider hydropower
development along the Chattahoochee.[29] On April 28, 1936, the Committee
on Rivers and Harbors requested that the corps compile and analyze their
data and recommend projects to improve the basin.[30]

In response, corps district engineer Colonel R. Park began work on a
detailed report on the geography, history, and potential development opportunities for the entire ACF basin.[31] The "Park Report," as it was later known,
became the basis for all future corps construction projects in the basin. The
report identified many different potential dam sites, including one named
the "Roswell" site. This Roswell plan, located sixteen miles north of Atlanta
and two and a half miles upstream from the Roswell highway bridge, was the
precursor to the project that would later be sited in Buford.[32]

The Park Report weighed the monetary significance of each of the following benefits: public transportation savings, hydroelectric power, national
defense value, commercial value, recreational value, and value as a source
of municipal water supply.[33] In the report, municipal water supply was val-
ued at $0 because "there is apparently no immediate necessity for increased
water supply in this area."[34] The report did note, however, that "the prospect
of future demand is not improbable."[35] It concluded that the benefits from
hydroelectric power and navigation would be the most significant.

If the Chattahoochee became navigable up to Atlanta, the city and its
local industries would benefit greatly from the availability of barge transportation. During the 1930s, when the Park Report was made, the railroad
was the only viable transportation industry servicing Atlanta; automobiles
and airliners hadn't yet become popular forms of interstate shipping. In
the absence of waterborne competition, rail's dominance over the shipping
market permitted it to artificially inflate freight rates in landlocked areas like
Atlanta. If someone were to ship a one-hundred-pound plate glass panel
from Philadelphia, for example, the cost of rail freight would be sixty-six
cents to Atlanta but only thirty-one cents to the nearby port city of Savannah.[36] With no other viable options aside from rail, Atlanta's industries suffered from high shipping rates and a competitive disadvantage in relation to
industries with a port.

Despite the significant benefits for Atlanta, however, the Park Report
concluded that the river's geography made navigation projects north of
Columbus, Georgia, too expensive to complete.[37] Like almost all rivers, the
Chattahoochee experienced the most significant elevation changes in the earliest, northernmost portions of the river. Between Gainesville and Columbus

alone, the river plummeted from an elevation of 371 feet to 190 feet.[38] To make this steep section navigable, the corps would have to build a series of smaller locks to act as a staircase for barge traffic. The locks were significantly more expensive than a single large dam, and the Army Corps believed that even substantial benefits to Atlanta's industries would not offset the additional cost.

Unsurprisingly, the decision to not pursue navigability above Columbus received a lot of criticism from Atlanta's business elite. Coca-Cola, Rich's Department Store, Gulf Oil, and many other large corporations stood to benefit greatly if Atlanta became a port, and these interests commanded a strong influence over Mayor Hartsfield's administration. "When Hartsfield had to make a tough decision," wrote Louis Williams, "he would gather the city's business and political leaders in Woodruff's private dining room at the Coca-Cola Company."[39] The CEOs of Rich's, Gulf Oil, Trust Company Bank, and First National Bank were among Hartsfield's closest personal friends and political allies.

At the urging of his friends, Hartsfield championed the further development of navigation to Atlanta. In an interview with *Atlanta Constitution* reporters, Mayor Hartsfield expressed his concern that Atlanta would become a "railway island" in the midst of other cities that had waterborne navigation.[40] At the time, only three cities with more than 300,000 residents were without water transportation: Dallas, Denver, and Atlanta.[41] "Wake up or we will be out in the cold," said Hartsfield.

Despite Hartsfield's protestations, the corps held firm to its original assessment. Another Army Corps report, which was supposed to be the final report on development of the ACF basin, was completed in April of 1945.[42] In it, the Army Corps recommended creating a nine-foot navigable channel from the Apalachicola Bay up to Columbus, but limited the project scope above Columbus to only flood control and power development.[43] The Army Corps estimated the total cost of the ACF project to be $200 million.[44] Adding navigation up to Atlanta would cost an additional $23.5 million for locks on the dams and blasting through the area's rocky riverbed.[45] The corps thought the additional cost would not be justified by the estimated increase in barge traffic to Atlanta.[46]

Before the corps could even officially release its report, Mayor Hartsfield and an army of Atlanta businessmen had already mounted a public campaign against it. In anticipation of the report's negative findings, Hartsfield and other industry representatives had written a petition for a restudy.[47]

Hartsfield, along with members of the Atlanta Freight Bureau, the Georgia Agricultural and Industrial Development Board, the Atlanta Chamber of Commerce, and other state agencies, descended upon the U.S. Board of Engineers for Rivers and Harbors on April 2, 1945, in Washington, D.C.[48] After hearing the Atlanta representatives' pleas, the board decided to refer the issue back to the Army Corp's Atlanta office for reexamination.[49]

Hartsfield convinced the Georgia Agricultural and Industrial Development Board to partially pay for a private survey on the Chattahoochee's navigation prospects.[50] The board hired the New York–based engineering firm Frederick H. Harris, Inc., to complete the survey.[51] This survey was never designed to be particularly impartial; one firm engineer described the company's goal saying, "We will leave no stone unturned to bring navigation to Atlanta."[52]

If Atlanta was going to convince the corps to extend its navigation channel, it would need to show that the benefits of the project would outweigh its hefty price tag. The Harris firm sent twelve engineers to Atlanta to interview area merchants and shipping companies.[53] They created a questionnaire that asked businessmen to estimate the total volume of waterborne traffic that they currently used, the destination of the traffic, and the volume that they expected to ship in ten years if the river were navigable.[54] The survey only took four months to complete.[55] By August, the engineers had selected areas in Atlanta for the future port site.[56]

The survey results were predictably in favor of the navigation channel. Harris's engineers concluded that developing a nine-foot navigation channel to Atlanta would be both "practical and profitable."[57] Their survey indicated that, if the channel were constructed, at least two and a half million tons of freight would be shipped on the river each year, saving area businesses a total of three million dollars annually.[58] The surveyors also found, however, that the corps had underestimated the project's total cost. Instead of $23.5 million, Harris's engineers concluded that the navigation channel would cost at least $40 million, plus an additional $5 million to construct a port in Atlanta.[59] Still, they argued, the benefits were so large that even a $60 million project would be justified.[60]

The same week that the Harris study was released, Atlanta officials scheduled a meeting with the corps.[61] They were joined by industry representatives and politicians from many of the small towns between Columbus and Atlanta.[62] At the meeting, only the railroad representatives spoke out against the project, arguing that the navigation channel would "subsidize" water transportation to an area that was already being served well.[63] Considering how many millions of federal dollars had subsidized railroad expansion, this argument was taken with a grain of salt.[64]

Atlanta was granted its navigation request but only for a flickering moment. After the meeting, the Army Corps's revised report declared that navigation was the primary purpose of the Buford Dam project.[65] The federal government agreed to blast the channel and build the locks; Hartsfield agreed that Atlanta would pay for port construction.[66]

The agreement, however, was short-lived. By 1946, many of the corps's initial reasons for developing navigation to Atlanta were beginning to become outdated. Since Park's report, other forms of transportation aside from barges had grown to compete with rail. Highway improvements had made trucks more viable, and Atlanta's Candler Airport had become the nation's busiest airport thanks to its status as a military airfield.[67] Furthermore, a 1940 Interstate Commerce Commission regulation had effectively required railroad companies to charge all eastern cities the same baseline rate for freight.[68]

Realizing that it had been strong-armed a little too forcefully by Hartsfield, the corps quickly backpedaled from its determination that navigation would be the project's primary purpose. In less than a year, the corps revised its report a final time, listing hydropower as the project's most important goal. Navigation above Columbus, the report concluded, was simply not feasible.

Not to be outdone, Atlanta's political leaders switched tactics. Instead of pushing for a complete project with a series of locks, they focused on getting a large dam that could make future navigational projects more feasible. The dam would still provide a number of benefits to Atlanta aside from navigability. It would generate enough hydroelectric power to significantly lower energy rates, and its reservoir and scheduled dam releases would add an additional element of predictability to the city's water supply and flood control planning.

The corps had already accounted for flood control, navigation, and energy production in its feasibility analysis; the only benefit that was inadequately recognized was the dam's contribution to the city water supply. If the corps wouldn't build a dam for navigational purposes, Hartsfield and his compatriots believed, perhaps Atlanta's water supply needs would persuade them?

In truth, the touted benefits to Atlanta's water supply were more than just a political ploy; the city actually was running out of water. When Atlanta first drew water from the river in 1893, city leaders believed that the Chattahoochee's natural flow would provide enough water for the city forever. After just fifty years of growth, however, Atlanta had already begun to reach the limits of the great river's natural water supply.

Residential uses accounted for most of Atlanta's increased demand. The city's infrastructure improvements brought running water to every household, and a new boom in population brought more and more water users into the city every day. In just thirty years, Atlanta's water works went from providing water to roughly three thousand homes to providing water to more than fifty thousand.

Aided by a booming wartime economy and the Hartsfield administration's pro-business atmosphere, the city's industrial and manufacturing sectors also grew significantly during and in between World War I and II. Marietta won a contract for a massive Bell Bomber plant that employed thirty thousand people.[69] Ford and GM opened car manufacturing plants, and Coca-Cola continued to expand its production in the city.[70] Other industries, like chicken processing and timber distribution, expanded rapidly in the area as well.[71] All of the industries relied on Chattahoochee water to operate.

By 1940, the city was drawing more water from the Chattahoochee than was available in the entire river during the area's worst recorded drought.[72] The city had doubled its water usage in just twenty years and was likely to do so again in the coming decades.[73] Atlanta consumed 12.6 billion gallons of water from the Chattahoochee that year and would draw even more from the river every year after that.[74]

Atlanta upgraded, expanded, and improved its waterworks to meet rising demands. The city constructed two additional massive water mains alongside the original pipe from the Chattahoochee pumping station to Hemphill treatment plant.[75] Hemphill's reservoir was expanded repeatedly, so that by the 1940s, it was three times its original size.[76] The plant pumped water into 675 miles of iron water mains that spread like capillaries across the city.[77] Above ground, meters calculated end user flow rates at sixty thousand different points in Atlanta and another ten thousand outside city limits.[78] Every year, another two thousand new meters were added to Atlanta's lines.[79]

In 1940, over three hundred thousand people lived in Atlanta's city center.[80] Population in the city's outer suburban ring was still just a fraction of the city's population, but these residential areas were growing quickly as well. Atlanta's water infrastructure was sufficient to support its inner-city residents, and the city worked cooperatively with the outer-ring communities to expand their suburban residential services.

Some Atlanta suburbs grew large enough to construct or expand their own waterworks independent from Atlanta's system. DeKalb County, home to many of the city's new northern suburbs, replaced its old Decatur City plant with a large-scale water treatment facility in 1941.[81] Like Atlanta's system, DeKalb also drew water from the Chattahoochee River.[82]

DeKalb's new pumping station piped water into a storage lake two miles north of Doraville, where a large purifying plant treated the water before diverting it into an adjacent thirty-acre reservoir.[83] One principal main took water from the plant to Decatur City, with offshoot lines flowing to the fast-growing communities of Doraville, Chamblee, Brookhaven, Druid Hills, Avondale, Scottsdale, and Panthersville.[84] The plant had a capacity of four million gallons a day and serviced forty thousand people when it went online.[85]

The suburban city of Marietta also required new infrastructure to meet its growing demand. By 1942, the town was consuming twenty million gallons of Chattahoochee water a month.[86] When the city won its bid to become home to the Bell Bomber plant, it needed to increase withdrawals by 50 percent to meet the new plant's demand.[87] Marietta entered into a contract to buy water from the City of Atlanta.[88] Atlanta agreed to extend its water mains to connect to Marietta's and developed plans to construct a new million-dollar filtering plant to supplement its existing Hemphill Station.[89]

Atlanta also entered into short-term contracts to supply water to the southern suburbs of East Point, College Park, and Hapeville.[90] Demand in these communities began exceeding their well water supply in 1940, and suburban taps periodically ran dry during droughts or freezes.[91] During long winters, the communities would tap into Atlanta's water lines for emergency relief.[92]

The metro water system's infrastructure was built so that sharing could occur easily. Fulton County, DeKalb County, Decatur City, Atlanta, and then Marietta all maintained water main connection points with other systems. If any system broke down, it could immediately receive water from a neighboring municipality by just opening a few valves.[93] As more suburban communities became reliant on Atlanta's water supply and the Chattahoochee River, the city's waterworks engineers began to advocate for a new water supply source outside the Chattahoochee River basin.

Even by the 1940s, Atlanta's average daily use was still nowhere near the average capacity of the river, but averages are deceptive. Atlanta's water use fluctuated greatly as did the river levels. The Chattahoochee's normal flow of 217 million gallons a day was five times greater than Atlanta's average withdrawals.[94] The Chattahoochee, however, was rarely "normal." It was prone to periods of extreme flooding and equally extreme drought.[95] River levels also fluctuated predictably with the seasons, reaching low summer flows of only 160 million gallons a day.[96]

At the same time, Atlanta's consumption spiked in the mornings and evenings and rose steadily during summer months. If the area experienced a drought, outdoor watering increases would drive the city's consumption even higher. If this peak demand occurred during low flow, Atlanta's pipes would need to withdraw more than half the river's water to keep pace with demand.

Even during normal days, the city was taking out enough water to impact downstream communities. Under Georgia common law, Atlanta was not legally allowed to withdraw water in a way that would materially interfere with other reasonable uses of the river.[97] Thus, if Atlanta took out so much water that other cities didn't have enough drinking water, or other industries couldn't operate, Georgia courts could potentially order Atlanta to decrease its water withdrawals.

Atlanta had not been sued by anyone downstream, but the waterworks officials felt that it was only a matter of time before Columbus pursued legal action against the city and its ever increasing water withdrawals. City engineers estimated that Atlanta would need to triple its available water supply to meet the city's long-term projected demand without impacting downstream use.[98]

In light of the city's increasing demand, Hartsfield began to investigate water supply. When the city and state hired the Harris firm to complete the navigation survey of the Chattahoochee, the firm was specifically asked to "devise means for adequate water supply in the future."[99] Hartsfield directed the firm to arrive at a plan to expand Atlanta's water supply to accommodate more than one million residents.[100]

The firm's study discussed the metro area water supply almost as much as navigation.[101] Operating a dam, the engineers argued, would cost Atlanta only a small fraction of what another comparable water supply project would cost.[102] The study found that the navigation channel would save Atlanta "several million dollars in capital investment" in reservoirs and other water supply improvements.[103]

Thus, when the corps began to deemphasize the navigational benefits of a northern Chattahoochee Dam, Hartsfield and his political allies switched tactics and began to advocate for the dam as a possible solution to Atlanta's water concerns. An additional benefit of a nine-foot-deep navigation channel in Atlanta, Hartsfield argued, was the "preservation of the flow of the Chattahoochee River, which at the present time is the only source of water supply for the state's largest city."[104] In another speech promoting the navigation

project, Hartsfield warned, "Within ten years, we must do something to provide an adequate water supply."[105]

Hartsfield issued a similar refrain during a 1947 Senate Appropriations
Committee meeting. In the event of a drought, he argued, Atlanta would face
severe shortages and be forced to ration water. Because the dam could release
additional water from the reservoir in times of low flow, Hartsfield felt that
the Buford Dam project was a necessary component of Atlanta's long-term
water supply strategy. The mayor's handwringing over water scarcity continued into the fall, when the Senate approved the first $250,000 in funding for
planning the Buford Dam.

The final report on development of the ACF was submitted to Congress
by Brigadier General James B. Newman Jr. in 1947.[106] The Newman Report
recommended extensive dam construction along the entire Apalachicola-
Chattahoochee-Flint River system and included plans for a dam north of
Atlanta.[107]

The report identified hydropower as the "principal value" of the corps
project but also specified the value of navigation improvements. The report
also acknowledged that municipal water supply improvements were an "incidental" benefit of the proposed reservoir, noting: "If the regulating storage
reservoir . . . could be located above Atlanta, it would greatly increase the
minimum flow in the river . . . thereby producing considerable incidental benefits by reinforcing and safeguarding the water supply of the metropolitan
area.[108] Importantly, however, the Newman Report concluded by listing only
three "authorized purposes" for the proposed Buford Dam: flood control,
navigation, and power.

Congress approved the corps's report and permitted dam construction
in the Rivers and Harbors Act of 1946.[109] Approval was only the first step,
however. Next, Atlanta would need to get federal funding for construction.

At this stage in the process, Atlanta politicos determined once again to
switch tactics. The project couldn't get full federal funding if the dam and
reservoir were seen as nothing more than a municipal water source.[110] By
1948, the federal government was requiring many cities to contribute funds
to Army Corps projects that were designed, in part, to assure a city's water
supply.[111] Atlanta Freight Bureau head J. M. Cooper warned Hartsfield that
emphasizing the water supply issue would be "a wide open invitation for
some of the Republicans up there to insist on Atlanta paying a good part of
the cost."[112]

Hartsfield and others tried to deemphasize the city's water supply concerns during a January 1948 House Subcommittee on Appropriations hearing.

Although he admitted that the city's water supply would benefit from the project, Hartsfield stressed that "Atlanta should not be put in the category of such cities in the arid places in the West or flat plain cities where there is one sole source of water."[113] In other words, Atlanta wasn't like the cities that had been forced to pay for their water projects.

Hartsfield also tried to frame the supply issue as an incidental benefit, saying once that "Atlanta's water supply is not an issue here. It is not water that we need but regulation of that water."[114]The difference between regulation and supply was fairly semantic, and many in the appropriations committee were reluctant to sponsor such a "special interest" project. The House of Representatives struck the dam's funding from its 1948 budget and threatened to stall the project indefinitely until Atlanta agreed to ante up for a significant portion of the project's cost.[115]

Still, Hartsfield pushed on with fervor and used his political savvy to reframe the debate over the dam. The next year, he came to the appropriation committee with a dozen local politicians and a folder of newspaper articles on recent winter floods in Georgia.[116] "Gentlemen," he said, holding up the articles, "I should like to show you the present interest of Atlanta."[117] He was also armed with a little extra leverage: a recent study had shown that the corps's Woodruff Dam project downstream from Atlanta would only achieve its maximum effectiveness if water was regulated from a point upstream.[118]

Hartsfield also enlisted the support of pivotal Georgia congressmen in his fight. Representative James C. Davis from Stone Mountain supported the dam from the start. Davis pushed through funding for an initial planning study and then used the funding as leverage for further appropriations the following years.[119] Georgia representative George Wood also campaigned for the project, although his support sometimes waned in response to opposition from constituents in his soon-to-be-flooded district.[120] On the Senate side, Hartsfield recruited both of Georgia's senators, Richard B. Russell Jr. and Walter George, to campaign for the project.

Senator Russell was particularly influential. He was an extremely popular politician and served on the subcommittee in charge of allocating funds for development of the corps's projects. When the project came in front of Russell's subcommittee, he was able to convince the group to recommend $2,000,000 to fund the dam.

When the House subcommittee refused to allocate any money for the dam, the issue was referred to a conference committee during the summer of 1949. The dam's biggest opponent was the chairman of the House Appropriations Committee, Clarence Cannon. Cannon was a die-hard fiscal conservative, and he wanted to slash funding for all corps projects across the southeast. He refused to budge from his position for months during the conference, much to the anger of the other congressmen involved. Discussions grew so tense that at one point, Senator Russell later said, most people on the conference committee were not on speaking terms with Cannon.

Finally, Russell wore Cannon down, and he agreed to allocate $750,000 to begin dam construction. The figure wasn't close to the $2,000,000 that Russell wanted, but it got the project underway and paved the path for future appropriations in the coming years. Over the course of the next decade, the federal government would pay for the entire project.

Eight months later, at the Buford Dam's official opening ceremony, Hartsfield would have been justified in feeling a bit smug. Atlanta had encountered so many obstacles and yet, against formidable odds, the city had persevered and emerged as the victor. Atlanta was getting its dam, along with a stable water supply and the promise of navigation, and the city was expected to pay absolutely nothing in return. To Hartsfield and his allies, this must have seemed like an excellent deal.

Later that night, as Hartsfield and his friends raised champagne toasts to the city, no one in the room had the faintest idea of how much trouble they had just caused. No one realized that their political maneuvering would later cripple the city they loved. No one anticipated that the dam's obscure authorizing document would embroil the city in decades of litigation. And no one foresaw that their refusal to pay a million dollars for the dam would cause a billion-dollar crisis in the future. And because they did not know, they raised their champagne flutes and drank to the future of Atlanta.

# 5

# URBANIZATION AND ITS DISCONTENTS

One spring morning in 1970, local resident and environmentalist Fritz Orr parked his car in a pull-off next to the Perimeter. Like he had so many mornings before, he slid his canoe off the roof and balanced it on top of his shoulders. Then he trudged down the steep bank to the water's edge. He dropped the canoe in the water, crawled into it, and pushed off from the bank into a narrow shoal of the Chattahoochee River.

Unlike his other trips on the river, this day was no simple recreational outing for Orr. Accompanying him were microbiologist and Georgia Canoeing Association founder Claude Terry, Georgia Conservancy member Dr. Bill Murdy, and a reporter from the *Atlanta Journal* named Hugh Nations. Together, the men planned to take a trip to a place that no boater ever planned to go, a place so dangerous to human health that the federal government would soon move to prohibit any human contact with it whatsoever.[1] It was a place described by one columnist as a "cancer," and yet it was surprisingly easy to get to. The men only had to float downstream.

Around the put-in at the Perimeter, the Chattahoochee was narrow, clear, and cold. Small rapids jostled the canoes around rock outcroppings in the center of the stream. Two muskrats tussled on driftwood at the shore, and a series of pointed stumps at the edge of the bank indicated that the area's beaver population was alive and well. "The upper reaches of the river are full of surprises," wrote Nations. "Horseshoe Bend gorge rises in unspoiled grandeur above the river, its crest and plunging flanks untouched by man."[2] On a cool morning, the occasional fly fisherman could be seen casting into one of the many holes and eddies at the river's edge.

Around a slow bend, Atlanta's riverside pumping station hummed softly as it drew water from a carved inlet. The intake structure was the first in a

long cycle of urban water use that would take the water through a series
of filtration tanks, into the cast-iron pipes of the city's downtown water
mains, and through its splintered connecting lines to the faucets, toilets, and
machines of Atlanta's homes and businesses. The men floated beyond a rock
retaining wall that prevented the river's downstream water from recirculating
up to the intake pipes and then, in an instant and with little warning, the men
and their canoes plunged into an abyss of filth.

At a point only a hundred yards from the city's intake pipes, the full
circle of Atlanta's urban water consumption came to a close. Here, raw sewage spilled like a waterfall from a massive underground pipe that jutted out
above the river from the center of its steeply sloped eastern bank. Every day,
Atlanta's R. M. Clayton sewage treatment plant used this pipe to dump eighty
million gallons of mostly untreated waste into the Chattahoochee in a continuous stream equal to 13 percent of the river's average flow.[3]

Beneath the outfall was a dead zone, a "frothing sewer" home to nothing but sludge worms, maggots, and flies.[4] The Chattahoochee's clear, cold
water turned tawny brown and was thick as a milkshake. Shiny, viscous sludge
coated the banks and rocks. Toilet paper and condoms hung from overhang-
ing branches. Sewage coated the top of the water and formed large, filmy
bubbles that expanded like balloons atop eddies at the edge of the bank.

Even from the relative comfort of his vessel, Nations was concerned.
"The sight of millions of gallons of sewage boiling just off the prow of
one's canoe can be unnerving," he wrote. He was right to be afraid: by one
measurement, the fecal coliform concentration in this section of the river
was 3,300 times greater than the amount considered safe for recreation.[5] The
slightest contact with the water could cause serious harm from infection and
maybe even death.

The men paddled to the shore and climbed out next to a paper repulping
plant. There was nothing left to see downstream, except more of the same
thing. For the next one hundred miles, according to state administrator Rock
Howard, the Chattahoochee was "devoid of life."[6]

From their perch on top of the bank, the men had a perfect view of one
of the greatest environmental catastrophes of their day. At any given time,
this single narrow section of river, from creek bank to creek bank, was host
to a full one-third of the state of Georgia's total waterborne pollution. Most
of it had arrived to the river via R. M. Clayton's sewage outfall pipe, but still
more had flowed in from the "grossly polluted" water of Peachtree Creek,
which merged into the Chattahoochee next to the city's sewage treatment

plant. Local industries contributed to the problem as well; as the men stood on the bank, they noticed a manhole at the paper plant that spewed a "swampy, evil-smelling" discharge that traveled in rivulets to the river below.[7]

This was the hell that Hartsfield's progress had wrought. Orr pointed to a spot across the river on the Chattahoochee's shore. "I used to slide down that bank with Ivan Allen and a lot of others," he said wistfully. "They've all forgotten about that now."[8]

In the thirty years prior to Orr's canoe trip, Atlanta's pro-business atmosphere had ushered in an era of unprecedented abundance and growth. Rural farmers had fled from the depressed countryside to the big city, lured by the promise of new manufacturing jobs. Atlanta's urban population ballooned from three hundred thousand to nearly half a million by 1970, and the surrounding metro region became home to more than a million more. In the state of Georgia, the 1950 census would be the last ever to record more rural residents than urban ones.[9] Historian Peter Daniel remarked that this massive urbanization—along with the changes in production, social organization, and lifestyle that accompanied it—was the single most revolutionary period in Southern history.[10]

For many, life in the city was a blessing. Hard-working men who had lost their farms in the Depression found new hope in manufacturing jobs in the city. Atlanta's industries provided relatively safe work, decent hours, and a real living wage. For the first time in their lives, blue-collar workers in Atlanta could afford to feed and clothe their families, buy a car, and pay the mortgage. They moved to tract homes in the suburbs, hosted backyard barbecues, and sent their kids to college. They lived the American dream.

And yet, amid the prosperity, a few early warning signs emerged. On the city's north side, a group of concerned parents complained that during the warmest months Piedmont Park was permeated with the odor of raw sewage.[11] Nearby, outside her Northside Drive home, Frances Smith noticed that toilet paper stuck to the grass in her backyard after heavy rains.[12] East of the city in Rockdale, the water in Charles Anderson's well turned a sickly yellow and caught on fire when he lit a match next to it.[13] But most days, there seemed to be little cause for concern.

In truth, however, the city of Atlanta had become an organism that hemorrhaged harmful toxins from every possible orifice. Throughout thirty years of growth, the city had built highways and interstates, added new schools, improved public parks, doubled its water supply intake system, planned a citywide rapid transit, and even added a couple professional sports teams and an international airport. One of the only aspects of urban infrastructure that hadn't been completely revolutionized or upgraded was Atlanta's method of controlling municipal pollution.

The city of Atlanta's waterborne discharges were particularly troubling. Atlanta had expanded sewer lines every year, but the pace of sewer expansion was not remotely close to the rapid pace of development. By the late 1960s, there was a huge gulf between the kind of sewer system that a city the size of Atlanta *should* have and the kind it actually possessed.

For starters, the city's sole treatment plant, R. M. Clayton, was woefully out of date and far too small. The facility was designed to handle a maximum of forty-two million gallons of sewage a day, but by 1969, Atlanta was producing an average of sixty million gallons a day and had peak flow days greater than one hundred million gallons.[14] The plant was running at full blast all the time, and yet close to half the city's sewage had to be bypassed around the overloaded treatment tanks and discharged directly into the river.

Even when sewage was treated at R. M. Clayton, the processes used left most of the sewage's harmful contaminants intact. Clayton used primary treatment only. During primary treatment, the sewage flowed through a screen to remove large objects and then passed through a settling tank to remove most of the remaining solids.[15] That's it. No digesters, no chemical treatments, no sanitizing of any kind: just a couple of screens and then the sewage was dumped into the river.

Making matters worse, not all of the city's sewage even reached R. M. Clayton at all. Twenty-two miles of Atlanta's downtown sewer lines were connected to the city's stormwater drainage system. When it rained, and even sometimes when it didn't, the pipes would reach maximum capacity and the mixture of sewage and rainwater would burst out of built-in escape hatches above natural drainage areas. The South River, Peachtree Creek, and Intrenchment Creek all contained these escape hatches, and these water bodies would flood with sewage during wet months.

Of course, sewage was only a part of Atlanta's water pollution problem. The entire nation, including the Chattahoochee basin, also struggled with waterborne industrial pollution. World War II's military-industrial production had had a devastating effect on American water quality. Extractive industries like iron, steel, oil, aluminum, and coal ramped up production to accommodate the skyrocketing wartime demand for manufactures of automobiles, ships, and aircraft carriers.[16] In the absence of regulation, many of the industries' by-products were expelled directly into the nation's waterways.

At the end of World War II, American manufacturing grew amid the nation's postwar economic boom, and industrial pollution outpaced sewage discharges to become America's leading source of water pollution.[17] Over the following decades, American industrial waste continued to increase exponentially along with production: "chemical production increased six times over, rubber and plastic production rose nearly five-fold, and aluminum production quadrupled. Furthermore, car sales doubled, phosphate detergents came into large-scale use, and pesticide usage climbed 168 percent."[18] By 1965, at least two-thirds of the liquid waste produced in America was discharged by industries.[19]

Nationally, organic animal and vegetable-based compounds were the largest category of industrial waste by volume.[20] Food processing plants, textile plants, and paper mills were the worst offenders. Below Omaha, Nebraska, discharges from the city's meatpacking plants literally stained the river red with blood.[21] In Washington, pulp pollution from paper mills threatened to destroy the Puget Sound ecosystem.[22] In Ohio, oil slicks on the Cuyahoga River infamously caught fire in 1969. Of course, at the time, it wasn't that big of a deal. The river had caught on fire many times before.[23]

The chemical revolution during World War II also created a new group of toxic wastewater discharges that were lethal even in small doses.[24] Both Allied and German forces used industrial techniques to manufacture chemical weapons. After the war, American producers found domestic uses for some chemicals, like DDT and dioxin, and repackaged them for retail markets within the United States. These inorganic wastes were discharged in smaller quantities than industrial organic waste but were no less frightening or harmful.[25] Industries also polluted waterways with radioactive waste and thermal discharges.[26]

Despite the state and federal governments' early feeble efforts at pollution control, most Georgia businesses still operated in a virtual state of lawlessness in regard to water discharges. Around Atlanta, a wide range of businesses used local waterways as their own personal trash can. In Smyrna, north of Atlanta, Lockheed Aircraft Corporation's manufacturing plant dumped millions of gallons of cyanide and other toxins into Nickajack Creek each year.[27] Area developments, like Fulton County's upscale Riverbend Apartments, eschewed expensive sewer hookup costs and instead discharged sewage directly into the river.[28] Every service station in town drained its grease, oil, and detergents into the city's stormwater grates,[29] and pieces of butchered chickens could be found floating in the Chattahoochee more than forty miles downstream from where Atlanta's poultry processors dumped bones, blood, and offal.[30]

Large-scale industrial accidents were also commonplace, and these incidents contributed to the growing public unease. A 1970 rail yard accident dumped thousands of gallons of diesel fuel into Proctor Creek near Atlanta, and the resulting oil slick extended for one hundred miles.[31] Periodically, the Bona Allen tannery in Buford would spill its leather tanning waste in amounts so large that the Chattahoochee would be stained an unnaturally deep color of indigo blue for days.[32] Several times, thousands of fish in a single water body died unexpectedly and from unexplained causes.[33]

Amid so many well-publicized incidents, public support for industrial interests began to wane. With every fish kill or oil spill, more people began to replace their pro-business World War II era patriotism with a deep-rooted skepticism about corporate motives and practices. Rachel Carson's book *Silent Spring* tapped into these emotions when it detailed a shocking laundry list of ecological degradation caused by the popular industrial compound DDT. Her book's massive commercial success stirred a nationwide political dialogue about the environmental consequences of the nation's relatively unchecked pollution problems, and it galvanized a new brand of American environmental activism.

Unlike previous clean water movements that were based on anthropocentric concerns like human health or navigation, this new American environmental ethic embraced wildlife and ecosystem health as its primary goal. Activists pushed for all American waterways to be returned to their natural state, and as industrial accidents and ecological degradation continued, this perspective transitioned from fringe to mainstream.

By the 1960s, the voice of the environmental movement was unified and strong enough to counterbalance some of the industrial favoritism that had plagued water pollution legislation in the prior decade. In Georgia, sportsmen, concerned parents, college students, and homeowner groups all formed their own grassroots conservation clubs and advocated for stronger water pollution control laws.[34]

Increasingly, the Atlanta Chamber of Commerce began to push for greater environmental protection as well.[35] Too much pollution, the Chamber of Commerce reasoned, was bad for business. A 1964 study by the Atlanta Region Metropolitan Commission found that Atlanta's municipal waste was "handicapping" industrial development downstream from the city.[36] Furthermore, in a nearly Shakespearian turn of events, the pollution spawned by Hartsfield's neglect threatened to destroy one of his most cherished pro-business projects. Atlanta could never become a port city, the Army Corps warned, because the city's pollution would turn the project's downstream lock-and-dam reservoirs into stagnant, disease-breeding sewage lagoons.[37]

The state was also pressured by its neighbors to clean up its act. Alabama and Florida experienced public pressure to improve state water quality standards, but the two states were unable to meet their water quality goals because Georgia's pollution upstream badly contaminated the water. The U.S. Public Health Service sponsored numerous interstate conferences between Alabama and Georgia to resolve pollution disputes about the Coosa River.[38]

In response to political pressure, Georgia's General Assembly enacted the Georgia Water Control Act in 1964. The old Georgia statutes permitted pollution so long as public health was not in jeopardy. The new act's stated objective, however, reflected the nation's new environmental conscience. The statute set the river's natural state as its goal.[39]

The act required every wastewater disposal system to get a state permit.[40] The state would compare each system's plans to ensure that the discharges did not violate other water quality regulations.[41] If the state found a violation, it was empowered to enter private property and to access personal records to investigate.[42] The state could make rules, issue injunctions, declare emergency orders, and take legal action through the attorney general.[43]

The statute created the Water Quality Control Board to oversee the state's permitting system.[44] Unlike previous governing groups, the board was not captive to industrial interests. And, unlike the previous groups, the board had a specific statutory mandate to take steps to improve water quality. The board was required to survey water, prepare a comprehensive pollution plan, and adopt rules and regulations "in accordance with the public interest in water supply and the conservation of fish, game and aquatic life."[45]

Perhaps most importantly, the board also hired Executive Secretary R. S. "Rock" Howard as its new chief pollution officer. Howard was a Savannah, Georgia, native and a graduate of both Clemson and Harvard's Sanitary Engineering schools. He wasn't an extreme environmentalist, but he wasn't about to kowtow to the state's largest polluters, either. "Howard's adversaries read like a list of 'Who's Who' in size and influence," wrote *Atlanta Journal* columnist Bob Hurt. In the Atlanta metro region, Howard filed suit against heavy-hitters Lockheed Aircraft, General Motors, and Ford Motor Company.[46]

The board also wasted no time regulating municipal sewage discharges like the ones from Atlanta's R. M. Clayton plant. Within the board's first four

months of existence, it issued an order requiring all municipal and industrial
sewage sources to provide secondary treatment.[47] In response to the order,
$11,666,000 of construction began on fourteen sewage treatment projects
across the state.[48]

Despite the new law, many of the state's municipalities—including
Atlanta—refused to act. No one wanted to raise water or sewer rates to fund
the pollution control projects. "It's almost a joke," board member Bob Cor-
bitt told reporters. "All the cities are doing is wasting time and letting things
ride as long as they can without paying more."[49] Rock Howard was slightly
more sympathetic, but he also implored the cities to raise the necessary revenue for upgrades. "Everyone wants things cleaned up, but who's going to
pay the bill?" he said to the *Atlanta Journal*. "What we need are some coura-
geous politicians."[50]

Howard could have forced municipal action by issuing sewer hookup
moratoriums for noncompliant areas, but it seemed he lacked the requisite
political courage, as well. Years later, when the Chattahoochee's horrible condition would become national headline news, Water Pollution Control Board
members would admit in private that they had been derelict in enforcement
of the act.[51] Behind closed doors, Atlanta's city leaders had pressured the
board to allow the city more time to get into compliance, and the board had
relented. Afterward, however, the city had openly flouted the rules, making
no discernible signs of improvement. R. M. Clayton remained in complete
noncompliance for six years, and Atlanta was never meaningfully punished.[52]
Rock Howard could take on the nation's largest Fortune 500 companies, it
seemed, but he couldn't touch Atlanta.

A federal movement was occurring, however, that would soon challenge Atlanta's untouchability. Sensing that environmentalism had gained
mainstream traction as a political issue, Lyndon Johnson's administration
embraced the movement and adopted a policy labeled "New Conservation"
to promote regulatory reductions in air and water pollution. The president
pushed his environmental agenda in a speech called "A Special Message to
Congress on Natural Beauty" in the spring of 1965. In a line that could have
been in direct reference to the Chattahoochee, Johnson warned, "Waterways
that were once sources of pleasure and beauty and recreation are forbidden to human contact and objectionable to sight and smell."[53] The president urged Congress to adopt legislation that would regulate pollution at the
source "rather than attempting to cure pollution after it occurs."[54]

When Lyndon Johnson gave his speech to Congress, the Senate had a
new clean water champion named Edmund Muskie. Muskie was born and

raised in Maine and returned to practice law there after graduating from Cornell Law School. In the 1940s, when Muskie was just starting his own sole practitioner law firm, the Androscoggin River in Maine became so polluted with paper mill pulp that downstream fumes from the river peeled the paint off of riverfront houses.[55] The affected homeowners successfully sued the paper companies, but the resulting court order didn't actually improve conditions on the Androscoggin.

Muskie's autobiography cited the Androscoggin case as a turning point in his political thinking.[56] Although his early career in the Maine House of Representatives did not reflect a deep passion for environmentalism, Muskie's gubernatorial speeches in the 1950s began to display his growing environmental consciousness. "Surely it is beyond argument," said Muskie in his 1956 election victory speech, "that an abundant supply of clean water is essential."[57] At his urging, Maine's legislature enacted its first water quality legislation a year later.

In the U.S. Senate, Muskie used his position as chairman of the Subcommittee on Air and Water Pollution to assail the Federal Water Pollution Control Act. Although the act had made some improvements in water quality, Muskie said, greater progress was urgently needed.[58] During his first two years in office, the senator hosted water quality hearings across the nation and poured over national data on pollution.

By the time Johnson gave his famous "Natural Beauty Message," Muskie had already passed a bill in the Senate that would give the federal government the power to establish national water quality standards.[59] Johnson endorsed Muskie's bill in his address, and the House Public Works Committee reported a modified version of Muskie's Senate bill three weeks later. The House version differed from Muskie's Senate bill in one very significant way: it eliminated the provision that allowed the federal government to set water quality standards if a state failed to do so.[60]

To win over House members, Muskie organized more field hearings in eight different cities that were experiencing severe water quality problems. One of these cities was Atlanta, whose municipal wastewater discharges were still on par with the worst of the worst. After reviewing thousands of pages of information collected from the field hearings in Atlanta and other cities, the joint committee agreed to recommend a bill that included a federal water quality provision.[61]

The final bill allowed the states to set water quality standards, but the federal government could enforce its own standards if the Department of Health, Education, and Welfare's (HEW) secretary determined that the state's regulations were inadequate.[62] The act created the Federal Water Pollution Control Administration within the HEW to administer the federal water quality program.[63] The bill passed both houses and became known as the Water Quality Act of 1965.

After President Johnson signed the act into law, his environmental agenda became even more ambitious. In 1966, he proposed new legislation to create river basin organizations to study and manage pollution on a watershed level.[64] Congress, however, was tired from the three-year struggle to pass the 1965 act and was also reluctant to "add another layer of government between the states and federal government."[65] Johnson's watershed management idea was never put into legislation.

Although the 1965 Water Quality Act had promise, it failed to meet environmental expectations. Legal historian William Andreen argues that the act's enforcement mechanisms contained too many loopholes and that the government's burden of proof was problematically high: "purely intrastate waters were not covered; actual endangerment to health or welfare had to be shown; and, even if interstate waters were involved, states had veto power where the offending discharge only affected persons in the same state."[66] The federal government also faced the difficult burden of proving which polluter caused the ambient water quality degradation.[67] With some water bodies absorbing a thousand polluting discharges or more, it was nearly impossible to isolate a single offender as the primary reason for decline in water quality.

Fortunately for the federal government, R. M. Clayton's discharges were one of the rare offenses that fit squarely within the scope of the 1965 act: the Chattahoochee was an interstate river, Clayton's discharges affected downstream users in other states, and the city's sewage could be easily isolated as a primary contributor to the river's degradation. Federal officials ordered Atlanta to obtain adequate secondary treatment for its sewage by July 1, 1971.[68] Despite the federal pressure, however, Atlanta still dragged its feet. Mayor Sam Massell paid lip service to the idea of pollution control but construction never began.[69]

In late fall of 1970, when President Nixon appointed William Ruckelshaus to head the newly formed Environmental Protection Agency (EPA), the agency was given a clear directive to crack down on recalcitrant municipalities like Atlanta. At Senate confirmation hearings in December, Ruckelshaus stated, "If we are to make progress in pollution abatement, we must have a firm enforcement policy at the federal level. That doesn't mean that this policy will be unfair . . . but it does mean that it will be firm."[70] Less than a week later, Ruckelshaus boarded a plane to Atlanta.

In a speech at the annual National League of Cities convention in the city, Ruckelshaus notified Atlanta and two other cities, Detroit and Cleveland, that their municipal sewage discharges were violating water quality standards and would be unable to receive a permit under the new Refuse Act regulations. The Chattahoochee, he said, was an "open sewer."[71] Ruckelshaus warned Atlanta, "Corrective steps must be taken within 180 days . . . or the EPA administrator can ask the Justice Department to file court action."[72]

With the full force of the federal government now on their side, Rock Howard and the Georgia Water Quality Control Board jumped into the fray as well. Howard ordered the city to accelerate work on R. M. Clayton and to approve sewer rate increases to provide funding for completion of the project. Until this was done, Atlanta was prohibited from making any sewer hookups without first obtaining the specific approval from the board.[73] Because the city's downtown construction projects all required sewer hookups, this meant that Atlanta might be forced to indefinitely halt most of its construction projects, which totaled an estimated $112 million at the time.[74]

Despite the heavy consequences of the threatened moratorium, some city officials still refused to raise rates. The mayor and the Chamber of Commerce endorsed a rate increase, but there were still enough holdouts among the city aldermen to block its implementation. The aldermen complained to *Atlanta Journal* reporter Jeff Nesmith that the EPA's order wasn't fair: "The Current City Hall regime is being told that in a few years it must clean up pollution that developed for a decade."[75] One alderman was particularly outspoken in his opposition to the rate increase. "Let the sludge flow, is what I say," Alderman Hugh Pierce remarked to reporters.[76]

In open meetings with city residents, EPA administrators were wholly unsympathetic. At one public meeting, EPA enforcement official Murray Stein blamed Atlanta's frivolous spending in other areas: "If you want to know what cities have major pollution problems, just look for the ones with major league sports teams. . . . Every time I drive by Atlanta's impressive stadium on the way in from the airport, I think about this. Waste treatment plants are low man on the totem pole for most cities, behind stadiums, coliseums, museums, and other facilities."[77] Atlanta, he said, had plenty of money; it just didn't want to spend it on pollution abatement.

Stein was right about Atlanta's priorities, but he should have added the state of Georgia in his critique as well. According to a complicated federal financing scheme, the EPA could pay for the majority of the abatement only if the state added money as well. Otherwise, the feds would only pick up a third of the tab, leaving Atlanta to pay more than $34 million for the project by itself.[78] Many Georgia legislators, a number of whom represented angry downstream communities, believed that Atlanta should bear the brunt of the abatement costs. Because they refused to allocate sufficient state funds for the project, Atlanta needed to pass a drastic 300 percent sewer rate increase to fully fund the construction.

As the clock wound down on Atlanta's 180-day deadline, the aldermen began to realize that the EPA wasn't bluffing. For the first time ever, the federal and state governments fully intended to punish the city if it willfully neglected to solve its sewage problems on time. A few days before Christmas, the mayor and the aldermen locked themselves in a marathon six-hour-long meeting to hash out a sewer rate deal. They clashed over details, and two men even came close to physically fighting, but the group emerged from the meeting with a significant rate increase on the books.[79] Soon thereafter, the city reached a settlement agreement with administrators.[80] With the new revenue from sewer rates, the city agreed to build two new treatment facilities and upgrade all of its existing filtering technology.

When Muskie finally pushed through his groundbreaking Clean Water Act (CWA) legislation a year later, it was hardly front-page news in Atlanta. For the city, the hard part was already over. Still, the act's regulatory scheme would have lasting repercussions on the way pollution was regulated in the state. Most importantly, the act made it unlawful to discharge any pollutant from a point source into a navigable waterway without a permit.[81] Under the act, a point source was defined as any discrete conveyance, like a pipe, canal, or ditch. The CWA required industry discharges to meet technology-based standards. In addition to technology standards, the act created an additional layer of standards based on water quality.

Like the other federal water quality acts before it, the CWA still involved the states in enforcement. But, unlike prior statutes, the CWA created a concurrent enforcement scheme that lessened the states' discretion. States could take control of permitting under the CWA, but the federal government could veto the state's permit or issue its own permits if it determined that the state was not doing an adequate job. In theory, the threat of a federal takeover set a floor, a national standard below which state regulations could not fall.[82] Muskie and other clean water advocates hoped that this level playing field would halt the states' "race to the bottom" and would instead foster innovation and collaboration on pollution control.

Chattahoochee water quality improved significantly after the wave of legislation in the sixties and early seventies. From a record low average of zero in 1972, low-flow dissolved oxygen levels have rebounded to five mg/L and are now sufficient to support a wide range of aquatic life.[83] Where only bacteria once thrived, fish have come back to the river below R. M. Clayton. A sample of species found at least seventeen different kinds of fish below the plant's discharge pipes in 1990; a similar study in 1970 didn't find a single one.[84]

Most of the improvement can be attributed to the adoption of advanced sewage treatment process in the entire Atlanta metro area. By 1974, all of Atlanta metro sewage treatment plants had upgraded from primary treatment to secondary treatment.[85] When Atlanta's R. M. Clayton plant switched to secondary treatment, it also expanded its capacity.[86] For the first part of the 1970s, the plant was still overloaded, and some sewage bypassed the system and discharged directly into the river. Further improvements in 1974, however, finally brought the treatment facilities' capacity up to the city's current production rates. After that upgrade, 100 percent of Atlanta's sewage-only pipes received secondary treatment before being discharged into the river.[87] Today, all of Atlanta's regional wastewater treatment plants must meet treatment requirements that exceed secondary treatment standards.[88] Many of the treatment plants also recycle wastewater for use on golf courses, landscaped lawns, and forestland.[89]

# 6

# SUBURBAN EXPLOSION

Muskie's Clean Water Act had a shockingly audacious goal: it aimed to return all American waterways to a natural state by 1985. As the clock began ticking on this thirteen-year deadline, however, it became obvious that the nation would fall drastically short of meeting the act's ambitious objective. Despite the improvements in municipal and industrial discharges, America's waters continued to suffer from unnaturally high levels of heavy metals, phosphates, fecal coliform, and many other contaminants.

Around Atlanta, the Chattahoochee was no longer an open sewer, but its condition remained far from a natural state. Even though there were no gushing sewage pipes in sight, the river's low nitrogen-to-phosphorus ratio indicated that sewage was contaminating the Chattahoochee south of Peachtree Creek.[1] The river also registered unnatural levels of other contaminants including copper, lead, zinc, phosphorous, nitrogen, and dissolved organic carbon, even though point sources accounted for only a tiny fraction of the contaminants' levels near the city.[2] If not from point sources, where was the pollution coming from?

The Chattahoochee, like many other rivers, was suffering from nonpoint source pollution. Nonpoint source pollution enters the waterway from diffuse sources. Instead of flowing through pipes and ditches, nonpoint pollution reaches a water body through rainwater runoff or groundwater percolation. It occurs when rain washes pesticides from farmland into a nearby stream, or when oil and grease from a road washes down into a curbside gutter. It happens when arsenic-contaminated groundwater flows into a hydrologically connected riverbed.

When the Clean Water Act was written, nonpoint pollution from mining, agriculture, construction, and sewer overflows was already recognized as a significant source of pollution in America's waterways.[3] Without effective regulation of these sources, it was apparent from the outset that the act's "natural state" goal would be unmet. Still, the final version of the Clean Water Act left this entire category virtually untouched.[4]

The reasons for doing so were both practical and political. Unlike point sources, which could be monitored and regulated at a clearly defined outfall point, nonpoint pollution can only be remedied by appropriate land use decisions. Historically, land use had been the purview of states and municipal zoning boards, not the U.S. Congress, and many on the Public Works Committee were philosophically concerned about federal intrusion into such a traditionally local issue.[5]

Federal regulation of nonpoint sources was also strictly opposed by the powerful agricultural lobbying force.[6] Because agricultural runoff was, and still is, one of the most significant contributors to nonpoint source pollution in America, any meaningful regulation of nonpoint sources would have to impact agricultural practices. The committee was concerned that compliance with nonpoint source regulations would bankrupt many of the country's already struggling small farming communities.[7]

The cost of nonpoint source regulation was also an issue. The feds would require a great deal of manpower to administer and enforce land use regulations and zoning laws in every municipality throughout the country, and many worried that the costs incurred would outweigh the benefits of such a program. Some of the land use changes would also be incredibly costly for cities and towns to implement. Federal officials estimated that fixing the country's urban combined sewer problem could cost up to $47 billion alone.[8]

Ultimately, Muskie and the Public Works Committee determined that nonpoint source regulation was too much of a political gamble, and they decided to leave land use and zoning regulation to local governments. Like it had so many times before, Atlanta exercised this freedom of self-governance in a reckless and environmentally harmful way. This time, however, the city of Atlanta was not the only perpetrator; the area's numerous suburbs contributed heavily to the problem as well.

As Georgia residents shifted from rural to urban communities after World War II, the city of Atlanta experienced a similarly titanic demographic shift within the metro area's boundaries. Atlanta's suburbs exploded with growth, and the majority of Atlanta's white population shifted almost completely from urban to suburban life. During the 1940s, the white suburban population in Atlanta increased by 67 percent as more than one hundred thousand white residents moved to the suburbs.[9] In following decades, millions more would move to the city's outer fringe.

Atlanta's white flight was the product of both concerted effort and mere accident. At first, it was spawned primarily from the development of the nation's interstate highway system. In a 1939 report, the Bureau of Public Roads announced that it planned to route three freeways through Atlanta.[10] Thereafter, the Georgia State Highway Department commissioned H.W. Lochner & Company to study traffic patterns and create a system of secondary roads to be completed at the same time as the construction of the highways.[11] The report concluded that traffic should be concentrated in a north-south direction to accommodate the growing northern suburbs.[12] With this in mind, the plan recommended that the new freeways run along the cardinal directions, with two freeways joining to run from the north to south of the city and another running from east to west.[13] All along the highways, Lochner planned exits to connect to new or expanded suburban thoroughfares.

Atlanta's highways were built according to Lochner's recommendations and were later transformed by Eisenhower's 1956 Federal Aid Highway Act into Interstates 85, 75, and 20. Commuting to the suburbs became easier and faster. Suburban drivers no longer had to lurch from stoplight to stoplight on their way into town, and the speed of interstate travel permitted residents to move farther geographically from the city center than they had before. At each interstate exit, businesses, strip malls, and restaurants sprouted from the ground like mushrooms, and before long, many of Atlanta's suburbs became autonomous communities capable of providing all their residents' retail and lifestyle needs.

Suburban growth was also triggered by competition between the city of Atlanta and its surrounding counties. Atlanta's 1952 Plan of Improvement expanded city boundaries to include upscale northern suburbs like Buckhead.[14] City leaders devised the boundary expansion plan as a means of maintaining a white voting majority inside city limits, but in public statements they claimed that the plan would help Fulton County accommodate its expanding population.[15] The plan tripled Atlanta's size from thirty-seven square miles to 118 square miles, and it added an additional one hundred thousand suburban residents to Atlanta's voting population.[16] It also extended city services to the new areas, encouraging even more growth in the annexed suburbs in Fulton County.

Not to be outdone by Atlanta and Fulton, DeKalb County commissioner Scott Candler promised to provide vital services to all residents of his county, including those that moved into unincorporated areas outside of DeKalb's existing suburban towns.[17] Wherever residents moved, no matter how remote, they could enjoy the same kind of water, power, and trash removal services as incorporated residents closer to town. During Candler's tenure in office from 1940 to 1960, DeKalb's population doubled.[18]

This early jockeying between DeKalb and Fulton was the opening salvo in a battle among suburbs that would last for decades. Prior to most of Atlanta's suburban growth, Georgia had adopted a "home rule" approach to urban planning, meaning that each of the state's individual municipalities maintained almost exclusive control of zoning and land use decisions within their own boundaries.[19] Home rule planning did have some positive attributes—Atlanta, for example, no longer had to get the state legislature's approval to increase the salaries of its municipal officers—but it also had a number of pitfalls as well.

Because Atlanta's suburban communities operated with nearly complete autonomy, the region suffered from the absence of a cohesive development plan. Without oversight, Atlanta's suburban communities participated in a sort of real-estate arms race with one another, competing fiercely to attract the most valuable business and residential development. In the place of thoughtful regional planning, Atlanta's metro communities strove to build and develop at all costs, even when their infrastructural development was unable to keep pace with growth.

From a theoretical perspective, Georgia's home rule environment had unintentionally created a classic case of what scientist Garrett Hardin calls the "tragedy of the commons."[20] Hardin's famous tragedy of the commons scenario features a hypothetical group of shepherds who graze their herds on a common piece of land. Each shepherd, Hardin argues, derives the greatest benefit from increasing his herd size and corresponding revenue, even though each additional animal contributes incrementally to the overgrazing of the communal rangeland. Without regulation or coordination among the shepherds, each man will act in his own self-interest and expand his herd size until the rangeland is completely destroyed. "Therein lies the tragedy," wrote Hardin. "Each man is locked into a system that compels him to increase his herd without limit—in a world that is limited."[21]

Just as the unregulated rangeland had locked Hardin's shepherds into a cycle of overgrazing, Georgia's home rule trapped Atlanta's metro communities in a cycle of overdevelopment. Each municipality, acting in its own self-interest, increased its tax revenue by approving more and more developments, even though each additional development contributed incrementally to the metro area's problems with pollution, congestion, and crowding.

In their quest to attract upper-income homeowners, many suburban communities enacted racist and classist zoning laws aimed at preventing the development of mixed income housing. These zoning laws set minimum lot sizes and square footage requirements, thereby creating residential neighborhoods that were prohibitively expensive for the vast majority of Atlanta residents.[22] As an unintended side effect of this zoning, the large homes and lots were also grossly inefficient. The big lawns required extensive watering, and the homes' many bathrooms and appliances drained hydroelectrically produced energy as well as municipal water.

In addition to problems with water consumption, the competition among Atlanta suburbs also led developers to rely excessively upon septic tanks. Across the nation, fast-growing suburbs experienced what policymakers called a "water-sewer time lag."[23] Faced with tight budgets and eager to promote growth, city governments built infrastructure necessary for development first. The governments built water mains and roads, but sewer lines weren't prioritized because developers could still build using septic tanks instead of municipal sewage. As a result of this time lag, large suburban communities became almost entirely reliant on septic tanks instead of municipal sewage services. Although official census statistics weren't available until 1950, historians estimate that the number of homes in America with a septic tank jumped from just four and a half million in 1945 to nearly fourteen million in 1960.[24] Most of the new septic tanks were installed in the suburbs, where as many as 70 percent of homes used septic.[25]

As in other growing suburbs around the country, Atlanta's suburban infrastructural development reflected this water-sewer time lag trend. When money became available for water infrastructure, communities invested first in the development of water supplies and only considered wastewater development as a distant afterthought. Although all of the fifty different Atlanta metro governments had public water systems by the 1960s, only sixteen had public sewer systems.[26] Fulton County's massive population growth was entirely dependent on septic systems, and in many other municipalities, the majority of residents relied on septic.

When functioning properly, septic tanks use bacteria to break down household waste into relatively harmless components.[27] Inside the tank, the waste separates into solids at the bottom, a greasy residue on top, and liquids in the middle.[28] Drainage pipes leach the liquid waste into the soil, where it is

disinfected naturally by microorganisms. Septic tanks, however, are extremely
finicky. If it rains, the system will overflow. If the soil is too compacted, the
system will back up into the house. If the tank is not cleaned periodically, it
will break. One survey of suburban septic tanks found that as many as one-
third of all systems failed within the first three years.[29]

Unlike R. M. Clayton's massive sewage discharges, septic pollution was
an invisible menace. Whenever a tank failed, raw sewage would discharge
from the septic pipes directly into the ground. From there, it would slowly
seep into groundwater and eventually into nearby surface water. Clayton polluted the waterways with a single, centralized sewage outfall pipe, but septic pollution oozed from a thousand different points along trickling springs,
streambeds, and river banks. Because it contaminated surface water from
diffuse sources and not clearly defined outfall points, septic tank seepage was
unlike R. M. Clayton's discharges in another important way: it was regulated
as a nonpoint source under the Clean Water Act, which is to say that it was
hardly regulated at all.

Of course, septic tank leachate was not the only pollution by-product of
Atlanta's suburban competition and growth. Although the Lochner report
had envisioned a clean, orderly system of commuter thoroughfares, Atlanta's
commuter traffic became a nightmare. The report itself had a fatal flaw: it
grossly underestimated Atlanta's suburban growth. Lochner assumed that
the metro area's population would grow modestly from 500,000 in 1940 to
750,000 in 1970. Instead, the metro population nearly tripled during that
period of time.[30] By 1970, Atlanta had twice as many residents as Lochner
had predicted.[31]

The new suburban commuters choked Atlanta's highway network every
rush hour. In response, the state highway department expanded highways on
the north side of town. By the time a road expansion was complete, however,
the road would already be overcrowded. The suburban road crews laid mile
upon mile of new road as fast as they could, but it never was enough. "Today,
we have a situation that is basically out of control," said state commissioner
of industry and trade George Berry.

As Atlanta struggled to resolve its traffic problems, the city's ground
became increasingly covered in asphalt, and the asphalt caused runoff. Runoff is rainfall that is neither absorbed nor evaporated. It is water that falls
onto a surface and then runs across the top of the surface to the lowest
nearby elevation point, which is typically a ditch or waterway. As it flows,
runoff can pick up any contaminants in its path and carry them into the
receiving water body.

Undeveloped land is composed of permeable surfaces like grassy fields, forestland, wetlands, or sandy soil. When rain falls onto undeveloped land, at least half of its volume is absorbed by this permeable ground.[32] Another 40 percent of the rainfall evaporates or is absorbed by plant roots.[33] Only 10 percent of rainfall on undeveloped land turns into runoff.

Suburban development replaces natural absorbent land with compacted construction sites and hard concrete surfaces. In the place of a grassy field or forest, suburbs have roads, box store roofs, and parking lots. Construction equipment rips out tree roots and compacts the soil. As a result, the dirt on the construction site also becomes less permeable and therefore less able to absorb rainfall. The EPA estimates that, on average, 55 percent of all rainfall in cities turns into runoff.[34] This water picks up contaminants, like grease, oil, trash, and chemicals, and deposits them into urban streams and rivers. In Atlanta's suburban "crabgrass frontier," runoff is also contaminated with fertilizer and pesticides from the residents' perfectly manicured lawns.

During its population boom, Atlanta covered acres of fields in new asphalt roads, shopping centers, and parking lots every day. And every day, new suburban developments created compacted earth construction zones where grassy fields and forest previously existed. The city's stormwater runoff increased at the same pace as development.

Metro suburban runoff flows from hard surfaces into a patchwork of "curbs, gutters, catch basins, storm sewers, and concretized channels."[35] Water from a parking lot or street flows into a gutter that connects to a series of ditches. Like tributaries, the ditches then flow into a main channel that carries the water to a natural stream or river. The suburban stormwater drainage systems are completely separate from the communities' municipal sewage systems.

When it rains, the water from a thousand parking lots washes into this centralized channel, all at once. The water is not filtered or treated, and so it still contains all the sediment, trash, and toxins that were in all of the parking lots, roads, and gutters of an entire neighborhood. Every cigarette butt, every puddle of grease or oil, every littered McDonald's wrapper—it all gets washed into the ditches and eventually into the river.

Stormwater pollution from Atlanta poisoned the Chattahoochee, and heavy rains after dry periods were the most damaging. During Atlanta's rainy summer in 1989, pollution from runoff killed 150 thousand young trout stocked in the river. Six tributaries and one segment of the river itself were declared unsuitable for fishing or swimming.[36]

One report found that stormwater runoff deposited twenty times more lead, twenty-five times more copper, and six times more zinc into Georgia's waterways than all of the state's industrial pollutant discharges combined.[37] City storm drains also released one hundred thousand gallons of oil and grease into the state's rivers.[38] Two-thirds of the state's streams and rivers did not meet water quality standards because of stormwater pollution.[39]

In addition to the stormwater channels, the drainage from the northern suburban septic fields also flowed directly into the Chattahoochee.[40] Atlanta's Hemphill Station pumping plant drew its water from a pipe on the river underneath the Marietta Boulevard Bridge, south of Fulton and other suburbs' septic discharges. The station had to add large amounts of alum, chlorine, ammonia, carbon, and lime to make the Chattahoochee water potable.[41] The increasingly complex treatment processes became prohibitively expensive. At the urging of Atlanta water providers, Fulton County raised money for a new $3.7 million treatment facility to service its fastest growing suburban areas in 1963.[42] Other municipalities followed behind Fulton County and constructed their own central wastewater treatment facilities.

Gwinnett County started with a decentralized sewage treatment system because it couldn't afford to construct a large wastewater treatment plant.[43] Instead, the county built small neighborhood treatment plants and oxidation ponds. As the population grew, the county added more ponds until there were at least eighty different small treatment systems scattered throughout the district.[44] Georgia's Environmental Protection Division required Gwinnett to build three centralized wastewater treatment plants in 1973.[45]

Like Gwinnett, Cobb County also didn't start with a centralized waste treatment system. Instead, each city within the county had its own small treatment pond. The ponds didn't treat the water thoroughly enough, and Cobb's population outgrew them by the sixties.[46] In 1967, Cobb created a countywide sewage treatment system and built three large treatment plants: R. L. Sutton and South Cobb on the Chattahoochee, and Noonday Creek Plant on Lake Allatoona.[47]

Unfortunately, Atlanta metro's septic problems did not end after the suburbs constructed centralized systems. Explosive development overburdened the new suburban facilities in less than a decade. Out of desperation, many communities continued to approve septic system developments as a means to avoid costly wastewater treatment upgrades.

By 1985, Gwinnett County had added two more plants, but five of their six facilities were still over capacity.[48] One Gwinnett plant, Beaver Run, was treating a million gallons per day over and above its design limit.[49] Georgia's

Environmental Protection Division put a moratorium on development in the area serviced by the plant.[50] Still, at the time the moratorium went into place, Gwinnett had already granted permits that would add another four million gallons of sewage into the system each day.[51]

Cobb County experienced similar problems with its R. L. Sutton plant, which serviced the fast-growing "Platinum Triangle" area around the Cumberland-Galleria mall. The county had to enforce an occupancy moratorium on four subdivisions until they could be hooked up to the county's sewage system. It also expanded the plant so that it could treat an additional twenty-five million gallons of sewage daily, but by the time the expansion was complete, the county had already granted permits that would nearly reach the facility's capacity.[52]

All of the county water and sewer systems are designed to connect with neighboring systems. If any provider experienced an emergency shortage or malfunction, it could link to other systems to avoid a service interruption. By the 1980s, however, the counties routinely used these emergency links and entered into sewage treatment contracts with their neighbors. "The region's tight resources have fostered a type of shell game among the counties," wrote *Atlanta Journal-Constitution* reporter Gail Epstein. "They trade off water and sewer capabilities like poker chips, hoping to win more time."[53]

When Gwinnett couldn't treat its sewage in 1985, it entered into a contract with Fulton County. Fulton's John's Creek Plant took two million gallons of Gwinnett's Crooked Creek Plant sewage for two years while the Crooked Creek facility was expanded.[54] Fulton County then diverted the sewage from the John's Creek plant to another Fulton treatment plant that had just expanded.[55] In exchange, parched Fulton County received ten million gallons of Gwinnett's drinking water from its Duluth production facility.[56] Two years later, by the time Gwinnett's Crooked Creek expansion was complete, Fulton had already exceeded its sewage facility's capacity. Gwinnett agreed to treat a million gallons of Fulton's sewage each day and cancelled another million-gallon sewage contract with another Fulton facility.[57] Despite the obvious infrastructural deficiencies, each of the suburbs continued to recruit businesses and developers to build in their area.

All of Atlanta's water problems, from water usage to septic seepage and stormwater runoff, could have been resolved by good development practices. To avoid water shortages, for example, the suburbs could have required water-efficient building designs and fixtures in new development projects. Similarly, the suburbs' planning boards could have also required sewer hook-ups as a condition of development to curb septic seepage. To prevent runoff, the suburbs could have enacted regulations that required developments to provide a riparian buffer between a construction site and the riverbank, or they could have required parking lots to be paved in permeable surfaces as opposed to impermeable concrete.

With Georgia's home rule still in effect, however, none of the municipalities wanted to be the first to adopt more stringent building and construction regulations. In fact, in the competitive environment fostered by the home rule, the opposite occurred. Atlanta's suburbs competed with one another in a race to the bottom to eliminate regulatory burdens on businesses and developers. After all, why would a developer build a store with a permeable parking lot in Marietta if he could build his store with a much cheaper asphalt parking lot a mile away in Roswell?

Georgia tried unsuccessfully for decades to coordinate development as a means of overcoming Atlanta's competitive home rule environment. Starting in 1947, the state legislature created the Fulton and DeKalb Metropolitan Planning District to create a coordinated development strategy for Atlanta and its northern suburbs.[58] Initially, the group played only an advisory role and had very little power to actually influence suburban development decisions.[59] Over time, however, the group expanded to include more counties and became a respected planning organization. In 1960, it was renamed the Atlanta Regional Commission (ARC).[60]

Despite the ARC's best efforts, suburban areas continued to develop at a frenzied pace. Construction along the Chattahoochee waterfront was particularly damaging. Runoff from construction sites on the waterfront did not collect in stormwater drains; instead, it ran in sheets from building sites into the waterway. Construction equipment compacted the soil, causing it to lose permeability. When rain hit the hardened construction surface, runoff carried topsoil from the site directly into the river. This caused massive erosion along the Chattahoochee's banks and contaminated the water with sediment.

To combat Atlanta metro's nonpoint source problems along the Chattahoochee, the Georgia legislature passed the Metropolitan River Protection Act (MRPA) in 1973. The act applied to the forty-eight-mile stretch of the Chattahoochee River between Buford Dam and Peachtree Creek in west Atlanta.

The MRPA gave the ARC power to review any construction within two thousand feet of the river.[61] It categorized and ranked the river's banks according to erosion risk based on bedrock, soil, vegetation, and slope data.[62] It also authorized the ARC to create guidelines for construction.[63] The act set minimum standards for building in the flood plain, including a 35-foot structural height limit, a 50-foot vegetated buffer, and a 150-foot river buffer.[64]

Despite the new guidelines, however, Atlanta suburbs continued to develop the waterfront irresponsibly. Waterside real estate was some of the most expensive property in town. Residential lots sold for half a million dollars, and high-rise office towers offered prime space for businesses.[65] The suburban communities competed with one another to attract high-profile developers to their waterfront spaces.

In their race to build, the suburbs often ignored the ARC's recommendations. On a rafting trip down the Chattahoochee in the 1980s, environmental activist Bob Kerr observed multiple violations of the MRPA. In one place, the riverbank was bulldozed "into a gash of raw earth about fifty feet wide and more than five hundred feet long."[66] In another supposedly protected ravine, one county had dug a massive sewer right-of-way.[67] Nearly every twist and turn of the river displayed a new host of flagrant MRPA violations.

A report for the nearby Chattahoochee National Recreation Area placed the blame on the ARC. "In general, local zoning has not been helpful in protecting key resources in the Chattahoochee corridor," claimed the report.[68] The report noted that, even though the MRPA authorized government agencies to file suit against developers that violated the act, very few actions had taken place.[69] The biggest problem was that the ARC was still limited to primarily an advisory role. The individual suburbs maintained ultimate decision-making authority. And, because the suburbs received revenue from property taxes on development, they had an overwhelming incentive to develop at all costs.

This shortcoming was thrust into the spotlight in 1985, when the city of Duluth approved a large development that clearly violated the goals of the MRPA. A local developer proposed to construct a 285-acre, one-hundred-million-dollar office park adjacent to the riverbank of the Chattahoochee in Duluth.[70] The proposal violated many of the MRPA standards for building height, riparian buffers, and good construction practices. Despite heated opposition to the development, the City of Duluth overrode ARC recommendations and approved the park for construction. "I am very concerned about Duluth being a precedent," said Warren Beach, superintendent of the Chattahoochee National Recreation Area, to *Atlanta Journal-Constitution* reporter David Corvette. "One little thing does not appear to be a disaster, but you start adding to it and there is a potential for a snowball effect."[71]

That year, the ARC voted to expand its development recommendations for the area.[72] The commission planned to develop a detailed land use plan to guide construction and development throughout the entire Chattahoochee corridor. "The idea is to go beyond designating this as an area of concern," said Paul Kelman, the chief environmental planner for the ARC. Without a land use plan, he admitted, corridor protection under the MRPA was merely symbolic.[73]

In response to the Duluth incident, the state legislature also expanded the MRPA's oversight controls in 1986. The revised statute made it more difficult for suburbs to override ARC recommendations. If the ARC opposed a project, then the suburb could only approve development if it also received approval from the state Environmental Protection Division director Leonard Ledbetter.[74]

Municipal planners were used to making completely independent zoning decisions, and they chafed under the new regulatory oversight. "It's ridiculous," said an outraged Duluth city clerk to reporters. "What the heck good is local government? Why not go straight to Ledbetter? He'll decide anyway."[75] Despite their protestations, however, the communities began to comply more often with the MRPA goals.

After the ARC developed a land use plan and the MRPA amendments went into effect, development along the Chattahoochee was better regulated. The ARC's Chattahoochee Corridor Plan created specific development guidelines that varied according to site's sensitivity to erosion.[76] Any development in the corridor required an ARC permit to certify that the development was in compliance with the plan. After only a few years of implementation, a 1989 study found that compliance with the plan was generally widespread, although minor violations still occurred.[77]

Although Georgia's MRPA curbed runoff problems directly along the banks of the Chattahoochee, the rest of the metro area was still unregulated. Atlanta's suburban developers continued to bulldoze forestland and replace it with asphalt parking lots, wide-lane roads, and box store roofs. In Gwinnett County alone, over thirty-four thousand wooded acres were cleared for houses, shopping centers, and offices between 1975 and 1985.[78] Although these sites were not adjacent to the Chattahoochee, many of them drained into stormwater systems that discharged into the river.

On the federal level, EPA stormwater regulations—and oftentimes their *lack* of regulation—landed the agency in court many times throughout the 1970s and 1980s. Most of the controversy centered on whether stormwater drains were a point source or not.[79] The Clean Water Act required all point sources to get a permit, but nonpoint sources did not require one. Stormwater drains were difficult to define because they were technically a "conveyance," or point source, but their discharges were composed entirely of nonpoint source pollution.

In 1973, the EPA proposed regulations that would exempt most stormwater drains from the NPDES permitting process.[80] The agency cited feasibility as its primary motivator and claimed that it would be too timely and costly to permit and monitor every stormwater drain in the country.[81]

After this first regulation was successfully challenged by the Natural Resources Defense Council (NRDC) in federal court,[82] the EPA issued a series of regulations in the 1980s that attempted to avoid a full permitting process for stormwater drains.[83] The regulation sparked criticism from industry and environmentalists alike. The NRDC challenged these regulations, too, and stormwater regulation seemed doomed to another decade of litigation.

Congress stepped in to help the EPA in 1987. It amended the Clean Water Act by adding a new section on stormwater discharges, Section 402(p). The new section required point source permits for all stormwater discharges by 1994.[84] It also required all stormwater drain owners to limit pollution to the "maximum extent practicable." Stormwater systems that served large populations, like the ones in Atlanta's suburbs, were on an abbreviated timetable; Congress required them to get permits by 1992.

Although the EPA dragged its feet again after the 1987 amendments, and was sued, again, by the NRDC, it promulgated a new rule that set the guidelines for stormwater drains' permitting on November 16, 1990.[85] The rule was, of course, promptly challenged in court by the NRDC. Still, by 1992, it looked like the EPA might actually get around to issuing permits.

For Atlanta's suburbs, the first step in the stormwater permitting process was fact-finding. None of Atlanta's municipalities could map their storm drains from start to finish, and no one knew what kind of pollutants were released at the end of each ditch.[86] Federal regulations addressed this issue and gave all metro Atlanta counties a year to map the thousands of ditches and drains in their stormwater systems and measure the pollutants at each pipe's end.[87] The next year, the EPA required each county to complete a stormwater pollution control plan and get permits for any stormwater pollution discharges from the county system.

The stormwater permits required all the metro municipalities to adhere to a list of minimum control measures.[88] At a minimum, the municipalities had to provide public education, detect illicit discharges, control construction runoff, and enact pollution prevention strategies.[89] According to state regulations, each municipality was required to outline their minimum control measures in a Stormwater Management Plan by 1992.

Cost was the biggest obstacle for implementing the new stormwater regulations. Gwinnett estimated that compliance with new stormwater regulations would cost the county an additional $10 million each year.[90] DeKalb County's long-term plan would cost $300 million.[91] To address these costs, most of the Atlanta metro counties created stormwater utilities. Like other utilities, they charged water users a fee each month for stormwater control. Fees were typically based on the area of impermeable surface owned by each property owner: the more asphalt, the higher the bill.[92]

Atlanta's metro counties also added additional zoning requirements for new development that placed limits on destruction of permeable land surfaces. Roswell proposed an ordinance to create a twenty-five-foot development buffer around all its streams.[93] Gwinnett adopted a "tree ordinance" that required developers to plant a certain number of trees at each project site.[94] Decatur required developers to construct stormwater detention areas on their sites.[95] Fulton even hired a tree arborist to inspect building sites to see if trees could be saved.[96]

In Roswell, the water authority created a 159-acre constructed wetland park with funds from an EPA grant. The park has three main structures that capture stormwater runoff from the area's suburban communities.[97] The captured stormwater is channeled to a large field, where it percolates down into a wetland area.[98] This natural filtering system separates the water from many of its contaminants. The wetland park has helped the city cut down on its stormwater pollution and increase its drinking water quality.

Despite these successes, Atlanta's suburbs still struggle with proper land use management. Prior to the 2008 economic downturn, the metro area replaced an estimated fifty-five acres of natural, permeable surface with hard concrete *every day*.[99] Although development slowed during the recession, tighter regulation of land use and stormwater prevention will be needed as construction returns to its prerecession pace.

The city's stormwater struggles are not the only problem spawned from Atlanta's urban sprawl. Today, Atlanta also lives with a lasting septic legacy from its period of suburban growth: one out of every four homes in metro Atlanta still uses a septic tank.[100] This percentage is higher than any other urban area in the country.[101] A recent study of the water quality around the Chattahoochee National Recreation Area found that septic tank leachate, in combination with other discharges, caused the Chattahoochee's fecal coliform levels to regularly exceed state and federal standards for drinking and recreational water quality.[102]

Another legacy from Atlanta's sprawl, however, has been much more devastating to the region. During Atlanta's home rule development frenzy, the suburbs' pattern of inefficient construction strained each municipality's existing water supply. The rapid pace of development, along with a sheer absence of coordinated long-term urban planning, placed Atlanta on a collision course toward the city's present water war.

Gwinnet was the first to run out of water. In 1975, the fast-growing county outgrew its source on the Chattahoochee and successfully petitioned the Army Corps for the short-term right to withdraw forty million gallons of water daily from Lake Lanier.[103] A year later, DeKalb began to run out of water as well, and without first clearing the increase with the Army Corps, Gwinnett agreed to withdraw more water from Lake Lanier and sell the surplus to DeKalb.[104] South Atlanta counties also experienced shortages, and the Army Corps contemplated altering the Buford Dam's flow regime to accommodate their needs.[105] Despite the water scarcity, none of the suburbs halted development in anticipation of shortages, and none of the communities adopted measures to increase residential and commercial water efficiency.

Throughout the 1970s and 1980s, the Army Corps issued short-term withdrawal permits to the following Atlanta-area water providers: the cities of Cumming, Gainesville, and Buford; Gwinnett, Fulton, and Hall counties; and the Atlanta Regional Commission.[106] The permitted withdrawals based on these contracts totaled 377 million gallons a day.[107] All of the contracts were scheduled to expire by 1989.[108]

No one was more dependent on Lake Lanier than Gwinnett County. Gwinnett's first water source was a small intake facility on the Chattahoochee in Duluth, Georgia, but county planners constructed the Lake Lanier Filter Plant as soon as the reservoir was constructed.[109] Of the total withdrawals, Gwinnett accounted for more than a quarter, or one hundred million gallons, of the region's daily water withdrawals from the lake. By the 1970s, the lake was by far the county's largest water source.

Because the withdrawal contracts could not interfere with the authorized purposes of the dam, the amount that each entity could withdraw from Lake Lanier was dependent upon the reservoir's water level. The contracts were also need based, meaning that the counties were permitted to withdraw water based only on their system's needs given the area's rainfall, water use, or seasonal conditions.[110]

Even though the Army Corps contracts allowed withdrawals of 377 million gallons from the Chattahoochee and Lake Lanier daily,[111] Georgia's state regulations limited the metro region to 300 million gallons.[112] This limit applied to Atlanta's seven suburban counties—Clayton, Cobb, DeKalb, Douglas, Fulton, Gwinnett, and Rockdale—as well as the Atlanta City system.[113] By 1985, the Atlanta metro area's average withdrawals equaled 99 percent of their total allotment, and several municipal water providers exceeded the limit during peak periods of use.[114] Even so, the region's suburban ring continued to grow with no endgame in sight.

# 7

# URBAN DECAY

While the region's suburban ring continued to expand, the inner core of Atlanta began to rot in neglect. During the 1990s, anyone who hooked their ball on the Ansley Golf Club's seventh hole would have encountered a shocking sight. Just feet from the rough, beyond a well-manicured line of trees, was a creek bed strewn with toilet paper, diapers, condoms, hypodermic needles, and even the occasional crack pipe.[1] It wasn't the club's fault; even if their course landscapers had cleaned the creek every morning, a new round of filth would've wash into the creek bed before nightfall.

The suburbs might have had septic seepage, but at least their creeks weren't a biohazard. The difference between Atlanta and its suburbs was a function of their wastewater infrastructural networks. Suburban stormwater systems were separate systems, meaning that sewers and stormwater drains were contained in separate pipes. The systems were also generally built to accommodate the volume of stormwater produced by the suburban communities they serviced. In Atlanta's city center, however, the stormwater drainage flowed into sewer pipes. These "combined sewers" were built prior to the New Deal projects of the 1930s, and they serviced all of the nineteen square miles of Atlanta's business district.[2] When it rained, water would flow from the city's hard concrete surfaces into the curbside drains that were connected to the combined sewer system.

Unlike modern stormwater ditches, which can naturally overflow in times of excess stormwater drainage, combined sewer systems use pipes. With only a finite volume of carrying capacity, these pipes require some kind of mechanism to prevent them from exploding or cracking when the stormwater exceeds the pipe's interior volume. Atlanta's system uses combined sewer

89

overflows (CSOs), which are thick horizontal pipes that stretch from the underground sewer connections to an outlet on a ditch or waterway. When it rains, pressure builds up in the sewer pipe and pushes sewage and stormwater over a barrier and out into the CSO, where it is then discharged directly into the ditch: "After a rain, toilet paper, condoms and other throwaways that people flush down their toilets hang thickly in trees or carpet Clear Creek's banks. Rotting raw sewage, laden with bacteria and viruses, can be smelled or seen bubbling in many places along the stream bed."[3] Although the visual impact of the sewage discharges was disturbing, the CSOs' invisible pollutants were the most harmful. In addition to the typical human sewage pollutants, CSOs also contain toxic industrial waste from industries that receive permits to discharge into the Atlanta sewer system.[4]

The city's CSO system was built to accommodate the urban landscape of the early 1900s, but much of the city has changed greatly since then. At the turn of the century, the city center still contained residential areas with absorbent, grassy lawns. Eighty years later, these lawns had all been replaced by dense urban development in the form of roads, buildings, and parking garages.

The city's new landscape was almost entirely composed of impermeable surfaces, and the amount of runoff produced within city limits increased exponentially. The overflow points were intended as a stopgap measure for extreme rain events, but the increased runoff made pipe overflows commonplace. Any time it rained in the city, the combined sewers would overflow. From 1988 to 1991, CSOs in the city overflowed into the South River and Chattahoochee River 1,925 times.[5]

Unlike the stormwater laws, which originated with state legislation, regulation of CSOs began at the federal level. Congress began studying CSO issues in 1964, but it did not act to regulate the CSOs for decades. Because CSO problems are very difficult to remedy, Congress was unwilling to place such a heavy burden on American cites, even though the discharges clearly endangered public health.

CSO overflows can only be fixed in one of three ways: a city can build a giant underground storage tunnel to store the overflow until the pipes are no longer overburdened, it can build a facility at each overflow point to clean the discharges, or it can rip out the old system and replace it with a new system that separates the sewage and stormwater pipes.[6] All of the possible solutions are exorbitantly expensive.

Congressional studies repeatedly concluded that CSOs were a major contributor of pollution to American waterways, but the federal government was hesitant to adopt regulations that would bankrupt city budgets.[7] Although CSOs should have required permits under the Clean Water Act starting in 1972, the EPA first promulgated its CSO permit regulations seventeen years later in 1989.[8]

In its 1989 *Final National Control Strategy for Combined Sewer Overflows*, the EPA set three goals for state implementation of the federal CSO law. The new regulations, the EPA claimed, would ensure that overflows result only when it rains, bring overflows into compliance with technology limitations and water quality standards, and minimize negative impacts from overflows.[9] In other words, the EPA wanted states to start treating CSOs like any other discharge of pollutants into water.

To get in line with federal regulations, Georgia amended its Water Quality Control Act in 1990 to permit and then gradually eliminate CSOs. The amendments required CSO operators to submit a plan to treat sewage overflows to the state Environmental Protection Division by the end of 1993.[10] Any municipalities that failed to follow the new CSO regulations would face daily fines and a possible sewer hookup moratorium.[11]

In May 1990, the city sent its first CSO plan to the state for approval. The plan called for overflow treatment plants at five of the worst offending CSO points in the business district.[12] The cost of the plants was estimated at $90 million. The city planned to construct treatment plants at two of the CSO points in Piedmont Park and Clear Creek in the first phase of its plan. These plants would inject chlorine into the water to kill bacteria and would screen solid debris before discharging the stormwater.[13]

The city's treatment plan was not popular with area residents. Environmentalists complained that the chlorine would only partially treat the water, leaving heavy metals, pesticides, and nutrients like phosphorous and nitrogen still in the stormwater stream.[14] Local citizens' groups in the business district also lashed out against the treatment plans. They believed the plants would take away land from valuable inner-city park space.[15] Of course, since the parks in question were strewn with fecal matter from the CSOs every time it rained, their "value" was debatable.

After fielding citizen complaints about the projects, the City Council voted unanimously to install separate pipes at Clear Creek instead of building a treatment facility.[16] The new city plan would replace the entire combined sewer pipe system with two separate pipe systems, one for sewage and another for stormwater. This would effectively remove sewage from the stormwater system's periodic overflows. The system, however, was much more expensive to construct than the treatment plant. Mayor Jackson cited budget concerns when he vetoed the plan, but the council voted unanimously to override his decision.[17] At the same time, however, the council didn't account for a way to fund the project.

At the Piedmont Park site, the City Council finally quelled resident opposition when it proposed to site the treatment facility on land adjacent to the park.[18] Because citizen opposition had delayed a decision, and because the new treatment facility site was farther away from the CSO outlet, the project cost $118 million as opposed to the originally planned $30 million.[19]

Citizen groups also opposed construction of a massive tunnel that would capture discharges from the Utoy Creek CSO. The tunnel would have connected the Utoy overflow point to the city's R. M. Clayton sewage treatment plant. Although R. M. Clayton had exceeded its capacity, the proposed eight-mile-long, twenty-five-foot-wide tunnel would provide storage and enable the plant to treat the CSO and other sewage from the city of Atlanta as well as Fulton, Gwinnett, and DeKalb counties.[20] The city spent $20 million to design the tunnel before citizen groups forced it to abandon the plan.[21]

By the time Atlanta reached its 1993 deadline, it had built treatment plants for only three out of five of its CSO points.[22] The two remaining points, at Clear Creek and Utoy Creek, still spewed untreated overflow. The city had begun construction on a treatment facility at Clear Creek, but it had not started work at all on the Utoy Creek sewer separation.[23]

Starting January 1, 1994, the state began to impose daily fines on Atlanta for the two untreated CSOs, and new sewer hookups in both sewer service areas were forbidden.[24] After two years of continued noncompliance, the daily fines were raised from one thousand to ten thousand dollars and would increase again to $100,000 a day if Atlanta failed to meet its projected completion dates for each project.[25]

On top of the CSO fines, Atlanta also faced fines for sewage spills. By 1996, Atlanta's R. M. Clayton plant was massively overburdened once again. In June, and again in January 1997, plant malfunctions spilled hundreds of thousands of gallons of raw sewage directly into the Chattahoochee.[26] The state fined the city $20,000 for the first spill and $100,000 for the second spill.[27] Although the cumulative fines were crippling, the city faced an even greater punishment for noncompliance. If the city didn't get its act together soon, Georgia officials warned, the state would enforce a construction moratorium for the entire area.

To compound the pressure on Atlanta, the environmental group Upper Chattahoochee Riverkeeper, along with downstream cities and counties, filed suit against Atlanta for violating the Clean Water Act.[28] The plaintiffs claimed

that Atlanta's three new CSO treatment facilities' discharges violated the act
by dumping heavy metals and fecal coliform into the Chattahoochee. At the
time, Atlanta's CSO discharges and sewage spills caused widespread contamination of the river and the fish living in it. Atlanta's section of the Chattahoochee ranked among the top five rivers in the United States in terms of
chlordane, PCB, mercury, and other toxic chemicals in fish tissue samples.[29]
The group was granted summary judgment.

Two years later, the EPA and EPD investigated Atlanta's wastewater
treatment system and found that the entire system was in need of a complete overhaul.[30] The lines were decaying and flowing at capacity. Even worse,
Atlanta was doing nothing to fix the problem. The two agencies joined with
the Upper Chattahoochee Riverkeeper in its suit against the city.[31]

Atlanta reached a settlement with the groups in September of 1998. The
city agreed to pay a $2.5 million fine, buy $25 million of Chattahoochee
River riparian land as a runoff buffer, and spend another $2.5 million on city
creek cleanup.[32] Even after the city complied with this agreement, however,
it would still need to find a permanent solution to eliminate combined sewer
overflows.

In addition to CSO concerns, the city also had to upgrade their decaying
water mains. In fact, the entire water supply system was falling apart. Atlanta
was still using the same pumping facility that was built off the Chattahoochee
a century earlier in 1897.[33] "We're afraid to touch anything here," said Atlanta's water chief. "If we try to undo a bolt or turn a valve, we could break it."[34]
The city had begun construction on a $36-million new pump station, but the
project was two years overdue and also over budget.[35] It seemed as though
every inch of the city's water system, from intake pumps to sewer outfalls,
was in need of costly repairs.

The entire burden of solving Atlanta's water and budget crisis fell on
one man: Bill Campbell. After Maynard Jackson decided not to run for a
fourth term in office, the city elected former city councilman Bill Campbell
as its new mayor in 1993. From the start, controversy surrounded the Campbell administration. During his election campaign, Campbell fought rumors
that he had taken bribes from airport businessmen in exchange for favorable
votes.[36] Scandal also dogged the Campbell administration after Atlanta hosted
the summer Olympics in 1996 and Campbell's friend received a multimillion-
dollar windfall from dubious management of the city's vending program.[37]

After the Olympic games, Campbell geared up for a difficult reelection campaign against City Council president Marvin Arrington.[38] Campbell
was far ahead in the polls, but the campaign rhetoric quickly devolved into

contentious mudslinging that damaged both men's reputations. Arrington accused Campbell of being a puppet for Atlanta's white elites, and both men accused each other of corruption. Campbell distributed a videotape of Arrington getting a $500 bribe, and Arrington distributed a cassette from local rapper Lil' Jon that criticized Campbell for living in the suburbs and sending his kids to private school.[39]

Bob Holmes, the director of the Southern Center for Studies in Public Policy, told reporters that Atlanta's mayoral campaign was the most negative campaign in Atlanta since the 1970s. "I've run into a lot of people who've said we ought to have 'none of the above' on the ballot," said Holmes.[40] The *Atlanta Journal-Constitution* editors agreed, and decided that neither candidate was worthy of the newspaper's endorsement that year.[41]

Although substantive issues received less attention during the campaign, the city's mounting water woes were also a stain on Campbell's record. Early in the campaign, Arrington blasted Campbell for city sewer problems during his administration. Closer to elections, drinking water quality also became an issue. At one of the televised debates, Arrington held up a jar of dark, discolored water that he claimed had come from an Atlanta kitchen faucet.[42] Campbell responded by casually sipping tap water during the next televised debate.[43] Nevertheless, it became clear to Campbell's reelection team that the mayor would need to at least begin to act to resolve the city's water problems.

Like Hartsfield before him, Campbell wanted to resolve Atlanta's water issues without footing the bill. Unfortunately for Campbell, the regulatory environment of the 1990s wasn't skewed in favor of large federal handouts like it had been for Hartsfield. The big dam era was long gone, and in its place was a post–Reagan era focus on limited federal spending and fiscal accountability. Local funding was equally unlikely, as tax hikes during an election year amounted to political suicide. The mayor would have to look outside the public sector for funds.

On December 6, 1997, Campbell held a press conference to release his "Blueprint for Atlanta," a plan which he claimed would solve all of Atlanta's water problems at once. His plan was both simple and revolutionary at the same time: Atlanta would sell its water and sewer system to a private company.[44]

Campbell's original plan was to privatize the system for a lengthy term; he wanted to privatize the city's water and sewers for at least twenty years.[45] The Georgia legislature, however, was hesitant. Despite Campbell's push the year before to change Georgia's old statutes, the legislature had failed to revise a law that placed limits on long-term sewer contracts.[46] Hampered by the state's unrevised statute, Campbell pushed for a long-term contract for the city's water but stuck to a short-term, five-year contract for municipal sewers.[47]

At first, selling the water system seemed like a great deal. Atlanta hired an engineering firm to calculate the amount of money that Atlanta could save by making the switch from public to private water systems. The firm found that the city could save up to $30 million annually, just by privatizing the water department.[48] Those profits, Campbell reasoned, would be funneled directly into projects to fix the city's serious stormwater and sewer issues.

Campbell encouraged the City Council to proceed as soon as possible in the summer so that the city could go ahead and start reaping the thirty-million-dollar-a-year savings from privatization.[49] This timeline, of course, would also ensure that the deal was complete just before the fall mayoral elections.

The city started the bidding process by issuing a 194-page "request for proposal," outlining the city's expectations.[50] Bidders were invited to send their technical and financial qualifications during the first round.[51] After the first round, bids were ranked based on six different qualification standards: compliance with the city's minority contracting requirements, performance, technical capabilities, plans to transfer Water Department employees to private payroll, cost, and the credentials and structure of the company's management teams.[52] Once the first-round rankings were assigned, those companies deemed qualified would have a chance to submit final proposals in the second round, which was also known as the "best and final offer" phase.[53]

Atlanta was not alone in its decision to privatize. Approximately 770 cities across the nation also used combined sewer overflow systems that needed to be replaced.[54] In 1996, the EPA estimated that $44.7 billion would be needed to control the nation's combined sewer overflow problems.[55]

Many of these cities also looked to privatization as a means of raising revenue for infrastructural repairs.[56] This trend increased after the U.S. tax code was revised in 1997 to allow municipalities to privatize and still maintain their tax-exempt status.[57] From 1997 to 2000, seventy cities across the United State entered into long-term contracts with private companies to operate their water supply systems.[58] By 2007, the number of privatized water systems in the United States had increased to over six hundred.[59]

Atlanta was on the cusp of this privatization wave. At the time the deal was brokered, Atlanta's system was destined to become the largest privately managed waterworks in the United States. International mega-corporations like Suez and Vivendi were eager to break into the American market with a high-profile success story, and Atlanta's long-term contract was a coveted prize. At the end of the first round of bidding, five companies had submitted formal proposals: OMI Atlanta, Atlanta Water Alliance, United Water, U.S. Filter, and Atlanta Water Corporation. Although many of the companies had quaint, local-sounding names, all five were backed by the largest global water corporations in the world.

OMI Atlanta was part of CH2M Hill, a multibillion dollar American engineering corporation.[60] At the time it bid, CH2M Hill already operated 120 water and sewer systems across the world, including facilities in Kuwait, Brazil, and Atlanta's suburbs.[61]

With total annual revenues of only $5 billion and $2.4 billion respectively, U.S. Filter and Atlanta Water Corporation were the smallest contenders in the group. The California-based U.S. Filter operated twelve water systems in the United States, including Fulton County's water plant in Atlanta's northern suburbs.[62] It was bought by Vivendi two years later.[63] Atlanta Water Corporation was owned by the SAUR Group, a Paris company that operated over seven thousand water systems across the world.[64]

United Water was partially run by Suez Lyonnaise des Eaux, and Atlanta Water Alliance was a subsidiary of Vivendi Environment.[65] Suez and Vivendi are the two largest water corporations in the world.[66] Together, the two companies operate systems in 120 countries and bring in annual revenues nearing $100 billion.[67] The two companies control over two-thirds of the private water market.[68] Vivendi, which changed its name to Veolia in 2003, now provides water to 110 million people around the world.[69]

Early on in the process, many citizens were concerned that the same cronyism and corruption that had marred other Campbell administration projects would also skew the city's choice of water companies. Civilians were particularly concerned about OMI, whose public relations team had close ties to the Campbell administration. The city's legal advisor during contract negotiations was local attorney Steve Labowitz, Campbell's former chief of staff.[70] Labowitz's wife, however, worked with the law firm advising OMI Atlanta's contract bid, and one of the firm's partners had also worked for the Campbell administration as the director of internal affairs.[71]

After the bids were submitted and evaluated, the city issued its ranking for the first round of proposals. OMI came out on top, followed by Atlanta Water Alliance, United Water, U.S. Filter, and then Atlanta Water Corporation. U.S. Filter had submitted the least expensive proposal; it offered to run Atlanta's water system for a little over $25 million each year.

When OMI was ranked first, despite filing a more expensive proposal, Campbell's political opponents claimed the fix was in. City Council president

Robb Pitts called a press conference in July and cinematically waved a sealed envelope in which he claimed to have written the name of the firm that had already bought and paid for Campbell's endorsement.

After the first round of rankings, the companies were then allowed to revise their original bids in the city's "best and final offer" phase. United Water dramatically undercut every other company's proposal in the second round; it offered to run the waterworks for just $21.4 million each year.[72]

At the end of August, Bill Campbell shocked and silenced his opponents with his surprising endorsement of United Water Services for the water-works contract. "Today is a victorious day for the people of Atlanta and our ratepayers," said Campbell at his press conference.[73] Unwilling to let previous slights go unnoticed, Campbell also invited Council president Pitts to reveal the contents of his infamous envelope so that Atlanta could see "if he is prophetic as he [had] claimed" to be.[74]

While Pitts might have been wrong about OMI, he was probably right about the Campbell administration's motivation. Years later, the federal government indicted Campbell for racketeering, bribery, and tax evasion. It alleged that Campbell had received tens of thousands of dollars in payoffs and free gambling trips to Tennessee from the winning water bidder.[75] At his trial, one of Campbell's mistresses testified that she had taken an all-expense-paid vacation to Paris with Campbell that had been allegedly paid for by United Water.[76] A jury later convicted Campbell for tax evasion.

Problems with Atlanta's water management started almost immediately after the United Water takeover. From the start, a number of issues arose from the ambiguities in the poorly written and vague water contract. The entire privatization process, from announcement to selection, lasted only eighteen months.[77] Other cities with much smaller markets and less complicated infrastructure problems had taken many years to broker a deal.[78] The hastily drawn contract left many unanswered questions, and in some cases, was flat-out wrong.

The city hadn't kept records to establish how many repairs needed to be made in an average year, and the city's contract grossly underestimated repair needs across the board.[79] In its contract, the city estimated that 1,171 water meters would break each year; in reality, 11,108 broke the first year United Water was in charge.[80] The city also estimated that 101 main breaks would occur, but 279 actually occurred.[81] The city estimated that 734 fire hydrants would need to be repaired, but 1,633 broke in the first year.[82]

The wording of the contract was also unclear about who would be responsible for over $115 million in capital improvements.[83] The final language stated that responsibility for these improvements, which included $37 million in necessary water main upgrades across the city, were "to be determined."[84]

Some of the contract's ambiguity arose from the overall structure of the deal itself. The contract did not fully privatize Atlanta's system; instead, it specified that United Water would "take over all water purification, delivery, maintenance, and customer service responsibilities."[85] The contract retained some rights and obligations for the city's municipal waterworks, including the obligation to finish system improvements that were under construction at the time the contract was signed.[86] This division of responsibility left city residents wondering which group was responsible for the infrastructural problems that they encountered in the upcoming years.

The city had also slacked on repairs during its year of negotiation with water companies.[87] At the time United Water took control over the system, it inherited a backlogged list of requested pipe repairs that contained nearly a thousand entries.[88] The city's aging infrastructure also caused frequent main breaks throughout the city. This problem was compounded by Atlanta's continued rapid growth, as construction crews would often accidentally break water mains while laying foundations or cutting in new roads.

In the first years that United Water was in control of the city's drinking water, Atlanta had a number of issues with drinking water quality. The pumps at the water production facilities, including the still-used original pumps at the city's first facility on the Chattahoochee, were prone to breaking down. Whenever they'd break, pressure in the pipes would drop, causing potential problems with "back siphonage."[89] Back siphonage, or backflow, occurs when a vacuum effect in the pipes sucks polluted wastewater from end users, like homes, hotels, hospitals, and businesses, back into the system.[90]

Almost every endpoint in the system has a cross-connection point where sewage water flows past clean water. When clean water pressure lowers to a certain point, sewage from the cross-connections can get mixed into clean water.[91] Whenever a drop in pressure would occur, the city's water was at risk of becoming contaminated with bacteria and other pollutants from sewage and residents would be asked to boil their water. One particularly bad failure at the Northside Pumping Station led to a boil water advisory for tens of thousands of North Atlanta residents.[92]

At other times, main breaks would cause residential water to become badly discolored. Rust and debris from the aging pipes would settle in times of low pressure during a disruption and would then be released once pressure was restored.[93] Residents around the city would periodically turn on their taps to find brown-colored water with tiny bits of sediment and debris floating in it.[94] "It's pathetic . . . like a Third World country," claimed one resident. "You go to run a load of laundry, and it comes out brown. You can't even bathe your kid."[95] At the height of Atlanta's water main problems, United Water received hundreds of complaints about discolored water around the city.[96]

Atlanta also never made as much money as it had planned. As part of the deal, Atlanta had planned to use money from water user fees to repair its decaying sewage treatment system. But, United Water's bill collection system was deeply flawed and, since the income from water bills went to Atlanta, the company had very little incentive to fix the meters and upgrade the billing system. The water usage statistics for many users were wrong; some meters were broken, and water main breaks caused inflated charges. When one apartment complex was cut off for a particularly egregious outstanding bill of $479,000, the condo association managers claimed that their meters were broken and pipes were leaking.[97] Another woman had her water cut off for failure to pay a $600 bill that had been erroneously charged to her as a result of a faulty meter.[98]

When Bill Campbell left office amid controversy, Atlanta elected Shirley Franklin as its new mayor. Franklin had been part of the negotiation team for U.S. Filter during its losing bid for the Atlanta contract, so she wasn't predisposed to overlook United Water's failings. She wasted no time in taking United Water to task for shortcomings in their performance. In June of 2002, Franklin announced that she was formally putting the company on probation.

Mayor Franklin requested $1 million from the City Council to conduct an audit of United Water's performance over the upcoming three or four months.[99] When the council balked at the expenditure, United Water agreed to pay for the audit itself in a last ditch attempt to regain favor with the public and repair its tattered image.[100] The company also agreed to improve its performance on a list of nearly one hundred benchmarks that the mayor's office would use to evaluate the company's performance.

United Water was eager to keep the contract, even though it was hemorrhaging money. The company's financial outlook was surprisingly bleak, even by today's post-recession standards: its assets were worth only 75 percent of its liabilities, and it had a debt-to-equity ratio of three to one.[101] In short, it was flat broke and it owed a lot of money. During the company's probationary period, it failed every single financial benchmark.

The Atlanta contract, however, was about more than just money. Suez, United Water's parent company, wanted to rely on its success in Atlanta when courting other American cities in future privatization deals. A highly publicized failure in Atlanta would be a lasting handicap for United Water's attempts to enter and dominate the U.S. market. The company launched a massive public relations campaign aimed at winning back the hearts and minds of Atlanta's water users, and it also began to perform its municipal functions fairly well. The internal audit showed improvements in many of Franklin's benchmarks during the company's probationary period.

Things were looking fairly good for United Water, until it made one huge tactical mistake. In October, during negotiations with Mayor Franklin, United Water's legal team sent Franklin a copy of letters, signed by Bill Campbell in the waning hours of his final term in office, which authorized an additional $80 million in city funds to be paid to United Water.[102] The letters were patently illegal; Campbell had no authority to approve such an enormous expenditure without first procuring the approval of the City Council.

When confronted with such a dubious document, Mayor Franklin bristled. Her entire campaign had been centered on her promise to end the Campbell administration's practice of shady backroom deals, and this document represented everything that she had sworn to fight against.

United Water had hoped to use the letters as leverage to negotiate a higher yearly payout for services, but the move angered Franklin and raised a new firestorm of criticism about corruption in the contract awarding process. United Water quickly backtracked, claiming that it would rather drop its claim for more money than fight with Franklin, but the damage to the company's image had already been done.[103] United Water, in the public's eyes, was just another poorly functioning remnant of the Campbell administration's corrupt deal-making process.[104] By the time United Water's probationary period was over in November, its $80 million letter from Campbell was subject to a federal investigation.[105]

The final auditor's report on United Water's probation performance was bleak. The company had failed to collect over $57 million in overdue accounts that were supposed to go back to the city's general fund.[106] Worse yet, the city hadn't seen anything like the $20 million annual savings that had been promised at the start of the deal. Atlanta had saved roughly $10 million each year, but a 1998 Georgia law required the city to pay back $9.8 million a year in franchise fees.[107] The small leftover amount went to the city's general fund and the sewer system never got a dime.[108] All in all, said auditor Leslie Ward, "The city appears to have come out about even."[109]

In a last-ditch attempt to regain favor, United Water offered to freeze costs for three years, but the proposal was too little and too late.[110] Franklin canceled the contract the next week.[111]

Atlanta's broken water deal left the city back at square one. Pipes were still breaking, pumps were failing, stormwater and sewers were still in noncompliance, and the city didn't have any money. By the end of Atlanta's private water debacle, the city hadn't spent a dime on infrastructural improvements. In 1998, the year that United Water's contract was terminated, Atlanta's leaking pipes received the dubious honor of being named one of *Popular Mechanics* "Top Ten Pieces of U.S. Infrastructure We Must Fix Now."[112]

By then, however, Atlanta's water problems extended far beyond its infrastructural flaws. The neighboring states of Alabama and Florida had sued to halt more than half of the Atlanta metro area's water withdrawals, and it looked as though they just might win.

# 8

# WATER WAR, PART I

The year 1990 will likely be remembered as a turning point in Atlanta's environmental and urban planning history. That year, a century of poor urban planning decisions came back to haunt the city's present leaders. Every shortcut or misstep that the city had made—the Jim Crow–era sewer overflow points, Hartsfield's dam-related frugality, the metro region's suburban sprawl—had contributed to the deteriorating condition of the Chattahoochee River downstream of Atlanta. Eventually the river, and the people who relied upon it, reached a breaking point.

If Atlanta just had one water problem, such as stormwater pollution or overconsumption, the Chattahoochee River might have been able to recover from the city's ill effects. Stormwater pollution could be diluted with downstream fresh water sources. Likewise, Atlanta's overwithdrawals from the river could be partially remedied by water storage in the river's downstream reservoirs. Unfortunately, however, Atlanta didn't just have one problem. It had many problems, and all of the problems interacted with one another to make problem-solving on the river much more difficult. The city's water usage depleted the amount of fresh water that could have diluted its stormwater and CSO pollution. The CSO pollution and stormwater made sewage-ridden water storage in reservoirs an unpalatable option.

Furthermore, because there were so many pressing needs competing for attention all at once, Atlanta's politicians were unable, or perhaps unwilling, to meaningfully address all the city's problems. Pipes leaked, stormwater drained into the river, combined sewers overflowed, septic tanks leached, and the metro region's water intake pipes drew an increasingly large amount of water from Lake Lanier and the Chattahoochee River every day. The entire system, from start to finish, was broken.

Although litigation over the Chattahoochee began in 1990, Atlanta's water supply problems had started long before then. The Buford Dam was supposed to accommodate the city's water needs for decades, but just thirteen years after its completion, the greater Atlanta metro area had already exhausted the Chattahoochee's available water supply.

Atlanta's fast-growing suburban communities were a significant part of the problem. Many of the attributes that were the hallmark of suburbia, like the large homes and the lush green lawns, also created the perfect recipe for water inefficiency. In the summer, when Atlanta's weather was characteristically dry, the city's suburban residents used excessive amounts of water to maintain their lawns and to fill backyard swimming pools. Inside the homes, large kitchen and bathroom appliances were a year-round drain on both water and energy supplies.

Atlanta receives most of its power from thermoelectric facilities that require a huge amount of water to operate. The Upper Chattahoochee Riverkeeper estimates that it takes two full bathtubs of water to produce enough electricity to run a single suburban refrigerator for a day.[1] Throughout Georgia, thermoelectric facilities used more than half of the total surface water withdrawals in the state.[2] Most of Atlanta's energy is produced by facilities along the Chattahoochee that compete with the city for water withdrawals.[3] In this way, excessive energy consumption also exacerbated existing water consumption problems.

The suburb's water-sewer time lag also wreaked havoc on the metro area's water supply management. In a system where every home is connected to municipal water and sewers, water is generally drawn from intake pipes, used in homes and businesses, and then returned to the same river as treated wastewater. Every home used municipal water, which was primarily sourced from the Chattahoochee basin. However, if a home was not connected to the municipal sewer system, it might return its used wastewater to another basin. Septic tank seepage returned water to the watershed where the tank was located and, in many cases, this would transfer water from the Chattahoochee basin to another watershed. This was especially problematic in Gwinnett County because the water supply was sourced entirely from the Chattahoochee but the land area was in the Ocmulgee River basin.[4] Thus, the Chattahoochee watershed experienced a 100-percent water loss on any withdrawals from the county's septic tank homes.

These two problems, inefficiency and septic tank water loss, strained Atlanta's Chattahoochee River water withdrawal limit. As early as 1974, the Atlanta Regional Commission began to seriously consider supplementing the metro area's Chattahoochee water supply with water from Lake Lanier.[5] At the time, Cobb County and Marietta drew water from Lake Allatoona, where citizen groups vehemently opposed adding more intake structures from the city of Atlanta or any other suburbs.[6]

With blocked access to Allatoona, Lake Lanier seemed like the city's most feasible option. Because Atlanta had not contributed to funding the Buford Dam, however, the city and the Army Corps had to undergo some complicated legal maneuvering to form the Lake Lanier water supply contracts.

From a legal standpoint, the main obstacle to a water supply deal was that the list of "authorized purposes" for the Buford Dam was limited to flood control, navigation, and power. Under the Flood Control Act of 1944, which had been in effect at the time the Buford Dam was funded, the provision of municipal water supplies was not a valid authorized purpose for any Army Corps project.[7] Theoretically, the Army Corps could enter into water supply contracts with municipalities, but these contracts could not "adversely affect" any of the projects' actual authorized purposes.[8] In practice, however, the corps had begun to award long-term water supply contracts, regardless of these contracts' effect on the dams' authorized purposes, to any municipality that contributed money to fund a project.

A year after construction on the Buford Dam ended, Congress passed the Water Supply Act of 1958. The act authorized the Army Corps to include municipal and industrial uses as an authorized purpose for future reservoir projects.[9] According to the act, municipalities that paid a portion of a reservoir's construction costs could create long-term water supply contracts with the Army Corps.[10] This essentially codified a practice that had been used informally by the corps for years; instead of creating individual cost-sharing agreements for each project, the corps could list municipal supply as an authorized purpose and divide costs with cities according to an established formula.

Thus, Atlanta missed the boat in two ways. Instead of the proverbial day late and dollar short, Atlanta was a few years early and about a million dollars short of obtaining a rock-solid legal foundation for its water withdrawals. Because Hartsfield had neither entered into a cost-sharing agreement under the 1944 act nor waited to pay a portion of the cost under the 1958 act, Lake Lanier remained subject to the Flood Control Act of 1944's provision limiting municipal water supply contracts.[11] Therefore, any municipal supply contracts that would "seriously affect" Lake Lanier's authorized purposes, or any contracts that involved "major structural or operational changes," would need congressional approval.[12]

For the Buford Dam and other projects in the same predicament, the Army Corps generally issued two different kinds of short-term water supply contracts: withdrawal contracts and storage contracts.[13] Withdrawal contracts allowed local governments to withdraw a certain amount of water from the reservoir for municipal and industrial uses.[14] Storage contracts allowed additional water to be released from a dam to supply downstream water users.[15]

Throughout the 1970s and 1980s, the Army Corps issued a number of short-term withdrawal and storage contracts to Atlanta metro municipalities.[16] All of the contracts were scheduled to expire in 1989.[17] Despite the precariousness of their water supplies, Atlanta's suburban municipalities continued to recklessly develop at a breakneck pace during this time, and the metro area's water consumption grew as well. By the 1980s, Atlanta's short-term contracts totaled 377 million gallons a day.[18]

Atlanta's excessive withdrawals began to take a toll on the city's downstream neighbors. Even though they fished hundreds of miles away from Atlanta's water intake pipes, Florida oystermen and fishermen in the Apalachicola Bay suffered every time the Atlanta metro area had a drought. When the water level of the Chattahoochee lowered in Georgia, oysters and shrimp would die in the bay.[19] Fishing was more than just a way of life for Apalachicola residents; it was also big business. The area's seafood industry pulled in eighty million dollars a year.[20]

Apalachicola's marine wildlife relies on the "perfect blend" of salty ocean water and nutrient-rich Chattahoochee River water.[21] When Atlanta drew too much water from the river during droughts, the downstream bay would receive less fresh water and fewer nutrients. In the salty infertile bay, oysters grew small, failed to reproduce, and suffered from disease and predators.[22] With less nutrient-laden river water mixed into the bay's salt water, the shrimp also began to move farther out into the Gulf, to choppy waters that were too dangerous for many of the local fishermen's tiny shrimp boats.[23]

Atlanta's pollution discharges also became more problematic in times of low flow on the Chattahoochee. By 1990, the city's combined sewers overflowed constantly, in wet weather and on dry days as well. The river water would hold a higher concentration of toxins in droughts because the river held less fresh water to mix with the city's sewage and stormwater discharges. During dry years, wrote one reporter, the Chattahoochee would turn into "an oxygen-poor drainage ditch downstream of Atlanta."[24] The longer Atlanta delayed action on its CSOs, the more the river's condition deteriorated.

The river's "drainage ditch" characteristics made things difficult for industrial water users downstream in Alabama as well. Two of the region's

largest industrial employers, a nuclear power plant and a paper mill, both suffered from water quantity and quality problems. The state also had difficulty
attracting new businesses to the area because of Atlanta's discharges.

At first, the three states attempted to work together to resolve the ACF
basin's water problems. To better manage the increasingly predictable basin-
wide shortages, representatives from Alabama, Florida, Georgia, and the
Army Corps of Engineers formed a Drought Management Committee in
1985.[25] Less than a year after forming, the group received its first massive
planning challenge. A terrible drought rocked the Atlanta area in 1986. The
first four months of that year were the driest months since Atlanta began
record-keeping over one hundred years before.[26] In March, the Drought
Management Committee issued a "shortage alert," which stated that Lake
Lanier water levels were so low that all users on the ACF basin would face
shortages in the foreseeable future.[27]

During the drought, municipal water providers scrambled to stay under
their withdrawal limits. Across Georgia, 453 communities faced shortages
and enacted water consumption restrictions.[28] Fayette, Cobb, and North Fulton had the greatest problems in the metro area.[29] Fayette's use exceeded
the capacity of its municipal reservoir, which stopped recharging during the
drought.[30] The city enacted emergency water use restrictions and began to
draw all of its water from Atlanta's treatment facilities.[31] The systems in Cobb
and North Fulton also lost pressure because their treatment facilities couldn't
keep pace with demand.[32]

That fall, Army Corps officials ran through worst-case-scenario analy-
ses for the upcoming year. The results of their data runs were panic induc-
ing. The corps found that, if the drought continued into the winter, Atlanta
metro's available water supply would be cut in half.[33] The entire city would be
forced to ration water, close factories, and layoff manufacturing workers.[34] A
shortage on that scale would be devastating to Atlanta's economy and would
have ripple effects on the entire nation's economic growth.

In the face of such dire findings, many of Atlanta's lawmakers revived
the decades-old idea of developing a reregulation dam downstream from the
Buford Dam. Unlike the Buford Dam, which releases water in spurts and
gushes for hydropower generation, a reregulation dam could release water
continuously to maintain consistent flow rates in the river at all times.[35] The
dam would "smooth out peak hydropower generating lease and intervening
low flows," according to a corps statement.[36]

A reregulation dam was first considered by Army Corps engineers in the
1950s as a way to maintain a reliable water flow for municipal water.[37] At the

time, Atlanta's water demands were much less than they are today, and the Army Corps engineers determined that the cost of the project would outweigh its benefits.[38] By the seventies, though, Atlanta was again concerned about its limited water supply and public interest in a reregulation dam was renewed.

The quest for a reregulation dam had hit a speed bump in 1978, when Congress passed legislation creating the Chattahoochee National Recreation Area along the banks of the river.[39] Original plans for the reregulation reservoir included inundating some land within the newly designated area. Those involved in the project became concerned that it would be vulnerable to legal challenges if it interfered with the federal recreation area land. Still, Atlanta pushed for the reregulation dam, and in November 1980, the city-sponsored Metropolitan Atlanta Resources Study recommended that the reregulation dam was the best way to address Atlanta's growing water needs.[40]

The study had been challenged by the Georgia Wildlife Federation, the Georgia Conservancy, and the Friends of the River.[41] Environmentalists were concerned that a reregulation dam would kill the area's prized trout runs by raising the Chattahoochee's temperature and dissolved oxygen levels in between dams.[42] They also worried about losing six miles of the Chattahoochee National Recreation Area to flooding from the dam.[43]

In 1982, a U.S. House of Representatives subcommittee held a public hearing on the dam. Despite the environmental opposition, representatives from all water districts supported the plan. It seemed as though their testimony paid off, and the project progressed quickly in the following months. In April of 1983, Congress eliminated the biggest legal obstacle for the reregulation dam: it passed a bill that amended the Chattahoochee Recreation Area Act so that the dam could legally flood small portions of the area. In May, it allocated $700,000 for preconstruction planning.[44]

The Omnibus Water Resources Bill was passed in Congress later in the fall of 1985. The appropriately named act was a tour de force of big-government pork barrel spending. It doled out more than eleven billion dollars in water projects throughout the country, including $24.5 million for Atlanta's reregulation dam.[45] The law, however, became one of the many laws that were vetoed during President Reagan's standoff with a Democratic Congress that year. Reagan vetoed the bill, and the OMB ordered the corps to discontinue its three-year study of the dam.[46]

Two months later, a more tempered Congress passed another bill that authorized the reregulation dam.[47] This time, though, the bill had one very big difference: if Atlanta wanted the dam, it would have to pay for it with local funds. Reagan signed it into law.

Atlanta metro area governments were divided about who should pay for the reregulation dam. As is often the case, local councilmen had very little political incentive to provide the funding for a large water project. The immediate costs were simply too great, and the benefits were spread out over too long of a term. Politicians feared that, if they approved funding, local headlines would tell of tax hikes instead of increased water security. Furthermore, the individual municipalities that composed Atlanta's metro area were still in competition with one another; no one wanted to be disadvantaged by an unfavorable cost-sharing agreement.

At first, Gwinnett County proposed that the big four providers—the City of Atlanta and Gwinnett, Cobb, and Fulton counties—all divide the cost equally.[48] The other three refused and argued that Gwinnett should pay for the lion's share because it was fastest growing county.[49] Atlanta countered with a suggestion that it would pay $3.1 million if Fulton paid $6.1 million and Gwinnett paid $6 million.[50] The four providers continued to squabble over cost until the fall of 1987, when Gwinnett was hit hard by a drought for the second year in a row and the county had to implement outdoor watering restrictions. Facing serious political backlash from angry residents, Gwinnett agreed to pay $7.2 million for the reregulation dam.[51]

Before metro water providers could reach a final agreement, however, the Army Corps changed its mind about the benefits of a reregulation dam. In July of 1988, the corps released a study that concluded that reallocation of Lake Lanier would produce greater benefits than the construction of a reregulation dam.[52] The Army Corps report proposed allocating two hundred thousand acre-feet of Lake Lanier for permanent municipal water supply.[53] If passed by Congress, the agreement would give Atlanta metro providers a permanent contract to draw roughly 160 million gallons every day from the reservoir.[54] In exchange, the reallocation would cut peak power production by 12 percent; it would also reduce the amount of water released by the dam for downstream uses, including navigation.[55]

The report was a first draft of an official Post-Authorization Change Report that the corps planned to submit to Congress. In the final report, the corps would recommend that Congress approve a permanent reallocation of water storage in Lake Lanier for Atlanta metro's water supply.[56]

The proposed reallocation agreement was the last straw for Alabama and Florida. Both states felt that their right to downstream navigation and electricity generation had already been compromised by the city's short-term withdrawal contracts, and neither was willing to risk even greater withdrawals in the future. Alabama governor Guy Hunt sent a letter to Georgia governor Joe Frank Harris the same week the report was released. "Until such time that it can be shown to our satisfaction that there are no significant economic and environmental impacts," wrote Governor Hunt, "we plan to oppose the reallocation."[57]

Alabama and Georgia's governors engaged in a tense standoff for the next six months. In a last-ditch attempt to avoid litigation, Harris sent two of his top aides to negotiate with Hunt's team that June. Later, the two sides would have conflicting accounts of what went on behind closed doors. Alabama officials wanted to seek additional water withdrawals for a nuclear power plant and paper mill on the Chattahoochee, and they reported that Harris's men had threatened to delay the request. A spokesman for Harris said that negotiators "made their interests known" but denied that any threats were made.[58]

The state of Alabama filed suit against the U.S. Army Corps of Engineers in Federal District Court for the Northern District of Alabama days later on June 28, 1990.[59] Soon thereafter, the state of Florida intervened as a plaintiff, and the state of Georgia and the Atlanta Regional Commission intervened as defendants.[60] In their suit, Alabama and Florida alleged that the corps's congressional request for permanent water supply contracts violated a host of statutes, including the Flood Control Act, the Water Resources Development Act, the Water Supply Act, National Environmental Policy Act (NEPA), and the Endangered Species Act.[61]

Plaintiffs claimed that the corps contracts violated NEPA, which requires agencies to conduct an environmental analysis before taking any action that would "significantly affect the quality of the human environment."[62] According to Alabama and Florida, the corps should have conducted NEPA analysis before allowing increased withdrawals.[63] Florida also alleged that the corps had violated the Endangered Species Act. The act contains a "no jeopardy" clause that applies to agencies. The clause obligates agencies to "insure that any action they undertake is not likely to jeopardize the continued existence of any endangered or threatened species."[64] Because the ACF basin is home to many endangered species, Florida argued that the corps should have consulted with the secretary of the interior to insure that their water withdrawal contracts did not harm the federally protected animals.[65]

The main crux of the suit, however, dealt with the Flood Control Act. The Army Corps violated the Flood Control Act, plaintiffs alleged, by entering into contracts that adversely affected Lake Lanier's other lawful uses.[66] According to the act, contracts for municipal and industrial uses on Lake Lanier could only allocate surplus water that was not used for the reservoir's other authorized purposes.[67] The plaintiffs alleged that Atlanta metro area water withdrawals unlawfully affected hydropower generation.[68] Additionally, the Army Corps had not conducted studies to determine what water was "surplus" and what was necessary for other functions.[69]

In a related claim, Alabama and Florida also alleged that the corps violated the Water Supply Act by entering into withdrawal contracts that would "seriously affect the purposes for which the project was authorized."[70] Because withdrawal contracts "seriously affected" hydropower generation, plaintiffs claimed, the Water Supply Act required the Army Corps to seek congressional approval before entering into contracts.[71]

The Water Supply Act also required congressional approval for any "major operational changes."[72] According to the corps's own regulations, any allocation of fifty thousand acre-feet or more of Lake Lanier reservoir water should have qualified as a major operational change.[73] The proposed contracts allocated more than 130,000 acre-feet—an amount far in excess of the corps's own regulatory cutoff.[74] For this reason, plaintiffs argued that congressional approval was required, even if the court found that the water contracts did not "seriously affect" hydropower.

Unlike other legal skirmishes that the city had fought in the previous decades, a negative outcome in this case was likely to have dire consequences for Atlanta's water supply. By 1990, Atlanta and its suburbs received at least 60 percent of their water supply from either the Chattahoochee or Lake Lanier. If the Army Corps water withdrawal contracts were temporarily halted, the entire region would immediately face an extreme water shortage. If the contracts were permanently invalidated, Atlanta would face the daunting and virtually impossible task of convincing Congress to approve reauthorization.[75]

For Atlanta officials, the possibility of losing Lake Lanier was nearly unthinkable. Atlanta Regional Commission executive director Harry West said that the city would continue using Chattahoochee water until "the federal government sends troops in to keep us out . . . or when the state of Alabama sends their National Guard over."[76] The Atlanta Regional Commission said that it would intervene in the suit as soon as it could raise $500,000 for a legal team.[77]

A week after Alabama filed suit, Georgia fired back with a warning to two of Alabama's largest industrial plants along the Chattahoochee. The Georgia

Department of Natural Resources commissioner, Leonard Ledbetter, sent letters to the Mead Paperboard Company and Alabama Power Company's nuclear power plant, warning the businesses to either apply for a Georgia pollution permit or face fines up to $50,000 a day.[78] "They're saying we'll try to block you from getting more water for Atlanta," said Ledbetter, "so we're saying we'll have to take a harder look at what they're doing to our waters."

The move was petty but it was also strategic. By harming Alabama's largest Chattahoochee industries, Georgia hoped that it could strong-arm the state into negotiating a favorable settlement. The plan backfired, however, and Alabama responded to the attack with hardened resolve.

Despite their tough-talking public face, metro water providers also scrambled to find new water sources. Gwinnett, which drew most of its supply from Lake Lanier, hired consulting company CH2MHill to conduct a comprehensive study of its projected long-term water needs.[79] The company's study looked to a number of unconventional projects within the state, including a plan to pump water from south Georgia's aquifers. All of the plans, however, were likely to face similar opposition from impacted communities. "There's no sympathy in my district for helping Atlanta solve its problem," said Jonesboro, Georgia, resident and U.S. representative Newt Gingrich. "I think everybody who is downstream from Atlanta is on the same side."[80]

By the end of 1990, it was clear: Alabama and Florida were going to fight any increased withdrawals from Lake Lanier, and Atlanta would not be able to quickly transition to another water supply source. The disagreement over withdrawal contracts had escalated into a full-blown interstate water conflict.

Although relatively rare on the East Coast, and previously unprecedented in the Southeast, interstate water disputes were nothing new on a national scale. Colorado, Utah, Wyoming, New Mexico, California, Arizona, and Nevada had been arguing over Colorado River resources for more than a century. Historically, an interstate water dispute is resolved in one of three ways: the Supreme Court can equitably apportion the basin resources, Congress can create its own apportionment scheme, or the states can enter into an interstate compact.

If the states choose to pursue a judicial equitable apportionment, the Supreme Court has discretion to choose whether or not to hear the states' claims. If the court agrees to hear the claim, the court appoints a special master to conduct proceedings and make recommendations on how to resolve the dispute. After extensive data collection, the special master determines an allocation formula that divides the resource benefits equitably among the states.[81]

Judicial equitable apportionment is an exorbitantly expensive and time-consuming process. The Supreme Court's apportionment of the Delaware River, for instance, lasted in some capacity from 1931 to 1954.[82] Because of the time and effort they require, the Supreme Court has displayed an unwillingness to enter into these lengthy interstate apportionments. Thus far, states have requested that the Supreme Court apportion eight interstate rivers, but the Supreme Court has granted the states' requests only three times.[83]

The Supreme Court would be especially unwilling to hear an Apalachicola-Chattahoochee-Flint (ACF) apportionment claim because the Army Corps was heavily involved in the dispute. In the past, the court has dismissed suits where the federal government was an indispensable party and refused to waive sovereign immunity.[84] Similarly, the court denied a South Dakota apportionment request because it involved an interpretation of the Army Corps's flood control responsibilities. The court's denial indicated that apportionment was not necessary because South Dakota could instead challenge the Army Corps's regulations in federal court.[85] Because the Army Corps was also central to the ACF basin disputes, it seemed likely that the Supreme Court would reject the states' request on similar grounds.

As an alternative to the Supreme Court, the states could ask Congress to apportion the interstate water resources under its constitutional power to regulate interstate commerce.[86] Like the Supreme Court, however, Congress rarely exercises this power; it has only done so twice.[87] Congressmen are generally unwilling to create allocation formulas for states other than their own. The process provides little political benefit for them, as their voters are not likely to care how water is allocated in another part of the country. Allocation formulas are also likely to anger at least some representatives from the states involved, and other congressmen are typically unwilling to alienate or strain their relationships with these representatives.

Congressional apportionment was especially unlikely to resolve the ACF dispute because the conflict involved reallocation of an Army Corps reservoir. Reallocation is a hotly debated issue in the western states, and any apportionment that reallocated reservoir water resources would engender great political controversy there.

Interstate compacts are, by far, the most frequently used means of resolving an interstate water dispute. Today, more than two dozen compacts are in force in the United States.[88] A compact typically begins with the states meeting together to negotiate an allocation formula. Once an agreement is reached, each state enacts legislation that codifies and adopts this agreement as state law. Then, the states take this law to the U.S. Congress, where it is ratified as federal law.[89] Once the compact becomes a federal law, it takes precedence over state law via the supremacy clause of the Constitution.[90] Thus, it becomes binding for all states involved.

Because the other options were so unlikely, an interstate compact was clearly the most viable means of resolving the ACF dispute. Throughout the summer, officials from Alabama, Georgia, and Florida met privately at Callaway Gardens, Georgia, to try to negotiate an agreement.[91] By fall, the three states had decided to enter into negotiation in lieu of litigation. Together, Alabama, Georgia, and Florida filed a Joint Motion to Stay Proceedings on September 19, 1990.[92] It was granted, and the first tristate water case was put on hold indefinitely so that the parties could negotiate their own interstate compact.

The states' first discussions were fruitless. Less than a month after the joint motion was filed, a representative for Georgia governor Joe Frank Harris claimed that communication between the states had "all but shut down."[93]

As the 1990 November elections approached, politicians on all sides folded the water war into their campaign strategies and rhetoric. Many speculated that Alabama's governor, Guy Hunt, was intentionally postponing an agreement until his reelection campaign ended.[94] Other politicians sought to fan the flames. "This water thing is no longer a problem, it is no longer a controversy," said Alabama congressman Glen Browder. "We are in a water war."[95]

The parties' biggest disagreement was over Atlanta's interim contracts with the Army Corps. Atlanta and two other Georgia towns wanted to take out additional water while the states negotiated an equitable division of ACF water.[96] Alabama and Florida were reluctant to allow any interim contracts and argued that the contracts might make future negotiations a "moot point."[97]

While negotiations stalled, Georgia began to move forward with plans to construct a chain of reservoirs across north Georgia.[98] The regional reservoirs were part of Governor Joe Frank Harris's plan to "drought proof" the metro region.[99] With the new reservoirs, the governor believed that Atlanta could continue to grow at the same pace for another sixty years before running out of water.[100]

The reservoirs were not technically in violation of the stay order, but they would impound rainwater that would otherwise flow into the Chattahoochee or the Tallapoosa, another shared river with Alabama.[101] Montgomery, Alabama, residents bused into Atlanta to oppose the project at Army Corps hearings, and an unlikely coalition of Alabama politicians, environmental groups, and the Alabama Power Company also fought the reservoirs' construction.[102]

In March of 1991, Alabama and Georgia reached their first agreement during the negotiating process. Georgia agreed to put their reservoir plans on hold for two years and in return, Alabama allowed two towns in northwest Georgia to enter into interim contracts for water.[103] The governors and their teams began to work together in earnest after this first small step toward cooperation.

After a year of discussion, the three states entered into a Memorandum of Agreement (MOA) in January of 1992. The three state governors and a corps representative met in Montgomery to ceremoniously sign the agreement and pose for photographs. "Not only is this event unprecedented," said Georgia governor Zell Miller, "it's vital to the future of our three states."[104]

The MOA stated that all parties would equally participate in a fact-finding study on water resources in the ACF basin.[105] The comprehensive study would do the following: (1) create a conceptual plan for water resource management; (2) evaluate existing and future water resource needs; (3) assess the water resources available for the basin; and (4) determine an appropriate mechanism for implementing the study's findings in a water agreement.[106]

In effect, the MOA was an agreement to later agree once all the facts were known. "After the first year of negotiations," said Alabama attorney Buddy Cox, "everybody realized that nobody was going to believe the other person's information. You know the sort of claim—Georgia was going to grow to a population of ten billion, [and] Alabama said it needed more water than the City of Atlanta."[107] The comprehensive study would solve this problem by providing a reliable source of information that everyone could agree upon.

The parties also agreed to a "live and let live" provision in the MOA. This permitted Atlanta to continue to withdraw water from Lake Lanier and the Chattahoochee while the parties conducted the comprehensive study. The clause also required new contracts for water to be approved by all three states before taking effect.[108]

The comprehensive study focused on four different study areas: water demands, water resources, comprehensive management strategies, and coordination mechanisms.[109] The water demand portion would study in-stream and out-of-stream past and present uses of the river, including agricultural, environmental, industrial, municipal, recreational, and power generation demands.[110] The water resources portion would study the past and present availability of surface and groundwater in the basin.[111] Based on the findings of the water demand and water resource sections, the study would then develop a list of possible strategies for implementing a basin-wide water management plan.[112] In the last phase, the study would recommend a permanent coordination mechanism to implement the management plan.[113]

The three states and the Army Corps worked on their shared comprehensive study from 1991 to 1998, but it was never completely finished.[114] The process took much longer, and was much more expensive, than any of the parties had anticipated.[115] Ultimately, the study cost the Army Corps twenty-five million dollars, as compared to an estimated four million, to complete most of its elements.[116]

Despite the incomplete findings, all three states wrote and adopted an interstate compact based on the study. The ACF Compact created an "ACF Basin Commission," composed of the three state governors, their alternates, and a nonvoting representative from the federal government.[117] The commission agreed to meet at least once a year and promised to arrive at a formula for equitably apportioning ACF water among the three states. The states agreed to determine the formula by December 31, 1998.

It was unusual for an interstate compact to leave to actual allocation formula out of the agreement. Other eastern compacts, like the Delaware River Basin Compact and the Susquehanna Compact, contained specific formulas.[118] But, the states were not yet ready to reach an agreement, and so the actual formula decision-making was postponed.[119]

Although the repeated "agreements to agree" frustrated the water-war-weary public, there was really no other way for the states to proceed. The process of divvying up an interstate waterway, with its complex hydrologic systems and poorly understood human impacts, is a painstaking and expensive endeavor. To do it right is to do it on a timeframe that is neither politically expedient nor practically helpful. Every impacted community wished for an immediate resolution to their water problems and yet none were available. There simply isn't a quick fix for interstate water conflicts.

As the process dragged into the latter part of the 1990s, however, all of the problems that had initially started the conflict began to worsen. Atlanta consumed an increasing amount of water and spewed an increasing amount of pollution into the ACF waterways. The relatively wet years of the mid-1990s kept the region's water resources in a tenuous balance, but the entire ACF waterway was poised on the brink of disaster.

The first formal stages of negotiation on the allocation formula began in September 1998. Georgia wanted to increase Lake Lanier withdrawals, and in exchange, promised to maintain a minimum of 4,500 cubic feet of flow at the Florida state line.[120] Alabama wanted more water to be released from Buford Dam.[121]

Despite the years of fact-finding, a number of information gaps remained that made compromise more difficult. One problem was the computer modeling system used to create equitable allocation formulas. The comprehensive study used two different modeling platforms, STELLA and HEC-5, to determine water resource needs and availability. The two platforms used slightly different mathematical formulas and arrived at different answers for every hypothetical situation. The negotiating parties constantly bickered over the accuracy of the two models, and each side supported whichever model favored their position at any given time.[122]

Another problem was uncertainty about agricultural irrigation on the Flint River. Like many other states, Georgia didn't require its farmers to get water withdrawal permits for agricultural irrigation. Without permit statistics, the state really had no clue how much water was being taken out or how much would be needed in the future. The states argued over the best formula to use to estimate Georgia's irrigation needs during droughts.[123]

One of the biggest issues, though, was disagreement over long-term projections. The compact was supposed to last for at least fifty years, but models could not accurately project growth and needs for the entire basin over such a long duration of time.[124] Just six months after the governors unveiled the compact, Georgia revealed that metro Atlanta's population was growing faster than anyone had predicted. By mid-1997, northern Georgia's population had already exceeded the tristate comprehensive study's projected population estimates for the year 2000.[125]

Georgia wanted to replace the comprehensive study's population estimates with projections based on Atlanta's 1997 population and growth.[126] Alabama and Florida balked at changing the study so late in the negotiation process. The December 31, 1998, negotiation deadline passed without an agreement, and the states agreed to extend the deadline for another year.

Another year, however, brought a new round of problems to the talks. As negotiations stalled, Atlanta officials became even more desperate for water. If Atlanta continued the same level of growth, officials argued, all the water from Lake Lanier and the Chattahoochee combined would not be enough for the city by 2035.[127] The city's attempts to find more water exacerbated existing problems in the negotiation process.

By early 1999, Gwinnett already needed more water for its short-term needs. The county asked Georgia for a permit to withdraw an additional one hundred million gallons a day out of Lake Lanier. This would bring Gwinnett's total withdrawals up to 250 million gallons, but the county promised to return 40 million gallons in treated wastewater back into the reservoir.[128] By 2000, the entire Atlanta metro region's withdrawals had increased. The city drew 442 million gallons of water every day from the Chattahoochee or Lake Lanier.[129] The region's consumption had increased by a full 33 percent in the ten years since the negotiation process had begun.[130]

After a decade of staying in the background during negotiations, Atlanta Regional Commission director Harry West spoke out in 2000 just before leaving office. "Perpetual drought will become the normal operating procedure for Metropolitan Atlanta," warned West, who added that a poorly planned settlement could be "disastrous" for the city.[131] In response to West's open letter, Alabama's new governor, Don Siegelman, was similarly defiant. In a letter to his chief negotiator, Siegelman allegedly wrote that, if Georgia doesn't change their position, "we will see them in court."[132]

In February of 2000, the states made a last-ditch attempt to reach a settlement before the newest deadline. The parties had already extended the deadline twice, and many began to feel that the states would never agree on an allocation formula. The latest sparring between West and Siegelman only heightened the tension more. At the same time, Alabama and Georgia negotiated over water resources in another shared basin, the Alabama-Coosa-Tallapoosa. Rancorous discussions from one negotiation would affect the other, and both appeared destined to return to litigation by early 2000.[133]

Just when it seemed that the mediation could not get worse, it did. Georgia officials, it seemed, had not learned any lessons from the region's 1989 drought. The state had not created an emergency drought management plan, and unchecked consumption turned a moderate drought from 1998 and 1999 into a full-on crisis by the summer of 2000.[134] The metro area imposed last-minute citywide outdoor watering restrictions, but the ordinances eliminated only a tiny fraction of the city's overall demand.[135] Lake Lanier water levels plummeted, and the normally thriving tourist industry there struggled through sluggish summer sales.

Although Georgia imposed last-minute statewide restrictions on outdoor water use that summer, most of the rivers in southern Georgia were reduced to about half their normal size.[136] On the Flint River, where agricultural uses strained limited water supplies, three stream gauges measured all-time-low daily flows.[137] The Chattahoochee and Apalachicola rivers didn't fare much better, despite strategic reservoir releases from Lake Seminole and the Walter F. George Reservoir.[138] "We're already seeing a lot of dead mussels in the tributaries of the Apalachicola," reported biologist Jerry Ziewitz to the *Atlanta Journal-Constitution*. "And the oysters in the bay are already in pretty bad shape."[139]

By August, the corps ran out of other ways to maintain a minimal flow of water at the Florida state line, and it was faced with a tough decision. If the Army Corps released more water from the Buford Dam, the water in Lake Lanier would reach its lowest level ever. If it did not release the water by December, then the Apalachicola's flow would drop below the rate considered necessary for the survival of the bay's most fragile species.[140] Representatives from Georgia and Florida disagreed bitterly on the proper course of action.

Although an unexpected rain alleviated some of the Army Corps's concerns that fall, it did little to alleviate the heightened tension between Florida and Atlanta. In the early spring of 2001, the water war once again returned to court. This time, however, Atlanta would have to fight the battle on two fronts.

# 9

# WATER WAR, PART II

The drought of 2000 had strained Atlanta's fragile water supply to its breaking point once again. The city was desperate, and yet compact negotiations continued at a cripplingly slow pace. When the compact deadline was reached in 2000, and negotiations were again extended, Georgia decided to move on Gwinnett's request for water. The state asked the corps to substantially increase the amount of water that could be drawn from Lake Lanier.[1] Georgia governor Roy Barnes filed a formal Water Supply Request with the corps, asking for enough water to meet Atlanta's projected water supply needs up to 2030.[2] If granted, Georgia's request would allow Atlanta-area water providers to increase their water withdrawals by 250 percent.[3]

As the drought continued, Atlanta officials grew impatient. When the corps took nine months to respond to Georgia's request,[4] the state filed a claim against the corps in Georgia's northern district federal court in 2001.[5] Georgia's suit sought to compel the corps to accept its request for more water.[6] After Georgia sued them, the Army Corps formally denied Georgia's request. In its denial letter, the corps explained that the substantial withdrawal increase "would affect authorized project purposes . . . and cannot be accommodated without additional Congressional approval."[7] In other words, the corps was using Alabama and Florida's legal argument from the water war cases and applying it to limit Atlanta's latest demands.

Also in 2000, Southeastern Federal Power Consumers filed suit against the Army Corps in Washington, D.C.'s district court.[8] The plaintiffs purchased hydroelectric power generated from the Buford Dam.[9] Their power rates were dependent, in part, on the revenue that the Army Corps collected from other reservoir uses, including municipal water supply.[10] In their complaint, the customers alleged that the corps was undercharging municipal water withdrawals, which, in turn, meant that the customers were overcharged for power.[11]

Georgia and the Atlanta metro water supply providers intervened in the D.C. case.[12] As in the Alabama federal claim a decade earlier, all of the parties in the D.C. case agreed to freeze litigation and enter into mediation.[13]

While Atlanta fought in two different court cases, the original negotiation process between the three states continued to sour. Georgia wanted Florida to set a minimum flow and allow upstream users to withdraw water up to that point.[14] Florida wanted the allocation agreement to instead use a "natural flow" theory for apportionment that would allow for increased river flow during peak spring time rains.[15] Although Florida's state representatives were willing to compromise, environmental groups from the Apalachicola Bay took a hard-line stance against decreased spring flows.[16] Their political clout kept Florida from working together with Georgia to reach a middle-ground allocation agreement.

Meanwhile, on the other side of litigation, the D.C. parties reached the end of successful settlement negotiations in 2003. The agreement provided, in part, that the corps and the water providers would enter into new contracts that would generate more revenue for the Army Corps and lower the cost of hydropower.[17] The agreement also specified that the corps would conduct a full NEPA analysis before entering into the new contracts.[18] As part of the agreement, the corps promised to execute interim ten-year contracts with water supply providers. After the contracts ran out, the water supply providers had an option to renew.[19] These contracts, if implemented, would have increased Lake Lanier's water storage for municipal withdrawals by 60 percent.[20]

Alabama and Florida were not invited to D.C. agreements, which were confidential.[21] Georgia's request for more water, combined with the secret D.C. agreement, pushed all three states back into litigation. Nine months after the corps reached a settlement in the D.C. case with power customers, Alabama renewed its 1990 litigation in Northern Alabama District Court. Alabama claimed that the settlement had violated the Alabama case's 1990 stay order.[22] According to the order, any new contracts for water withdrawal from the Chattahoochee or Lake Lanier required approval from Florida and Georgia.[23] By agreeing to form interim contracts without approval from other states, Alabama argued, the Army Corps had violated the court's order.[24]

In the following years, lawyers from both sides engaged in procedural wrangling in a number of different venues. The laundry list of courts, judges, and suits involved mirrored the complexity of the issue at hand. First, a D.C.

court overruled Alabama and Florida's objection to the D.C. settlement, and the two states appealed the decision.[25] Since the same issues were being tried in two courts at once, the Alabama district court agreed to stay all activity until the D.C. appeal was settled.[26] Other litigation related to the tristate water allocation bounced around venues as well.

Eventually, the tangled web of litigation was once again streamlined into two distinct, separate cases: the D.C. power customer case and the tristate water allocation case. The D.C. power customer case was tried in D.C. circuit court in front of Judge Paul Rogers. The tristate water allocation cases were consolidated into a two-phase appeal in the U.S. District Court in Jacksonville, Florida, in front of Minnesota judge Paul Magnuson. The first phase of Magnuson's appeal was set to analyze the corps's ability to operate Lake Lanier as a water supply source, and the other would focus on Florida's Endangered Species Act claims.

At first, neither case went well for Atlanta. On February 5, 2008, D.C. circuit judge Rogers invalidated the D.C. settlement agreement. Noting that the agreement would reallocate more than 22 percent of Lake Lanier's water for municipal supply, Rogers held that the settlement agreement constituted a "major operational change" under the Water Supply Act and therefore required congressional authorization.[27] The D.C. case was then transferred to Magnuson's tristate water war court. Georgia appealed the D.C. circuit's ruling to the U.S. Supreme Court, but the court declined to hear the case on January 12, 2009.

Seven months later, the tristate water war judge ruled against Georgia, and his decision was even more demoralizing for the city. In his first phase ruling, Magnuson held that the Army Corps of Engineers could not withdraw any water from Lake Lanier for Atlanta's water supply. The court's ruling was critical of Atlanta's shortsighted planning: "Too often, state, local, and even national government actors do not consider the long-term consequences of their decisions. Local governments allow unchecked growth because it increases tax revenue, but these same governments do not sufficiently plan for the resources such unchecked growth will require."[28] Starting with Hartsfield's refusal to pay for the dam, and continuing with the area's reckless and unchecked growth, Atlanta had made poor decisions about its water needs and resources.

Magnuson allowed Georgia three years to work out a water-sharing agreement with Alabama and Florida. If an agreement was not reached by then, he ordered the Army Corps to cut off Atlanta's Lake Lanier withdrawals entirely. In his ruling, Magnuson wrote, "The court recognizes that this is a draconian result. It is, however, the only result that recognizes how far the operation of the Buford Dam project has strayed from the original authorization."[29] Under Magnuson's order, if Georgia didn't reach a settlement agreement by 2012, Atlanta would have to find an alternative water supply source for 3.5 million residents.

In response to Magnuson's ruling, local and state officials from Georgia were nearly apoplectic. Governor Sonny Perdue held a press conference where he vowed to "fight to the death" to draw water from Lake Lanier.[30] Sam Williams, president of the Metro Atlanta Chamber of Commerce, told reporters that if Atlanta lost access to Lake Lanier water, "it would perhaps have a Katrina-sized effect on the metro economy."[31]

The next week, the governor called upon 130 industry leaders, politicians, and bureaucrats to form "a multi-pronged impact team" or, as the *Atlanta Journal-Constitution* called it, a team of Water Warriors.[32] Although Purdue didn't specify their goal at the press conference, the warriors would be waging battle on a number of fronts. Some would lobby for Congress to reauthorize the Buford Dam to include the municipal water supply as an authorized purpose, others would work with their counterparts in Alabama and Florida to reach a tristate agreement prior to Magnuson's 2012 deadline, a few worked on the court appeal, and still more worked to develop alternative water resources in the event that all else failed.

The threat of a post-Katrina-style economic meltdown in Atlanta made congressional action incrementally more likely. However, an agreement with the other two states was still the most feasible option for Atlanta. Alabama and Florida, too, had an incentive to compromise while they still had the upper hand, since a successful appeal of Magnuson's ruling would probably make Atlanta's negotiators more aggressive in their demands. After the bluster and bombast that immediately followed Magnuson's decision, representatives from all three states quickly shifted gears and began to issue conciliatory public statements that hinted toward compromise.

Negotiation began again soon thereafter and, by most accounts, was proceeding more smoothly than before. "The two states [Georgia and Florida] are continuing to negotiate, where that really wasn't happening before," said a spokesperson for Alabama governor Bob Riley. "That's a positive."[33] Still, the states were a long way away from reaching an agreement.

At the start of 2010, Atlanta got a few glimmers of good news. That January, the 11th Circuit held that Magnuson's ruling was appealable and agreed to hear the case. While representatives continued to work to broker a tristate water agreement, some of Georgia's legal Water Warriors prepared to spend the summer in court. The spring weather was also cause for celebration; it rained so much that Lake Lanier and Lake Allatoona remained filled to capacity during the summer, despite Atlanta's continued withdrawals. In July, Judge Magnuson issued a favorable ruling for Atlanta on the second phase of litigation over the Endangered Species Act.

If the first half of 2010 was forgiving to Atlanta, however, then the second half was equally punishing. In September that year, under an order from Magnuson, the Army Corps issued an updated operating manual for Lake Lanier. In his ruling, the judge had also heavily criticized the Army Corps for their failure to manage the reservoir effectively. He said that corps's failure to update its fifty-year-old reservoir operation manual was "beyond comprehension." In the corps's new manual, it rejected Atlanta's request to include water usage in the operating manual and focused only on the lake's official water uses: flood control, navigation, and hydropower. The corps, it seemed, was now on Alabama and Florida's side.

Negotiation among the three governors also became tense. By coincidence, all three men planned to retire from office at the end of their terms in January. Their negotiating teams, who were doing the majority of the day-to-day work, would continue to meet together in the following years, but the change in leadership in all three states added an extra element of volatility to the region's already uncertain relationships. Many speculated that the states would either reach a deal by January or never reach a deal at all.

January came and went, however, and the states remained far from an agreement. With no end of litigation or negotiation in sight, and one year until Magnuson's deadline, the city had made only incremental steps toward reducing its water consumption. After nearly a century of pushing for greater water supplies to meet consumption demands, and after suffering through the uncertainty of a decade of water litigation, local and state leaders had finally begun to consider reductions in water consumption as a pathway to water supply stability. Atlanta wasn't used to tackling its issues from the supply side, however, and its first major attempts at conservation were tepid.

There were some success stories. The Clayton County Water Authority began an innovative leak detection program to identify and fix pipe leaks in the system.[34] The county used computer sonar equipment to find underground leaks. In 2000, when the project began, Clayton was losing almost 20 percent of its drinking water withdrawals through leaks.[35] The system has saved at least six billion gallons of water in its first six years.[36]

A year after Clayton began detecting leaks, the Georgia General Assembly passed the Metropolitan North Georgia Water Planning District Act, which required Atlanta's sixteen metro counties to coordinate and plan their future water needs.[37] The district, which encompassed fifteen counties and over ninety cities, would create unified management plans for stormwater, wastewater, and water supplies.

The regional coordination of water resources was certainly an improvement over Atlanta metro's chaotic home rule environment. The act, however, also had serious flaws. The biggest problem was that the act permitted, and even promoted, interbasin water transfers. District boundaries did not correspond to any single watershed. Instead, the metro district encompassed portions of the Chattahoochee, Coosa, Flint, Ocmulgee, Oconee, and Tallapoosa River basins.[38] The new metro district could decide to withdraw water from any basin for use in another basin without having to get approval from affected downstream communities. Interbasin transfers continue to cause water loss on the Flint and the Coosa rivers, as well as losses of forty-seven million gallons from the Chattahoochee every day.[39]

Still, the metro district implemented a number of conservation measures according to the act, including: using conservation pricing, replacing old plumbing fixtures, implementing irrigation rain-sensor systems and irrigation meter pricing, installing submeters on apartments, detecting and repairing pipe leaks, performing residential and commercial water audits, creating low-flow residential retrofit kits, installing efficient plumbing in government buildings, educating the public about conservation, and recycling water from car washes.[40]

The state also began to engage in coordinated drought management. The 2004 Comprehensive Statewide Water Management Planning Act directed the state Environmental Protection Division (EPD) to create a statewide drought management plan to manage "water resources in a sustainable manner to support the state's economy."[41] The EPD enacted short-term conservation initiatives as necessary during dry periods, and its aggressive actions managed to prevent shortages that might have otherwise occurred.[42]

Around the same time in the City of Atlanta, Mayor Shirley Franklin began to repair the damage done by Bill Campbell's failed privatization scheme. When the United Water contract was cancelled, the city's water infrastructure problems were thrust into the political spotlight. "Sewers became as sexy a subject as sewers can become," wrote one *Atlanta Journal-Constitution* reporter.[43] By the year 2000, Atlanta had already paid out $23.1 million in fines and was certain to pay more unless the city sewer system received a major upgrade.[44]

The compounding fines and system leaks required immediate attention, and Mayor Shirley Franklin had no choice but to act. In total, the city estimated that it would need at least three billion dollars to fix the city's water system.[45] Franklin began immediately to campaign for tax increases and rate hikes to pay for the city's infrastructural repairs.

Many cities across America are also experiencing the exact same growing pains as Atlanta. Built in the late 1800s, the water pipes in many urban areas are crumbling with age. Instead of selling their waterworks, as Atlanta did in the 1990s, some cities have issued municipal bonds. In the early 2000s, San Francisco residents voted on a $1 billion bond; California held a $3.4 billion bond issue at the same time.[46] Nationally, bonds for water projects total more than $26 billion each year.[47] Bonds for water infrastructure aren't always popular, though, because paying off the interest can require water rate hikes for consumers. "For the typical municipality, this is a cost," said one bond analyst. "No one gets elected because they have clean water."[48]

Originally, Franklin proposed to raise funds through increased property taxes. The measure, however, was fiercely fought by area developers. The city also planned to triple water rates from 2004 to 2010. Before the rate increases, Franklin held a number of town hall meetings to talk to residents about the city's ambitious plans to overhaul the water system. No one wanted to talk about the improvements, however, and most of the residents came armed with their water bill statements in hand.[49]

In lieu of the controversial property tax, Franklin was able to push through a one-cent sales tax to raise city funds for the water system. Residents were still unhappy about the plan, but many considered the sales tax to be the lesser of evils. "We've got to get money somewhere," said one resident. "Even though I don't like it, I'll probably hold my nose and vote for it."[50]

The sales tax went into effect, and Atlanta also began to increase water rates in increments. With this money, Atlanta began to address many of the city's long-standing water issues. The city separated one of its combined sewers into separate stormwater, sewage, and drinking water pipes. The city also used a tunnel boring machine to construct two eight-mile tunnels to store flows from another combined sewer in lieu of overflow points. As a result of these two projects, the city reduced the volume of its sewer spills by 80 percent.

The metro area's improvements helped somewhat, but their impact fell far short of the kind of drastic reductions in pollution that were needed to restore the ecosystem health of the Chattahoochee and Apalachicola rivers. Below Atlanta, sections of the Chattahoochee continued to exceed the fecal coliform levels considered safe for fishing, drinking, or recreation.[51] The new conservation laws also fell short of stabilizing the city's water supply. At one point during a drought in 2007 and 2008, city officials reported that Atlanta's current supply of water would run out in just three months unless the region received a heavy rain.[52]

# CONCLUSION

Although the Metropolitan North Georgia Planning District Water Supply Plan featured a number of innovative programs, the plan was unable to meet its full potential because the city and state didn't provide adequate funding for it. The state has chosen instead to focus the majority of its interest, discussion, and funding into schemes to develop greater water supplies. As a result, only a handful of municipalities have created toilet rebate programs, the region's conservation incentive programs are still in development, and the municipal conservation pricing schemes could be much more effective.[1] In response to the lack of buy-in, Georgia's 2010 Water Stewardship Act made four programs mandatory, but these initiatives continue to be underfunded.

Although these conservation measures seem like small steps, other cities faced with similar struggles have experienced dramatic reductions in water consumption after implementing conservation programs. When confronted with the potential for future water shortages, Boston opted to spend forty million dollars on conservation projects instead of spending five hundred million dollars to expand its water supply. Using retrofits, leak repairs, and water audits, the city managed to cut its consumption from more than three hundred million gallons a day in 1987 to just over two hundred million in 2006.[2] Today, Boston uses less water than it used a hundred years ago.[3]

In Seattle, conservation projects have reduced per capita water consumption by more than a third since 1980.[4] Over the past decade, Seattle's "Regional 1% Program" has also successfully reduced the region's overall water consumption by 1 percent every year.[5] The program encourages conservation using a blend of regulation, rebates, conservation pricing, and improved system operations.[6]

In order for Atlanta to break its cycle of consumption and pollution, the city should follow the lead of Seattle and Boston. It should begin to grow smart instead of simply growing big. For the past century, Atlanta has aggressively promoted development at all costs—development of industries, development of the Chattahoochee, development of subdivisions, and the development of reservoirs. These developments have brought about prosperity, no doubt. But the development, without more, has also contributed to the growing magnitude of Atlanta's water woes.

If Magnuson's "draconian" ruling had stood, if the intake pipes on Lake Lanier had truly been turned off, it's likely that Atlanta would have enacted more meaningful conservation programs. It's possible that Atlanta would have been forced to break its cycle of endless development. We can never know for sure. In June of 2011, Magnuson's decision was overturned by the 11th Circuit.

The U.S. Supreme Court's 2012 decision to not hear an appeal put an end to the water war debate, at least in one respect.[7] The municipal water supply is now an authorized use of Buford Dam. The day after the Supreme Court denied cert, the Army Corps issued a press release that it would consider the city's request to withdraw a total of 705 million gallons from the reservoir daily.[8] Environmental groups are already planning to challenge the withdrawals on other grounds,[9] but really, at this point, it hardly even matters anymore.

Atlanta's insatiable demand has already moved beyond Lake Lanier. Even if the city drained every drop from the reservoir, its projected future population would still go thirsty. The Metropolitan North Georgia Water Planning District anticipates that its service population will grow from just under 5.3 million people in 2015 to nearly 9 million by 2050.[10] With this growth, the district anticipates that the region will use at least 1.2 billion gallons of water *every day*.[11]

Georgia's new governor, Nathan Deal, has proposed to spend at least $300 million over the next three years to construct a chain of new reservoirs in northern Georgia.[12] In an executive order, Deal directed the Georgia Environmental Finance Agency (GEFA) to investigate potential reservoir sites across the state.[13] Since then, at least twenty proposed dam and reservoir projects have been planned, seven of which have already reached the permitting stage.[14] In addition to the state grant money, local Georgia taxpayers are likely to pay a total of $10 billion for the proposed projects.[15]

In the Metropolitan North Georgia Water Planning District alone, there are eleven proposed reservoirs. Hall County plans to build an 850-acre reservoir on a tributary of the Chattahoochee upstream from Lake Lanier.

Because the tributary is too small to fill the reservoir by itself, the majority of the water supply will be pumped directly from the river.[16] In south Fulton, the county plans to construct a 440-acre reservoir that will pump water from the Chattahoochee as well.[17] Other plans include dams on the Etowah and Ocmulgee rivers, and a massive reservoir project is also proposed for the main stem of the Flint River.[18]

These dams and reservoirs may supply Atlanta's foreseeable water needs, but what will their long-term impacts be? Throughout the city's history, Atlanta's politicians have suffered under the delusion that somewhere, somehow, an inexhaustible regional water supply can be achieved. But, such a supply does not exist. The Chattahoochee's natural currents ran dry, the Buford Dam did not bring everlasting prosperity, and the state's new reservoir plans will undoubtedly meet the same fate. The dream of an unlimited supply is certainly alluring, but it is merely a dream nonetheless.

Perhaps in recognition of this fact, Atlanta has also begun to look far beyond the Chattahoochee for its future water reserves. Already, a new water war is rising to fill the place of the tristate dispute, and it promises to be every bit as divisive and damaging as the first conflict. Georgia and Tennessee are now bickering over a tiny slice of their shared border, a scrap of land that would be completely insignificant to either state if not for the fact that it contains a one-acre sliver of Tennessee River riparian land.

If Georgia is able to claim this tiny section of river bank, along with the water use rights associated with it, state legislators want to build an intake pipe there that would withdraw one billion gallons of water from the Tennessee River every day.[19] Like the Apalachicola oystermen and the Alabama businesses before them, Tennessee's municipal water users, recreational groups, and local industries are bound to put up a fight. And perhaps, this time, they will win.

For now, however, Atlanta seems to be a nearly unshakable force, bulldozing its way outward in an ever-expanding ring of impact. With the Chattahoochee's supply now relatively secure, the metro area's intake pipes won't run dry for many more years. By the time the city's existing water sources are expended, many more battles will probably have been waged and won, and Atlanta will have built a new host of reservoirs to quench itself. The thirsty city continues to churn forward, while never looking back.

# NOTES

## CHAPTER 1. LIFE BEFORE THE CHATTAHOOCHEE

1. The state had so few contacts in the Piedmont region that the Governor had to ask Long for assistance in planning the removal of Cherokees. According to Richard G. Wood's biography of the engineer, Long replied that soldiers should be stationed on the border between Cherokee and Creek land to prevent the two tribes from joining forces. Richard G. Wood, *Stephen Harriman Long, 1784–1864: Army Engineer, Explorer, Inventor* (Glendale, CA: A. H. Clark, 1966), 7.
2. Wood 195.
3. United States Secretary of War, *Transmitting the Report of the Survey of the Western and Atlantic Railroad of the State of Georgia* (Washington, DC: Blair & Rives, 1837).
4. Ga. Laws, 1836, 214.
5. Ga. Laws, 1837, 210.
6. Franklin M. Garrett, *Atlanta and Environs: A Chronicle of Its People and Events*, vol. 1 (Athens: U of Georgia P, 1969), 150.
7. Wood 198.
8. Pioneer Citizens' Society of Atlanta, *Pioneer Citizens' History of Atlanta, 1833–1902* (Atlanta: Byrd Printing, 1902), 13.
9. Metropolitan North Georgia Water Planning District, *Watershed Management Plan 2009*, 4-4.
10. Metropolitan North Georgia Water Planning District, 4-30.
11. Wallace Putnam Reed, *History of Atlanta, Georgia: With Illustrations and Biographical Sketches of Some of Its Prominent Men and Pioneers* (Syracuse: D. Mason, 1889), 1–3.

12. Charles Rutheiser, *Imagineering Atlanta: The Politics of Place in the City of Dreams* (Brooklyn: Verso, 1996), 17.

13. Richard Peters, letter to Lemuel P. Grant, 26 July 1846, Lemuel P. Grant Papers, Atlanta History Center, Atlanta.

14. David F. Weiman, "Urban Growth on the Periphery of the Antebellum Cotton Belt: Atlanta, 1847–1860," *Journal of Economic History* 48.2 (1988): 263.

15. Reed 30.

16. Gary M. Pomerantz, *Where Peachtree Meets Sweet Auburn: The Saga of Two Families and the Making of Atlanta* (New York: Scribner, 1996), 35.

17. Weiman 263.

18. Suellen Hoy, *Chasing Dirt: The American Pursuit of Cleanliness* (New York: Oxford UP, 1995), 13.

19. Hoy 13.

20. Thomas Martin, *Atlanta and Its Builders* (Atlanta: Century Memorial, 1902), 100.

21. Garrett 329.

22. Garrett 330.

23. Pioneer Citizens' Society of Atlanta 239.

24. James M. Russell, *Atlanta, 1847–1890: City Building in the Old South and the New* (Baton Rouge: Louisiana UP, 1988), 73.

25. Sam Richards, *Sam Richard's Civil War Diary: A Chronicle of the Atlanta Home Front*, ed. Wendy Haman Venet (Athens: U of Georgia P, 2009), 205.

26. Lawrence Harold Larson, *The Urban South: A History* (Lexington: UP of Kentucky, 1990); Pomerantz 61.

27. Pomerantz 50.

28. Pomerantz 40.

29. Pomerantz 50.

30. Martin 505.

31. *Atlanta Daily Intelligencer*, 26 August 1864.

32. Pomerantz 51.

33. Pomerantz 51.

34. Rutheiser 20.

35. William T. Sherman, *Memoirs of General W. T. Sherman*, ed. Charles Roster (New York: Penguin Books, 1885), 929.

36. Garrett 662.

37. Garrett 662.

38. Sidney Andrews, *The South since the War* (Boston: Ticknor & Fields, 1866), 340.

39. Clara Mildred Thompson, *Reconstruction in Georgia: Economic, Social, Political, 1865–1874* (New York: Columbia UP, 1915), 331.

40. Pioneer Citizens' Society of Atlanta 303–305.

41. "The Great Railroad Chase!" *Southern Confederacy* 15 April 1862, 2.

42. Anthony Murphy, "Proposals for Water Works," *Daily Intelligencer*, 10 October 1866: 1.

43. See, e.g., "An Error Corrected," *Weekly Constitution*, 16 November 1875: 1 (refuting the claim by the *Columbus Enquirer Sun* about fire insurance rates and building ratings).

44. "City Council Proceedings," *Atlanta Daily Herald*, 4 September 1873: 4.

45. "City Council Proceedings," *Atlanta Daily Herald*, 4 September 1873: 4.

46. Russell 180.

47. Russell 181.

48. Rendigs Fels, "The Long-Wave Depression 1873–97," *Review of Economics and Statistics* 31.1 (1949): 69.

49. Russell 202.

50. Russell 201.

51. Russell 202.

52. Russell 202.

53. Garrett 916.

54. Garrett 916.

55. Reed 288.

56. "Water At Last," *Atlanta Constitution* 10 August 1875: 3.

57. Garrett 917.

58. "Our Water Works," *Atlanta Constitution*, 12 September 1875: 3.

## CHAPTER 2. TAPPING THE 'HOOCH

1. Contagious waterborne disease was systematically underreported as a cause of death during this time period. Official figures place Atlanta's typhoid death rate at twenty-five per three-month time period in 1899. See "The City's Health: The Board of Health Makes Its Report," *Atlanta Constitution*, 2 August 1888: 8.

2. Organization for Economic Co-Operation and Development, *Energy: The Next Fifty Years* (Paris: OECD Publishing, 1999), 48.

3. "For Rent," *Atlanta Daily Herald*, 5 February 1876, 3.
4. Franklin Garrett, *Atlanta and Environs: A Chronicle of Its People and Events*, vol. 2 (Athens: U of Georgia P, 1969), 210.
5. Garrett 210.
6. "The Poisoned Waters," *Daily Constitution*, 12 May 1877, 1; *Reid v. City of Atlanta*, 1884 WL 2412, *1 (Ga. 1884).
7. "The Poisoned Waters," *Daily Constitution*, 12 May 1877: 1.
8. "Our Streets," *Daily Constitution*, 7 January 1881: 1.
9. "Our Streets," *Daily Constitution*, 7 January 1881: 4.
10. "Our Streets," *Daily Constitution*, 20 December 1878: 4.
11. James M. Russell, *Atlanta 1847–1890: City Building in the Old South and the New* (Baton Rouge: Louisiana State UP, 1988), 205.
12. Russell 205.
13. Russell 205; "The Poisoned Waters," *Daily Constitution*, 12 May 877: 1.
14. "The Poisoned Waters," *Daily Constitution*, 12 May 877: 1.
15. Russell 205.
16. "Water! Water! Everywhere! But Is It Good to Drink?" *Atlanta Constitution*, 16 December 1888: 13.
17. Garrett 15.
18. "The Canal Scheme," *Atlanta Constitution*, 8 August 1882: 5.
19. "Death of Col. Frobel," *Atlanta Constitution*, 13 July 1888: 5.
20. "The Canal Project," *Atlanta Constitution*, 3 November 1881: 4.
21. "The Chattahoochee Canal," *Atlanta Constitution*, 18 October 1893: 7; "The Canal Scheme," *Atlanta Constitution*, 8 August 1882: 5.
22. "The Chattahoochee Canal," *Atlanta Constitution*, 18 October 1893: 7; "The Canal Scheme," *Atlanta Constitution*, 8 August 1882: 5. See "Water! Water! Everywhere! But Is It Good to Drink?" *Atlanta Constitution* 16 December 1888: 13 (Atlanta's old reservoir had a capacity of two million gallons per day).
23. "The Canal Scheme," *Atlanta Constitution*, 8 August 1882: 5.
24. "No Chattahoochee Canal," *Atlanta Constitution*, 24 April 1884: 7.
25. "No Chattahoochee Canal," *Atlanta Constitution*, 24 April 1884: 7.
26. Garrett 77.
27. Russell 255.
28. Russell 255.
29. "The Artesian Well: A Talk with Colonel Baum About What He's Doing," *Atlanta Constitution*, 17 January 1886: 9.
30. "Atlanta's Waterworks: What Engineer Herring Has to Say About It," *Atlanta Constitution*, 7 November 1889: 3.
31. Russell 255.

32. Russell 255. "Water! Water! Everywhere! But Is It Good to Drink?" *Atlanta Constitution*, 16 December 1888: 13.

33. "The Board of Health," *Atlanta Constitution*, 31 October 31 1891: 5.

34. Russell 255.

35. Russell 255.

36. "Timely Suggestion," *Atlanta Constitution*, 19 May 1891: 7.

37. "Timely Suggestion," *Atlanta Constitution*, 19 May 1891: 7.

38. "More Water and Better," *Atlanta Constitution*, 24 August 1890: 15.

39. "Atlanta's Waterworks," *Atlanta Constitution*, 7 November 1889: 3.

40. "More Water and Better," *Atlanta Constitution*, 24 August 1890: 15.

41. Wilson Stanbeck, "Our Water Supply," *Atlanta Constitution*, 29 August 1890: 6.

42. "The Water Supply," *Atlanta Constitution*, 18 September 1885: 7.

43. Wilson Stanbeck, "Our Water Supply," *Atlanta Constitution*, 29 August 1890: 6; John Rauschenberg, "Chattahoochee Water and Broilers," *Atlanta Constitution*, 11 October 1890: 4; "For New Waterworks," *Atlanta Constitution*, 29 December 1890: 2; "The Waterworks Question," *Atlanta Constitution*, 30 December 1890: 4.

44. Howell C. Erwin, A. Haas, Z. H. Smith, and George Winship, "New Waterworks," *Atlanta Constitution*, 2 June 1891: 5.

45. Erwin, Haas, Smith, and Winship, "New Waterworks," *Atlanta Constitution*, 2 June 1891: 5.

46. "Down to Work," *Atlanta Constitution*, 27 January 1892: 2.

47. Carolyn McKenzie, "Atlanta Leads Dixie in Pure Water Supply," *Atlanta Constitution*, 16 July 1940: 3.

48. "Tour of Inspection," *Atlanta Constitution*, 7 April 1893: 7.

49. "Tour of Inspection," *Atlanta Constitution*, 7 April 1893: 7.

50. "Tour of Inspection," *Atlanta Constitution*, 7 April 1893: 7.

51. "Break in Main Floods Avenue," *Atlanta Constitution*, 20 December 1943: 9.

52. "Atlanta Water Works Hemphill Avenue Pumping Station," *Artery*, HAS, n.d., Web, 30 January 2013.

53. "They Were In It," *Atlanta Constitution*, 12 January 1893: 5.

54. "Did You Feel It?" *Atlanta Constitution*, 26 July 1893: 7.

55. "The Waterworks," *Atlanta Constitution*, 10 April 1892: 2.

56. "Tour of Inspection," *Atlanta Constitution*, 7 April 1893: 7.

57. "Tour of Inspection," *Atlanta Constitution*, 7 April 1893: 7.

58. "Atlanta Water Works Hemphill Avenue Pumping Station," *Artery*, HAS, n.d., Web, 30 January 2013.

59. "The Waterworks," *Atlanta Constitution*, 10 April 1892: 2.

60. "The Waterworks," *Atlanta Constitution*, 10 April 1892: 2.

61. "Tour of Inspection," *Atlanta Constitution*, 7 April 1893: 7.

62. "Gushing Waters," *Atlanta Constitution*, 2 July 1893: 15.

63. "To Flood Atlanta," *Atlanta Constitution*, 25 July 1893: 5.

64. "Atlanta Water Works Hemphill Avenue Pumping Station," *Artery*, HAS, n.d., Web, 30 January 2013.

65. Metropolitan North Georgia Water Planning District, *Water Supply and Water Conservation Management Plan* (2009), ES-2.

66. Seth Rose and Norman E. Peters, "Effects of Urbanization on Streamflow in the Atlanta Area: A Comparative Hydrological Approach," *Hydrological Processes* 15 (2001): 1442.

67. United State Geological Survey, *How Much Water Is in the Apalachicola, Chattahoochee, and Flint Rivers, and How Much Is Used?* (Washington, DC: Government Printing Office, 2007), 2; "Monthly and Yearly Streamflow Patterns: An Example," *U.S. Geological Survey*, U.S. Department of Interior, 10 January 2013, Web, 30 January 2013.

## CHAPTER 3. WATER TO THE PEOPLE

1. Kerry A. Odell and David F. Weiman, "Metropolitan Development, Regional Financial Centers, and the Founding of the Fed in the Lower South," *Journal of Economic History* 58.1 (Cambridge: Cambridge UP, 1998), 108.

2. Urban Institute, *Urban Sprawl: Causes, Consequences, and Policy Responses*, ed. Gregory D. Squires (Washington, DC: Urban Institute P, 2002), 171. Peters was a particularly successful developer. His land is now known as Midtown.

3. Charles Rutheiser, *Imagineering Atlanta: The Politics of Place in the City of Dreams* (New York: Verso, 1996), 143.

4. "Gem of All Suburbs," *Atlanta Constitution*, 18 March 1804: 7.

5. "Gem of All Suburbs," *Atlanta Constitution*, 18 March 1804: 7.

6. Franklin M. Garrett and Harold H. Martin, *Atlanta and Environs*, vol. 2 (New York: Lewis Historical, 1987), 459.

7. Garrett and Martin 455.

8. *Present Routes: City of Atlanta* (New York: Beeler Organization Consultants, 1924), Map.

9. See Eric Foner, *Reconstruction: America's Unfinished Revolution, 1863–1877* (New York: Harper & Row, 1988), 535–536; David F. Weiman,

"Economic Emancipation of the Non-Slaveholding Class: Upcountry Farmers in the Georgia Cotton Economy," *Journal of Economic History* 45 (1985): 74; Peter Termin, "Patterns of Cotton Agriculture in Post-Bellum Georgia," *Journal of Economic History* 43 (1983): 664.

10. "Feeling the Pulse, Scanning the Tongue of, and Probing the Hygienic Conditions in Atlanta," *Atlanta Constitution*, 2 August 1908: 7.

11. "Feeling the Pulse," *Atlanta Constitution*, 2 August 1908: 7.

12. "Feeling the Pulse," *Atlanta Constitution*, 2 August 1908: 7.

13. "Feeling the Pulse," *Atlanta Constitution*, 2 August 1908: 7.

14. "Negros Live and Play in Germ-Laden Filth Then Sow Germs Through Homes of Atlanta," *Atlanta Constitution*, 19 April 1914: B5.

15. "Negros Live and Play in Germ-Laden Filth," *Atlanta Constitution*, 19 April 1914: B5.

16. "Negros Live and Play in Germ-Laden Filth," *Atlanta Constitution*, 19 April 1914: B5.

17. Cliff Kuhn, Harlon Joye, Bernard West, and Radio Free Broadcasting Foundation, *Living Atlanta: An Oral History of the City, 1914–1948* (Athens: U of Georgia P, 1990), 233.

18. "Comparative Death Rate of Atlanta for Each Important Disease," *Atlanta Constitution*, 2 August 1908: 7.

19. Based on an estimate population of 120,000 and death rates reported in "Comparative Death Rate," *Atlanta Constitution*, 2 August 1908: 7.

20. "Comparative Death Rate," *Atlanta Constitution*, 2 August 1908: 7.

21. L. L. Knight, "Atlanta's Health," *Atlanta Constitution*, 9 July 1893: 12.

22. "No Fever in Atlanta," *New York Times*, 21 September 1897: A1.

23. "No Fever in Atlanta," 21 September 1897: A1.

24. "Feeling the Pulse," *Atlanta Constitution*, 2 August 1908: 7.

25. Department of Health Created, 1903 Ga. Laws 72.

26. Department of Health Created, 1903 Ga. Laws 72.

27. See "Dr. C. F. Benson May Head Board," *Atlanta Constitution*, 6 January 1904: 7 (discussing the city health board composition).

28. "Member Board of Health and Leading Physicians Voice Sanitary Appeal," *Atlanta Constitution*, 16 September 1909: 5.

29. Charles Crowe, "Racial Violence and Social-Reform: Origins of the Atlanta Riot of 1906," *Journal of Negro History* 53.3 (1968): 235.

30. "Law of Nature Being Violated," *Atlanta Constitution*, 29 December 1909: 1.

31. "Law of Nature Being Violated," *Atlanta Constitution*, 29 December 1909: 1.

32. "Whites and Negroes May be Segregated," *Atlanta Constitution*, 15 February 1913: 1.

33. "Whites and Negroes May be Segregated," *Atlanta Constitution*, 15 February 1913: 1.

34. "Disease Crosses Over Race Line While City Dozes," *Atlanta Constitution*, 3 February 1914: 1.

35. See, e.g., "Disease Crosses Over Race Line," *Atlanta Constitution*, 3 February 1914: 1 (C. G. Lambert contracting disease from cook).

36. "Disease Crosses Over Race Line," *Atlanta Constitution*, 3 February 1914: 3.

37. Rutheiser 30.

38. "Negro Minister Tells of Danger from Disease Among Blacks," *Atlanta Constitution*, 5 February 1914: 4.

39. "Negroes Live and Play in Germ-Laden Filth, Then Sow Germs Through Homes of Atlanta," *Atlanta Constitution*, 19 April 1914: B5.

40. "Temporary Place Provided for Care of Negro Patients," *Atlanta Constitution*, 5 February 1914: 1.

41. Ronald H. Bayer, *Race and the Shaping of Twentieth-Century Atlanta* (Chapel Hill: U of North Carolina P, 1996), 54.

42. Kuhn 37.

43. Bayer 55.

44. Kuhn 37.

45. Bayer 132.

46. Douglas L. Smith, *The New Deal in the Urban South* (Baton Rouge: Louisiana State UP, 1988), 108.

47. Joel Tarr, *The Search for the Ultimate Sink: Urban Pollution in Historical Perspective* (Akron: U of Akron P, 1996), 174.

48. William Andreen, "The Evolution of Water Pollution Control in the United States—State local and Federal Efforts, 1789–1972: Part I," *Stanford Environmental Law Journal* 22.145 (2003): 181.

49. Andreen 172.

50. Andreen 173.

51. Jamie Benedickson, *Culture of Flushing: A Social and Legal History of Sewage* (Vancouver: U of British Columbia P, 2007), 165.

52. W. Harrison Moore, "Misfeasance and Non Feasance in the Liability of Public Authorities," *Law Quarterly Review* 30 (1914): 416; Benedickson 48 (by 1905, eight states—Connecticut, Massachusetts, New Hampshire,

New York, New Jersey, Minnesota, Vermont, and Pennsylvania—had enacted statutes creating "right" of access to unpolluted water).

53. See 18A McQuillin Mun. Corp. §53.137 (3rd ed.), FN1-2. (2010).

54. Robert Troxler, Debra Reinhart, and Alan Hallum, "Metro Atlanta Water Pollution Control: A Decade of Progress," *Journal of Water Pollution Control* 55 (1983): 1121.

55. Troxler, Reinhart, and Hallum 1121.

56. *Reid v. City of Atlanta*, 1884 WL 2414 (Ga. 1884); *Holmes v. City of Atlanta*, 39 S.E. 498 (Ga. 1901); *City of Macon v. Roy*, 130 S.E. 700 (Ga. App. 1925); see also *Harrison v. City of Atlanta*, 107 S.E. 83 (Ga. App. 1921) (municipality not liable when pollution results from "error of judgment").

57. *Watkins v. Pepperton Cotton Mills*, 134 S.E. 69 (Ga. 1926).

58. Smith 108.

59. "Columbus Protests Against Atlanta Sewage Pollution of Chattahoochee," *Atlanta Constitution*, 16 December 1930: 8.

60. "Mayor Urges Bonds for Public Improvement," *Atlanta Constitution*, 8 January 1929: 1.

61. "Mayor Urges Bonds for Public Improvement," *Atlanta Constitution*, 8 January 1929: 1.

62. "Municipal Improvements in 1929 Reach $2,208, 569; Important Work Scheduled," *Atlanta Constitution*, 29 December 1929: 2.

63. Jamil S. Zainaldin, "Great Depression," *The New Georgia Encyclopedia*, Georgia Humanities Council, 3 June 2011, Web, 30 January 2013.

64. Smith 108.

65. Smith 108.

66. Smith 108.

67. Smith 109. Georgia had elected an anti–New Deal governor, Eugene Talmadge, in 1933, and his forceful, inflammatory anti-federal rhetoric made many of the federal program administrators uneasy.

68. Smith 109.

69. Smith 109.

70. Kuhn 229.

71. Photograph by Boyd Lewis, on file with the Kenan Research Center, Atlanta History Center, catalogue number VIS 101.604.002, available at http://album.atlantahistorycenter.com.

72. John Lear, "Atlanta to Clear Slums with Help of PWA Fund," *St. Joseph News-Press*, 28 August 1938: 9B.

73. John Lear, "Atlanta to Clear Slums with Help of PWA Fund," *St. Joseph News-Press*, 28 August 1938: 9B; Charles F. Palmer, *Adventures of a Slum Fighter* (Atlanta: Tupper and Love, 1955), 113.

74. John Lear, "Atlanta to Clear Slums with Help of PWA Fund," *St. Joseph News-Press*, 28 August 1938: 9B.

75. "Slum Condemnation Begun to Make Way for New Flats," *Portsmouth Times*, 7 May 1934: 20.

76. John Lear, "Atlanta to Clear Slums with Help of PWA Fund," *St. Joseph News-Press*, 28 August 1938: 9B.

77. John Lear, "Atlanta to Clear Slums with Help of PWA Fund," *St. Joseph News-Press*, 28 August 1938: 9B.

78. "Slum Clearing Good Business in Atlanta," *Sunday Morning Star* (Wilmington, DE) 15 February 1942: 16.

79. Palmer 113.

80. Palmer 113.

81. Palmer 114.

82. "Atlanta Slum Clearance Move Seen by Sec. Ickes as End of Gangsters," *New London Evening Day*, 29 September 1934: 1.

83. Palmer 114.

84. "Atlanta Slum Clearance Move Seen by Sec. Ickes as End of Gangsters," *New London Evening Day*, 29 September 1934: 1.

85. John Lear, "Atlanta to Clear Slums with Help of PWA Fund," *St. Joseph News-Press*, 28 August 1938: 9B.

86. John Lear, "Atlanta to Clear Slums with Help of PWA Fund," *St. Joseph News-Press*, 28 August 1938: 9B.

87. "Says Money Squandered to Spread New Deal Propaganda," *Meriden Daily Journal*, 28 September 1936: 8.

88. "Slum Clearing Good Business in Atlanta," *Sunday Morning Star* (Wilmington, DE) 15 February 1942: 16.

89. "Reporter Starts Slum Cleanup," *St. Petersburg Times*, 30 November 1947: 31.

90. "Reporter Starts Slum Cleanup," *St. Petersburg Times*, 30 November 1947: 31.

91. "Reporter Starts Slum Cleanup," *St. Petersburg Times*, 30 November 1947: 31.

92. "Reporter Starts Slum Cleanup," *St. Petersburg Times*, 30 November 1947: 31.

93. "Albert Riley Is Dead at 84," *Waycross Journal-Herald*, 9 April 1984: P2.

94. "Reporter Starts Slum Cleanup," *St. Petersburg Times*, 30 November 1947: 31.

95. "Reporter Starts Slum Cleanup," *St. Petersburg Times*, 30 November 1947: 31.

96. "Reporter Starts Slum Cleanup," *St. Petersburg Times*, 30 November 1947: 31.

97. "It Can Be Done," *Miami News*, 11 September 1947: 14A.

98. "It Can Be Done," *Miami News*, 11 September 1947: 14A.

99. "It Can Be Done," *Miami News*, 11 September 1947: 14A.

100. "It Can Be Done," *Miami News*, 11 September 1947: 14A.

101. "It Can Be Done," *Miami News*, 11 September 1947: 14A.

102. Roy C. Hurd, "Slum Clearance National Issue," *Sunday Morning Star*, 11 January 1948: 30.

103. LeeAnn Lands, *The Culture of Property: Race, Class, and Housing Landscapes in Atlanta* (Athens: U of Georgia P, 2009), 174.

## CHAPTER 4. TAMING THE FLOW

1. Robert David Coughlin, *Lake Sidney Lanier: A Storybook Site* (Atlanta: RDC Productions, 1998), 38.

2. "New Buford Dam to Open Feb. 1," *Palm Beach Post*, 15 January 1956: 17.

3. "New Buford Dam to Open Feb. 1," Palm Beach Post, 15 January 1956: 17.

4. "Giant Buford Dam Is Dedicated Today," *Rome News-Tribune*, 9 October 1957: 1.

5. David P. Billington, Donald C. Jackson, and Martin V. Melosi, *The History of Large Federal Dams: Planning, Design, and Construction in the Era of Big Dams* (Denver: Bureau of Reclamation, 2005), 458.

6. Billington, Jackson, and Melosi 462.

7. *National Inventory of Dams*, Army Corps of Engineers, n.p., n.d., Web, 31 January 2013.

8. Arthur Maass, *Muddy Waters: The Army Engineers and the Nation's Rivers* (Cambridge: Harvard UP, 1974), 20; Daniel A. Mazmanian and Jeanne Nienaber, *Can Organizations Change?* (Washington, DC: Brookings Institution, 1979), 8.

9. Mazmanian and Nienaber 8.

10. Mazmanian and Nienaber 8.

11. Mazmanian 10.
12. Mazmanian and Nienaber 10.
13. Lori Coleman, "Our Whole Future Is Bound Up in This Project: The Making of the Buford Dam," Dissertation, Georgia State U, 2008.
14. Army Corps of Engineers, *Apalachicola River Basin Reservoir Regulation Manual: Appendix B, Buford Reservoir, Chattahoochee River, GA*, unpublished, December 1959, B-4.
15. Mazmanian and Nienaber 10.
16. Maass 21.
17. Mazmanian and Nienaber 10.
18. See Arthur E. Morgan, *Dams and Other Disasters* (Boston: P. Sargent, 1971), 252–257.
19. This resistance could be traced back to a series of reports in the 1870s and 1880s that argued that dams would never work for flood protection of the Mississippi. The reports argued that dams and reservoirs were simply not feasible. This may have been true because modern dam construction innovations (like Portland cement and earth-moving machinery) had not yet been invented at the time the reports were made. However, the corps continued to reference these findings long after the report had become seriously outdated. Morgan 252–257.
20. Morgan 281.
21. Morgan 282.
22. Morgan 282.
23. Morgan 277.
24. See Herbert Hoover, "Hoover Outlines Steps for Control of Floods," *Atlanta Constitution*, 12 June 1927: 9.
25. See, e.g., "Army Engineers Get Flood Blame," *Telegraph-Herald and Times-Journal* (Dubuque, IA), 17 June 1927: 1.
26. Herbert Hoover, "Hoover Outlines Steps for Control of Floods," *Atlanta Constitution*, 12 June 1927: 9.
27. Morgan 301.
28. Coleman.
29. See River & Harbor Act of 1925, Pub. L. No. 68-585, ch. 467, 43 Stat. 1186, 1186, 1194 (March 3, 1925).
30. Coleman 21.
31. See H.R. Doc. No. 76-342, at 9-87 (1939).
32. See H.R. Doc. No. 76-342, at 9-87 (1939), at 66.
33. See H.R. Doc. No. 76-342, at 9-87 (1939), at 77; see also *In re Tri-State Water Rights Litigation*, 639 F.Supp.2d 1308, 1311 (M.D.Fla., 2009).

34. H.R. Doc. No. 76-342, at 80 (1939).

35. H.R. Doc. No. 76-342, at 80 (1939).

36. Hon. Philander C. Knox, "Regulation of Railroad Rates," United States Senate, 1st Session, 59th Congress, 28 March 1906.

37. Coleman.

38. Coleman 27.

39. Louis Williams, "William Berry Hartsfield: The Reluctant Accommodationist and the Politics of Race in Atlanta," Dissertation, Georgia State U, 1996, 127.

40. See "'Waterfront' for Atlanta Imperative, Officials Say," *Atlanta Constitution*, 1 April 1945: 2A.

41. Gladstone Williams, "Apalachicola Restudy Sought by Hartsfield," *Atlanta Constitution*, 3 April 1945: 5.

42. Gladstone Williams, "Apalachicola Restudy Sought by Hartsfield," *Atlanta Constitution*, 3 April 1945: 5.

43. "'Waterfront' for Atlanta Imperative," *Atlanta Constitution*, 1 April 1945: 2A.

44. "United Drive to Be Made to Get Reappraisal of River Project," *Atlanta Constitution*, 17 May 1945: 1.

45. "River Fun Request to Go to Council," *Atlanta Constitution*, 21 May 1945: 2; "Dupont Wright, Big Shippers Cool on Chattahoochee Plan," *Atlanta Constitution*, 31 May 1945: 3; "'Waterfront' for Atlanta Imperative," *Atlanta Constitution*, 1 April 1945: 2A.

46. "United Drive to Be Made," *Atlanta Constitution*, 17 May 1945: 1.

47. "'Waterfront' for Atlanta Imperative," *Atlanta Constitution*, 1 April 1945: 2A.

48. "'Waterfront' for Atlanta Imperative," *Atlanta Constitution*, 1 April 1945: 2A.

49. Gladstone Williams, "Apalachicola Restudy Sought by Hartsfield," *Atlanta Constitution*, 3 April 1945: 5.

50. M. L. St. John, "City Asks Navigable Chattahoochee to Gulf," *Atlanta Constitution*, 31 March 1945: 1.

51. "United Drive to Be Made," *Atlanta Constitution*, 17 May 1945: 1.

52. "Engineers Are Enthusiastic Over City's Port Prospects," *Atlanta Constitution*, 10 July 1945: 10.

53. Herman Hancock, "Shippers' Aid Needed to Make Chattahoochee Project Success," *Atlanta Constitution*, 29 May 1945: 1.

54. "Engineers Begin River Survey for Atlanta Business Men," *Atlanta Constitution*, 17 June 1945: 2A.

55. Wellington Wright, "Report on River Survey Ready September 18," *Atlanta Constitution*, 9 September 1945: 6A.

56. "River Navigation Plans Reach Final Stage," *Atlanta Constitution*, 26 August 1945: 6A.

57. "Great News from the River Survey," *Atlanta Constitution*, 19 September 1945: 6.

58. "Great News from the River Survey," *Atlanta Constitution*, 19 September 1945: 6.

59. Wellington Wright, "Engineers Call River Navigation Justified," *Atlanta Constitution*, 19 September 1945: 1.

60. Wellington Wright, "Engineers Call River Navigation Justified," *Atlanta Constitution*, 19 September 1945: 1.

61. "Atlanta Groups to Meet Army in Hearing on Chattahoochee," *Atlanta Constitution*, 16 September 1945: 16A.

62. "Atlanta Groups Meet Army in Hearing," *Atlanta Constitution*, 16 September 1945: 16A.

63. Wellington Wright, "Engineers Call River Navigation Justified," *Atlanta Constitution*, 19 September 1945: 1.

64. Wellington Wright, "Engineers Call River Navigation Justified," *Atlanta Constitution*, 19 September 1945: 1.

65. Coleman 38.

66. Wellington Wright, "Engineers Call River Navigation Justified," *Atlanta Constitution*, 19 September 1945: 1.

67. "Airport History," *Hartsfield Jackson International Airport*, City of Atlanta, n.d., Web, 11 March 2010.

68. Coleman 36.

69. Coleman 30.

70. Coleman 30.

71. Coleman 30.

72. Coughlin 38.

73. Willard Cope, "Atlanta Told to Act on Water Expansion," *Atlanta Constitution*, 7 March 1942: 1.

74. "Muddy River Water Yields City $1,250,000 Profit," *Atlanta Constitution*, 4 January 1940: 14.

75. See "Break in Main Floods Avenue," *Atlanta Constitution*, 20 December 1945: 9 (specifying that there were three mains connecting the two pump stations).

76. See Carolyn McKenzie, "Atlanta Leads Dixie in Pure Water Supply," *Atlanta Constitution*, 16 July 1940: 3 (reservoir is 150 acres).

77. Herman Hancock, "City's Largest Industry Serves Atlanta Faucets," *Atlanta Constitution*, 2 December 1945: 2A; Carolyn McKenzie, "Atlanta Leads Dixie in Pure Water Supply," *Atlanta Constitution* 16 July 1940: 3.

78. Herman Hancock, "City's Largest Industry Serves Atlanta Faucets," *Atlanta Constitution*, 2 December 1945: 2A.

79. Herman Hancock, "City's Largest Industry Serves Atlanta Faucets," *Atlanta Constitution*, 2 December 1945: 2A.

80. C. A. McMahan, *The People of Atlanta: A Demographic Study of Georgia's Capital City* (Athens: U of Georgia P, 1950), 194.

81. "DeKalb's Huge Water Project Gets Under Way," *Atlanta Constitution*, 30 January 1941: 24; Ralph T. Jones, "Making Water Supplies Safe for Consumption," *Atlanta Constitution*, 14 March 1944: 14.

82. "DeKalb's Huge Water Project," *Atlanta Constitution*, 30 January 1941: 24.

83. "DeKalb's Huge Water Project," *Atlanta Constitution*, 30 January 1941: 24.

84. "DeKalb's Huge Water Project," *Atlanta Constitution*, 30 January 1941: 24.

85. Ralph T. Jones, "Making Water Supplies Safe for Consumption," *Atlanta Constitution*, 14 March 1944: 14.

86. "Million-Dollar Waterworks Extension Seen," *Atlanta Constitution*, 4 February 1942: 1.

87. "Million-Dollar Waterworks Extension Seen," *Atlanta Constitution*, 4 February 1942: 1.

88. "Million-Dollar Waterworks Extension Seen," *Atlanta Constitution*, 4 February 1942: 1.

89. "Million-Dollar Waterworks Extension Seen," *Atlanta Constitution*, 4 February 1942: 1.

90. "Atlanta's Southern Suburbs Plan Water Problem Study," *Atlanta Constitution*, 1 February 1940: 2.

91. "Atlanta's Southern Suburbs Plan Water Problem Study," *Atlanta Constitution*, 1 February 1940: 2.

92. "Atlanta's Southern Suburbs Plan Water Problem Study," *Atlanta Constitution*, 1 February 1940: 2.

93. Ralph T. Jones, "Making Water Supplies Safe for Consumption," *Atlanta Constitution*, 14 March 1944: 14.

94. Herman Hancock, "City Studies Water Expansion Plan to Cost $20,000,000," *Atlanta Constitution*, 2 November 1941: 10A.

95. Coughlin 21.

96. Herman Hancock, "City Studies Water Expansion Plan to Cost $20,000,000," *Atlanta Constitution*, 2 November 1941: 10A.

97. See *Pyle v. Gilbert*, 265 S.E.2d 584 (Ga. 1980).

98. Herman Hancock, "'Giant' Water System Proposed for Atlanta," *Atlanta Constitution*, 11 June 1944: 6A.
99. Herman Hancock, "Port Proposal at Top of City's Postwar List," *Atlanta Constitution*, 6 April 1945: 18.
100. "Hartsfield Sees City of Million in Plan for Chattahoochee Port," *Atlanta Constitution*, 27 April 1945: 21.
101. See M. L. St. John, "Channel Would Save Business $3,000,000," *Atlanta Constitution*, 22 November 1945: 1.
102. M. L. St. John, "Channel Would Save Business $3,000,000," *Atlanta Constitution*, 22 November 1945: 1.
103. M. L. St. John, "Channel Would Save Business $3,000,000," *Atlanta Constitution*, 22 November 1945: 1.
104. "'Waterfront' for Atlanta Imperative," *Atlanta Constitution*, 1 April 1945: 2A.
105. "'Waterfront' for Atlanta Imperative," *Atlanta Constitution*, 1 April 1945: 2A.
106. See *In re Tri-State Water Rights Litigation*, 639 F. Supp. 2d 1308, 1312 (M.D. Fla., 2009).
107. See Rivers and Harbors Act of 1946, 59 Stat. 10, §10–11 (1946).
108. H.R. Doc. No. 80-300, at 28–29 (1947); see also *State of Florida First Amended Complaint, Alabama v. Army Corps of Engineers*, 382 F. Supp. 2d, 2003 WL 24859220.
109. *State of Florida First Amended Complaint, Alabama v. Army Corps of Engineers*, 382 F. Supp. 2d, 2003 WL 24859220.
110. Coughlin.
111. Coleman 58.
112. Coleman 59.
113. Civil Function, Department of the Army Appropriation Bill 1949: Hearing before the Subcommittee of the Senate Committee on Appropriations, 80th Congress, 644 (statement of William B. Hartsfield, Mayor, Atlanta, Georgia), cited in *In re Tri-State Water Rights Litigation*, 639 F. Supp. 2d 1308, 1314 (M.D. Fla. 2009).
114. Coughlin.
115. Coughlin.
116. Coughlin 38.
117. Coughlin.
118. Coughlin.
119. Coughlin.
120. Coughlin.

## CHAPTER 5. URBANIZATION AND ITS DISCONTENTS

1. Prentice Palmer, "State Disagrees with U.S. on River," *Atlanta Journal*, 29 April 1971: 2A.

2. Hugh Nations, "No Song of Chattahoochee," *Atlanta Journal*, 6 May 1970: 3.

3. Environmental Protection Agency, *Progress in Water Quality: Technical Report* (Washington, DC: Government Accountability Office, 2000), 10-6.

4. Hugh Nations, "No Song of Chattahoochee," *Atlanta Journal*, 6 May 1970: 3.

5. Hugh Nations, "All That Filth in the Chattahoochee," *Atlanta Journal*, 5 May 1970: 1A.

6. Eugene W. Smith, "Lanier's 'Folly' Grimly Real," *Atlanta Journal*, 11 January 1968: 1A.

7. Hugh Nations, "All That Filth in the Chattahoochee," *Atlanta Journal*, 5 May 1970: 1A.

8. Hugh Nations, "All That Filth in the Chattahoochee," Atlanta Journal, 5 May 1970: 1A.

9. Harold Paul Henderson, *Ernest Vandiver: Governor of Georgia* (Athens: U of Georgia P, 2000), 17.

10. Numan V. Bartley, *The New South: 1945–1980* (Baton Rouge: Louisiana State UP, 1995), 125.

11. "Sewage in Creek Held Menace to Northsiders," *Atlanta Journal*, 2 December 1948: 40.

12. "Northsiders Complain: City Says Lack of Funds Blocks Sewer Solution," *Atlanta Journal-Constitution*, 19 April 1964: 16.

13. E. Neaders, *Atlanta Journal*, 13 December 1957: 17.

14. William B. Williams, "Sewage Battle Escalates," *Atlanta Journal*, 4 March 1969: 12A; Bill Shipp, "Sad Song of Sewage and the Chattahoochee," *Atlanta Journal*, 3 November 1963: 1C.

15. W. Eugene Smith, "How Pollution Is Fought," *Atlanta Journal*, 9 January 1968: 1A.

16. William L. Andreen, "The Evolution of Water Pollution Control in the United States: State, Local, and Federal Efforts," *Stanford Environmental Law Journal* 22 (2003): 188.

17. *See* Andreen 188 (Industrial pollution at the end of the war exceeded municipal sewage in a ratio of seven to six).

18. Andreen 189.

19. Gladwin Hill, "New U.S. Agency and New Policy," *New York Times*, 21

December 1965: 27.

20. N. William Hines, "Nor Any Drop to Drink: Public Regulation of Water Quality, Part I: State Pollution Control Programs," *Iowa Law Review* 52 (1966–1967): 192.

21. Hines 186.

22. *See* "State Paper Mills Urged to End Stream Pollution," *Spokesman-Review*, 7 October 1967: 9.

23. Jonathan H. Adler, "Fables of the Cuyahoga: Reconstructing a History of Environmental Protection," *Fordham Environmental Law Journal* 14 (2003).

24. William L. Andreen, "Water Quality Today: Has the Clean Water Act Been a Success?" *Alabama Law Review* 55 (2004): 554.

25. Hines 192.

26. Hines 186.

27. Bob Hurt, "Pollution Control Looks Good for State," *Atlanta Journal*, 7 December 1969: 2A.

28. Hugh Nations and Leonard Ray Teel, "State's Pollution Problem Real but Solvable," *Atlanta Journal*, 3 May 1970: 1C.

29. Paul Vesiland, "Awareness Key to Pollution Control," *Atlanta Journal*, 14 September 1969: 12H.

30. George V. R. Smith, "Will Man Be Modern Dinosaur?" *Atlanta Journal*, 5 March 1970: 23A.

31. "Nature Clears Up Massive Oil Slick," *Atlanta Journal*, 19 January 1970: 2A.

32. Raleigh Bryans, *Atlanta Journal*, 18 February 1971: 1A.

33. John Pennington, "Where Man Came to Pollute Rivers, He Now Must Labor to Clear Them," *Atlanta Journal*, 30 September 1955: 27.

34. See Jim Mann, "Chattooga to Seek Curb on Pollution," *Rome News-Tribune*, 31 December 1961: 3.

35. The Atlanta Chamber of Commerce, for example, endorsed a plan to raise sewer rates to increase revenue for renovations to R. M. Clayton. In an editorial, the chamber stated, "a serious pollution problem has a bad effect and is bad for business." Ed., "Forward Atlanta," *Atlanta Journal*, 13 August 1966: 2.

36. Bill Shipp, "River Pollution Found Slowing Industry," *Atlanta Journal*, 1 January 1964: 2C.

37. Richard Matthews, "Port Plans Here Stalled by Pollution," *Atlanta Journal*, 3 March 1970: 10A.

38. "Officials Set Progress Meet on Pollution," *Rome News-Tribune*, 15 January 1964.

39. Ga. Code. Ann. Sec. 17-502 (Supp. 1970) ("insure that all the waters of the state are protected, maintained, and restored to a state of purity for the maximum benefit of all Georgians").

40. Ga. Code Ann. Sec. 17-510(2) (Supp. 1970).

41. Ga. Code Ann. Sec. 17-410(3) (Supp. 1970).

42. Ga. Code Ann. Sec.17-514 (Supp. 1970); Ga. Code Ann. Sec. 17-516 (Supp. 1970).

43. Earl B. Benson, "Georgia's Environmental Law: A Survey," *Mercer Law Review* 23 (1972): 644.

44. Ga. Code Ann. Sec. 17-504 (Supp. 1970).

45. Ga. Code Ann. Sec. 17-505(b) (1)-(9) (Supp. 1970).

46. Bob Hurt, "Pollution Control Looks Good for State," *Atlanta Journal*, 7 December 1969: 2A.

47. Gladwin Hill, "Southeast Steps Up Drive to End Water Pollution," *New York Times*, 6 March 1965: 54.

48. Gladwin Hill, "Southeast Steps Up Drive to End Water Pollution," *New York Times*, 6 March 1965: 54.

49. Priit Vesiland, "Water Board Facing an Uphill Fight," *Atlanta Journal*, 11 September 1969: 10D.

50. Priit Vesiland, "Water Board Facing an Uphill Fight," *Atlanta Journal*, 11 September 1969: 10D.

51. Leon W. Lindsay, "Atlanta Told Clean Water Runs High," *Christian Science Monitor*, 2 February 1971: 14.

52. See Leon W. Lindsay, "Atlanta Told Clean Water Runs High," *Christian Science Monitor*, 2 February 1971: 14 (state board threatened Atlanta with sewer hookup moratorium immediately before federal intervention).

53. "A Special Message to Congress on Natural Beauty," 9 February 1965, PPP: Lyndon Baines Johnson, 1965, Book 1 (Washington, DC: Government Printing Office, 1966).

54. "A Special Message to Congress on Natural Beauty," 9 February 1965, PPP: Lyndon Baines Johnson, 1965, Book 1 (Washington, DC: Government Printing Office, 1966), 155–65.

55. Robert F. Blomquist, "'To Stir Up Public Interest': Edmund S. Muskie and the U.S. Senate Special Subcommittee's Water Pollution Investigations and Legislative Activities," *Columbia Journal of Environmental Law* 22 (1997): 6.

56. Edmund S. Muskie, *Journeys* (Garden City, NY: Doubleday, 1972), 80.
57. Blomquist 9.
58. Hearings before a Special Subcommittee on Air and Water Pollution, Committee on Public Works, United States Senate, 88th Cong., 1st Sess. 1 (1963).
59. Blomquist 37.
60. H.R. 215, 89th Cong., 1st Sess. (1965).
61. Blomquist 54–55.
62. Water Quality Act of 1965, Pub. L. No. 89-234, 79 Stat. 903 (1965) (superseded 1972).
63. Water Quality Act of 1965, Pub. L. No. 89-234, 79 Stat. 903, §2 (1965) (superseded 1972).
64. Andreen, "Evolution of Water," 251.
65. Andreen, "Evolution of Water," 251.
66. Andreen, "Evolution of Water," 253.
67. Andreen, "Evolution of Water," 253.
68. William B. Williams, "Sewage Battle Escalates," *Atlanta Journal*, 4 March 1969: 12A.
69. Harry Murphy, "Atlanta Steps Up Pollution Battle," *Atlanta Journal*, 9 March 1970: 2A.
70. "Origins of the EPA," *The Guardian*, Spring 1992.
71. "Pollution Pact Set by U.S. and Three Cities," *New York Times*, 11 June 1971: 40.
72. "U.S. Warns Three Cities to Halt Pollution," *New York Times*, 11 December 1970: 31. See also Stanley W. Schroeder, "Pollution in Perspective: A Survey of the Federal Efforts and the Case Approach," *Natural Resources Law Review* 4 (1971): 421.
73. Raleigh Bryans, "Stop Raw Sewage in River, City Told," *Atlanta Journal*, 10 December 1970: 1A.
74. Hugh Nations, "Action on Pollution Demanded by Board," *Atlanta Journal*, 17 December 1970: 1A.
75. Jeff Nesmith, "Atlanta: The Squeezed Turnip," *Atlanta Journal*, 13 December 1970: 1A.
76. Hugh Nations, "'Let the Sludge Flow' May Be a Classic," *Atlanta Journal*, 17 December 1970: 23A.
77. Leon W. Lindsay, "Atlanta Told Clean Water Runs High," *Christian Science Monitor*, 2 February 1971: 14.
78. Leon W. Lindsay, "Atlanta Told Clean Water Runs High," Christian Science Monitor, 2 February 1971: 14.

79. Hugh Nations, "City Votes Hike in Sewer Fees," *Atlanta Journal*, 22 December 1970: 1A.

80. "Pollution Pact Set by U.S. and Three Cities," *New York Times*, 11 June 1971: 40.

81. 33 U.S.C. 1344 (1972).

82. Many scholars have questioned the efficacy of this provision in practice. The threat of federal takeover has been a hollow one. The EPA lacks the funding to properly enforce the CWA without the individual states, and so it has been reluctant to take over state programs, even when it would have been completely appropriate to do so.

83. Environmental Protection Agency, *Progress in Water Quality: Technical Report*, 10-17.

84. Environmental Protection Agency, *Progress in Water Quality: An Evaluation of the National Investment in Municipal Wastewater Treatment* (Washington, DC: Government Accountability Office, 2000), 10-18.

85. Environmental Protection Agency, *Progress in Water Quality: An Evaluation*, 10-18.

86. Environmental Protection Agency, *Progress in Water Quality: An Evaluation*, 10-18.

87. Environmental Protection Agency, *Progress in Water Quality: An Evaluation*, 10-18.

88. Environmental Protection Agency, *Progress in Water Quality: An Evaluation*, 10-11.

89. Environmental Protection Agency, *Progress in Water Quality: An Evaluation*, 10-11.

## CHAPTER 6. SUBURBAN EXPLOSION

1. J. K. Stamer, R. N. Cherry, R. E. Faye, and R. L. Kleckner, "Magnitudes, Nature, and Effects of Point and Nonpoint Discharges in the Chattahoochee River Basin, Atlanta to West Point Dam, Georgia," *Geological Water Supply Paper* 2059 (Washington, DC: Government Accountability Office, 1979), 23.

2. Stamer et al. 33.

3. Paul Charles Milazzo, *Unlikely Environmentalists: Congress and Clean Water* (Lawrence: UP of Kansas, 2006), 208.

4. See 33 U.S.C. §1251 (b) (2006) ("It is the policy of the Congress to

recognize, preserve, and protect the primary responsibilities and rights of States to prevent, reduce, and eliminate pollution, to plan the development and use . . . of water resources.").

5. Milazzo 208.

6. Milazzo 209.

7. Milazzo 209.

8. Milazzo 209.

9. LeeAnn Lands, *The Culture of Property: Race, Class, and Housing Landscapes in Atlanta* (Athens: U of Georgia P, 2009), 194.

10. H. W. Lochner & Co. and De Leuw, Cather & Co., *Highway and Transportation Plan for Atlanta, Georgia* (1946), 9.

11. H.W. Lochner & Co. xi.

12. H.W. Lochner & Co. 5 (graph of predicted traffic patterns).

13. H.W. Lochner & Co. 18 (map of proposed expressway system).

14. Larry Keating, *Atlanta: Race, Class, and Urban Expansion* (Philadelphia: Temple UP, 2001), 71.

15. Keating 72.

16. "Atlanta History: From Railroad Hub to International City," *Atlanta Convention & Visitors Bureau*, n.p., n.d., Web, 31 January 2013, 6.

17. Urban Institute, *Urban Sprawl: Causes, Consequences, and Policy Responses*, ed. Gregory Squires (Washington, DC: Urban Institute Press, 2002), 176–77.

18. Urban Institute 177.

19. Frank S. Alexander, "Inherent Tensions between Home Rule and Regional Planning," *Wake Forest Law Review* 35 (2000): 543.

20. Garrett Hardin, "Tragedy of the Commons," *Science* 162.3859 (1968): 1243–48.

21. Hardin 1244.

22. Lands 169.

23. See "Atlanta Water, Sewer Conditions Reported," *Atlanta Daily World*, 12 January 1964: A1.

24. Adam Ward Rome, *The Bulldozer in the Countryside: Suburban Sprawl and the Rise of American Environmentalism* (Cambridge: Cambridge UP, 2004), 88.

25. Rome 88.

26. "Atlanta Water, Sewer Conditions Reported," *Atlanta Daily World*, 12 January 1964: A1.

27. Rome 90.

28. Rome 90.

29. Rome 93.

30. Harry Nicolas Coccassis, "Cornell Dissertations in Planning: The Shape

and Structure of Metropolitan Areas: An Application of Centrographic Analysis to Atlanta, Georgia," Dissertation, Cornell U, 1980, 117.

31. Coccassis 117.

32. Environmental Protection Agency, "Protecting Water Quality from Urban Runoff," Bulletin 941-F-03-003 (February 2003).

33. Environmental Protection Agency, "Protecting Water Quality from Urban Runoff."

34. Environmental Protection Agency, "Protecting Water Quality from Urban Runoff."

35. Joel B. Elsen, "Toward a Sustainable Urbanism: Lessons from Federal Regulation of Urban Stormwater Runoff," *Washington University Journal of Urban and Contemporary Law* 48 (1995): 13.

36. Douglas Lanvin, "County Confronts Cost of Treating Dirty Stormwater," *Atlanta Journal-Constitution*, 5 September 1990: J01.

37. Carrie Teegardin, "Study: Runoff a Major Villain in Pollution," *Atlanta Journal-Constitution*, 3 July 1991: D3.

38. Carrie Teegardin, "Study: Runoff a Major Villain in Pollution," *Atlanta Journal-Constitution*, 3 July 1991: D3.

39. Carrie Teegardin, "Focus: Cleaning Up Our Water," *Atlanta Journal-Constitution*, 4 April1991: D3.

40. "County Sewer Bond Projects Said 'Must' for Health," *Atlanta Daily World*, 11 April 1963: 4.

41. Gladwin Hill, "Atlanta Loses Ground in Fight on Pollution," *New York Times*, 2 March 1965: 21.

42. "County Sewer Bond Projects Said 'Must' for Health," *Atlanta Daily World*, 11 April 1963: 4.

43. Robert Troxler, Debra Reinhart, and Alan Hallum, "Metro Atlanta Water Pollution Control: A Decade of Progress," *Journal of Water Pollution Control* 55 (1983): 1125.

44. Troxler et al. 1123.

45. Troxler et al. 1123.

46. Troxler et al. 1123.

47. Troxler et al. 1123.

48. Gail Epstein and Ron Taylor, "New Dam Debated," *Atlanta Journal-Constitution*, 23 June 1985: D1.

49. Gail Epstein and Ron Taylor, "New Dam Debated," *Atlanta Journal-Constitution*, 23 June 1985: D1.

50. Maria Saporta, "Atlanta's Development Problems Grow in Rising Tide of Water Woes," *Atlanta Journal-Constitution*, 15 September 1985: M4.

51. Gail Epstein and Ron Taylor, "New Dam Debated," *Atlanta Journal-Constitution*, 23 June 1985: D1.

52. Gail Epstein and Ron Taylor, "New Dam Debated," *Atlanta Journal-Constitution*, 23 June 1985: D1.

53. Gail Epstein and Ron Taylor, "New Dam Debated," *Atlanta Journal-Constitution*, 23 June 1985: D1.

54. Gail Epstein and Ron Taylor, "New Dam Debated," *Atlanta Journal-Constitution*, 23 June 1985: D1.

55. Gail Epstein and Ron Taylor, "New Dam Debated," *Atlanta Journal-Constitution*, 23 June 1985: D1.

56. Gail Epstein and Ron Taylor, "New Dam Debated," *Atlanta Journal-Constitution*, 23 June 1985: D1.

57. John McCosh, "Water Board to Supervise New Facility," *Atlanta Journal-Constitution*, 5 June 1986: H1.

58. Fulton and DeKalb Metro. Planning Dist. and Comm., 147 Ga. Laws 849.

59. Fulton and DeKalb Metro. Planning Dist. and Comm., 147 Ga. Laws 849.

60. Atlanta Regional Metro. Planning Dist., 1960 Ga. Laws 3102.

61. John McCosh, "Feelings Run Deep Over Development of the Chattahoochee," *Atlanta Journal-Constitution*, 2 May 1985: H1.

62. John McCosh, "Feelings Run Deep Over Development of the Chattahoochee," *Atlanta Journal-Constitution*, 2 May 1985: H1.

63. John McCosh, "Feelings Run Deep Over Development of the Chattahoochee," *Atlanta Journal-Constitution*, 2 May 1985: H1.

64. David Corvette, "Balance of Nature at Stake as Developers Flock to River," *Atlanta Journal-Constitution*, 16 December1985: A1.

65. David Corvette, "Balance of Nature at Stake as Developers Flock to River," *Atlanta Journal-Constitution*, 16 December1985: A1.

66. Bob Harrell, "Environmental Laws Often Fail to Protect Chattahoochee," *Atlanta Journal-Constitution*, 6 April 1986: B4.

67. Bob Harrell, "Environmental Laws Often Fail to Protect Chattahoochee," *Atlanta Journal-Constitution*, 6 April 1986: B4.

68. John McCosh, "New Park Service Report Outlines Expansion of River Recreation Area," *Atlanta Journal-Constitution*, 26 September 1985: H1.

69. John McCosh, "New Park Service Report Outlines Expansion of River Recreation Area," *Atlanta Journal-Constitution*, 26 September 1985: H1.

70. David Corvette, "Balance of Nature at Stake as Developers Flock to River," *Atlanta Journal-Constitution*, 16 December1985: A1.

71. David Corvette, "Balance of Nature at Stake as Developers Flock to River," *Atlanta Journal-Constitution*, 16 December1985: A1.

72. Gale White, "Panel Votes to Extend River Controls," *Atlanta Journal-Constitution*, 15 March 1985: A25.

73. Gale White, "Panel Votes to Extend River Controls," *Atlanta Journal-Constitution*, 15 March 1985: A25.

74. Metro. River Prot. Act, 1986 Ga. Laws 321.

75. Ray Weiss, "House Gets Senate-Passed Bill to Put Teeth in ARC River Plan," *Atlanta Journal-Constitution*, 20 February 1986: A10.

76. James M. Sant, *Stream Corridor Protection in the Atlanta Region: The Metropolitan River Protection Act and the Chattahoochee Corridor Plan.* Proceedings of the Georgia Water Resources Conference, May 1989, U of Georgia.

77. Sant.

78. Carrie Teegardin, "Preservationists Take a Stand for Trees," *Atlanta Journal-Constitution.* 12 June 1989.

79. Elsen 37.

80. Elsen 37.

81. Elsen 39.

82. *NRDC v. Costle*, 568 F.2d 1369 (D.C.Cir. 1972).

83. Elsen 40.

84. Clean Water Act, §402(p).

85. Elsen 40.

86. Carrie Teegardin, "Focus: Cleaning Up Our Water," *Atlanta Journal-Constitution*, 4 April 1991: D3.

87. Carrie Teegardin, "Study: Runoff a Major Villain in Pollution," *Atlanta Journal-Constitution*, 3 July 1991: D3.

88. Environmental Protection Agency, *Stormwater Phase II Final Rule: An Overview* (Washington, DC: Government Accountability Office, 2005), 1.

89. Environmental Protection Agency, *Stormwater Phase II*, 1.

90. Douglas Lavin, "County Confronts Cost of Treating Dirty Stormwater," *Atlanta Journal-Constitution*, 5 September 1990: J01.

91. Carrie Teegardin, "Focus: Cleaning Up Our Water," *Atlanta Journal-Constitution*, 4 April 1991: D3.

92. See Carrie Teegardin, "Cost of Stormwater Cleanup Still Sinking In," *Atlanta Journal-Constitution*, 27 March 1991: J1.

93. Diane R. Stepp, "Officials Target Big Creek Pollution," *Atlanta Journal-Constitution*, 12 August 1993: H1.

94. Carrie Teegardin, "Preservationists Take a Stand for Trees," *Atlanta Journal-Constitution*, 12 June 1989.

95. "Decatur May Strengthen Storm Drainage Ordinance," *Atlanta Journal-Constitution*, 8 November 1990: A09.
96. Carrie Teegardin, "Preservationists Take a Stand for Trees," *Atlanta Journal-Constitution*, 12 June 1989.
97. "Our Water, Our Future," *Atlanta Regional Commission* (2006).
98. "Our Water, Our Future."
99. "Our Water, Our Future."
100. "Tapped Out," *Upper Chattahoochee Riverkeeper*, n.p., 2009, Web, 30 January 2013.
101. "Tapped Out," *Upper Chattahoochee Riverkeeper*, n.p., 2009, Web, 30 January 2013.
102. Adrienne Funk, "Water Quality Study Addresses Pollution Questions at Chattahoochee River National Recreation Area," *Natural Resources Year in Review: 1999* (Washington, DC: Government Accountability Office, 2000).
103. John Reetz, "Lake Battle about Water: Mountains vs. the City," *Atlanta Journal*, 19 February 1976: 1A.
104. John Reetz, "Lake Battle about Water: Mountains vs. the City," *Atlanta Journal*, 19 February 1976: 1A.
105. Barbara Casson, "Area Running Short of Water," *Atlanta Journal*, 30 November 1973: 1A.
106. *State of Florida First Amended Complaint, Alabama v. Army Corps of Engineers*, 382 F. Supp.2d, 2003 WL 24859220.
107. *State of Florida First Amended Complaint, Alabama v. Army Corps of Engineers*.
108. *State of Florida First Amended Complaint, Alabama v. Army Corps of Engineers*.
109. James H. Scarbrough, ed., *Sustainable Water Resources for Gwinnett County, Georgia*. Proceedings of the Georgia Water Resources Conference, April 2005, Athens: U of Georgia, 2005.
110. Robert David Coughlin, *Lake Sidney Lanier: A Storybook Site* (Atlanta: RDC Productions, 1998).
111. *State of Florida First Amended Complaint, Alabama v. Army Corps of Engineers*, 382 F. Supp.2d, 2003 WL 24859220.
112. David Corvette, "Growth Not Helping Metro Area to Weather Drought," *Atlanta Journal-Constitution*, 1 May 1986: A1.
113. Mike Christensen, "Special Report: Atlanta's Water Future," *Atlanta Constitution*, 21 December 1986: T1

114. Gail Epstein, "The Drought of 1986," *Atlanta Journal-Constitution*, 20 July 1986: A8.


## CHAPTER 7. URBAN DECAY

1. Charles Seabrook, "River in Peril: How Atlanta's Sewers Threaten the Chattahoochee," *Atlanta Journal*, 29 June 1997: C6.
2. Laurel A. David, "The EPA's Combined Sewer Overflow Abatement Methods: Do They Comply with the Clean Water Act?" *Urban Law* 35 (2003): 533.
3. Charles Seabrook, "Raw Sewage Still Flowing as Plans Languish," *Atlanta Journal-Constitution*, 24 November 1991: A1.
4. David 543–44.
5. Charles Seabrook, "Raw Sewage Still Flowing as Plans Languish," *Atlanta Journal-Constitution*, 24 November1991: A1.
6. Peter Crane Anderson, "The CSO Sleeping Giant: Combined Sewer Overflow or Congressional Stalling Objective," *Virginia Environmental Law Journal* 10 (1991): 392.
7. Anderson 385 ("some of the reasons cited for excluding CSOs from an overall, system-wide POTW pollution abatement effort relate to the unpopularity of large-scale expenditures").
8. Anderson 392.
9. Anderson 392.
10. Ga. Code Ann. Sec. 12-5-29.1(c)(2)(C) (Supp. 1995). Originally, the legislature set the deadline at December 31, 1993, but it was extended after it became clear that municipalities across the state needed more time. See Ga. Code Ann. Sec. 12-5-91.1 (2001) (setting original deadline).
11. Ga. Code Ann. Sec. 12-5-29.1(c)(2) (2001).
12. David 533.
13. Charles Seabrook, "Raw Sewage Still Flowing as Plans Languish," *Atlanta Journal-Constitution*, 24 November1991: A1; see also David 550.
14. Charles Seabrook, "Raw Sewage Still Flowing as Plans Languish," *Atlanta Journal-Constitution*, 24 November1991: A1.
15. Scott Bronstein, "City Panel Recommends Halting Proposed Combined Overflow Plant," *Atlanta Journal-Constitution*, 11 May 1993: C1.
16. Editorial, "Mayor Should Accept Sewer Verdict," *Atlanta Constitution*, 14 July 1993: A12.

17. Editorial, "Mayor Should Accept Sewer Verdict," *Atlanta Constitution*, 14 July 1993: A12.

18. David Pendered, "Panel: Local Sewage Plant Next to Park Backed by Neighborhood Advocates," *Atlanta Journal-Constitution*, 28 September 1993: E2.

19. David Pendered, "Panel: Local Sewage Plant Next to Park Backed by Neighborhood Advocates," *Atlanta Journal-Constitution*, 28 September 1993: E2.

20. David Pendered, "Fulton Urges New City Sewerage Site," *Atlanta Journal-Constitution*, 16 December 1993: D3.

21. Editorial, "How Can Atlanta Solve Water, Sewer Problems?" *Atlanta Journal-Constitution*, 11 February 1997: A08.

22. Laurel A. David, The EPA's Combined Sewer Overflow Abatement Methods: Do They Comply with the Clean Water Act? 35 Urb. Law. 533, 552 (2003).

23. *Upper Chattahoochee Riverkeeper Fund, Inc. v. Atlanta*, 986 F. Supp. 1406, 1412 (1997).

24. Laurel A. David, The EPA's Combined Sewer Overflow Abatement Methods: Do They Comply with the Clean Water Act? 35 Urb. Law. 533, 552 (2003).

25. Laurel A. David, The EPA's Combined Sewer Overflow Abatement Methods: Do They Comply with the Clean Water Act?, 35 Urb. Law. 533, 552 (2003).

26. Charles Seabrook and Charmagne Helton, "City Faces Another Sewage Spill," *Atlanta Journal-Constitution*, February 1, 1997: D.

27. Charles Seabrook & Charmagne Helton, "City Faces Another Sewage Spill," *Atlanta Journal-Constitution*, February 1, 1997: D.

28. *Upper Chattahoochee Riverkeeper Fund, Inc. v. Atlanta*, 986 F. Supp. 1406 (1997).

29. An Olympic Hurdle: Chattahoochee River Pollution, *Living on Earth* (June 28, 1996). Public Radio International. Audio.

30. Laurel A. David, The EPA's Combined Sewer Overflow Abatement Methods: Do They Comply with the Clean Water Act? 35 Urb. Law. 533, 555 (2003).

31. *Upper Chattahoochee Riverkeeper Fund v. Atlanta*, 98 F. Supp. 2d 1380 (N.D.Ga. 2000).

32. David 556.

33. Alan Parenteau, "Atlanta's Historic Watering Hole," *Atlanta Journal-Constitution*, 8 June 1986: H1.

34. Alan Parenteau, "Atlanta's Historic Watering Hole," *Atlanta Journal-*

*Constitution*, 8 June 1986: H1.

35. "Water Plant Fix Mire in Blame: Atlanta's Main Pump Station in Trouble," *Atlanta Journal*, 22 April 1998: A01.

36. Peter Applebome, "Scandal Casts Shadow Over Atlanta Mayoral Race," *New York Times*, 18 November 1993.

37. "Olympic Vendors Go Home with Empty Pockets While City Cashes In," *Waycross Journal-Herald*, 25 September 1996: P11.

38. Charmagne Helton, "Atlanta's Sewer Problems," *Atlanta Journal-Constitution*, 4 March 1997.

39. Russ Bynum, "A Dirty Campaign Down South," *Free Lance-Star* (Fredericksburg, VA), 31 October 1997: A15.

40. Russ Bynum, "A Dirty Campaign Down South," *Free Lance-Star* (Fredericksburg, VA), 31 October 1997: A15.

41. Russ Bynum, "A Dirty Campaign Down South," *Free Lance-Star* (Fredericksburg, VA), 31 October 1997: A15.

42. Darryl Fears, "Election '97: Water Safety Debate Stirs Mayor's Race," *Atlanta Journal-Constitution*, 18 November 1997.

43. Darryl Fears, "Election '97: Water Safety Debate Stirs Mayor's Race," *Atlanta Journal-Constitution*, 18 November 1997.

44. "Campbell Unfurls Blueprint, Vowing to 'Finish the Job,'" *Atlanta Journal-Constitution*, 6 December 1997: C3.

45. Charmagne Helton, "Privatizing to Affect Water," *Atlanta Journal-Constitution*, 16 January 1998.

46. Charmagne Helton, "Privatizing to Affect Water," *Atlanta Journal-Constitution*, 16 January 1998.

47. Charmagne Helton, "Privatizing to Affect Water," *Atlanta Journal-Constitution*, 16 January 1998.

48. Charmagne Helton, "Privatizing to Affect Water," *Atlanta Journal-Constitution*, 16 January 1998.

49. Carlos Campos and Julie B. Hairston, "Wading into Private Waters," *Atlanta Journal-Constitution*, 27 March 1998.

50. Carlos Campos and Julie B. Hairston, "Wading into Private Waters," *Atlanta Journal-Constitution*, 27 March 1998.

51. Julie B. Hairston, "Bidders Get OK to Seek Atlanta Water Contract," *Atlanta Journal-Constitution*, 22 May 1998.

52. Carlos Campos and Julie Hairston, "City Withholds Data on Water Bids," *Atlanta Journal-Constitution*, 21 July 1998.

53. Carlos Campos and Julie Hairston, "City Withholds Data on Water Bids," *Atlanta Journal-Constitution*, 21 July 1998.

54. David 533.

55. Kevin B. Smith, "Combined Sewer Overflows and Sanitary Sewer Over-flows: EPA's Regulatory Approach and Policy under the Federal Water Pollution Control Act," *Environmental Law Reporter* 26 (1996): 10297.

56. Douglas Jehl, "As Cities Move to Privatize Water, Atlanta Steps Back," *New York Times*, 10 February 2003.

57. Avital Louria Hahn, "Water Wars: How Do You Finance a Broken Down System?" *Investment Dealers' Digest* (2002): 232600.

58. Craig Anthony Arnold, "Water Privatization Trends in the United States: Human Rights, National Security, and Public Stewardship," *William and Mary Environmental Law and Policy Review* 33 (2009): 793.

59. Arnold 793.

60. Charmagne Helton, "Atlanta's Sewer Problems: Trio of Contenders Still the Ones in the Lead to Take Over All of Atlanta's Water and Sewer Operations," *Atlanta Journal-Constitution*, 4 March 1997.

61. Charmagne Helton, "Atlanta's Sewer Problems: Trio of Contenders Still the Ones in the Lead to Take Over All of Atlanta's Water and Sewer Operations," *Atlanta Journal-Constitution*, 4 March 1997.

62. Charmagne Helton, "Atlanta's Sewer Problems: Trio of Contenders Still the Ones in the Lead to Take Over All of Atlanta's Water and Sewer Operations," *Atlanta Journal-Constitution*, 4 March 1997.

63. Charmagne Helton, "Atlanta's Sewer Problems: Trio of Contenders Still the Ones in the Lead to Take Over All of Atlanta's Water and Sewer Operations," *Atlanta Journal-Constitution*, 4 March 1997.

64. Charmagne Helton, "Atlanta's Sewer Problems: Trio of Contenders Still the Ones in the Lead to Take Over All of Atlanta's Water and Sewer Operations," *Atlanta Journal-Constitution*, 4 March 1997.

65. See Charmagne Helton, "Atlanta's Sewer Problems: Trio of Contenders Still the Ones in the Lead to Take Over All of Atlanta's Water and Sewer Operations," *Atlanta Journal-Constitution*, 4 March 1997 (at the time, Vivendi Environment was known as "Compagnie Generale de Eaux").

66. Vandana Shiva, *Water Wars: Privatization, Pollution, and Profit* (Cambridge, MA: South End Press, 2002), 97.

67. Shiva 97.

68. Ann-Christin Sjölander Holland, *The Water Business: Corporations Versus People* (London: Zed Books, 2005), 16.

69. Holland 16.

70. Editorial, "Bid Process Better, But Still Has Flaws," *Atlanta Journal-Constitution* 27 July 1998.

71. Julie B. Hairston, "Water Privatization Bidder Will Face Debt, Backlog,

Major Upgrades," *Atlanta Journal-Constitution*, 23 August 1998.

72. Julie B. Hairston, "A Winner in Water War," *Atlanta Journal-Constitution*, 28 August 1998.

73. Julie B. Hairston, "A Winner in Water War," *Atlanta Journal-Constitution*, 28 August 1998.

74. Carlos Campos and Julie B. Hairston, "Privatizing Atlanta's Water System," *Atlanta Constitution-Journal*, 28 August 1998..

75. Richard Whitt and Alan Judd, "Campbell Indicted," *Atlanta Journal-Constitution*, 31 August 2004.

76. Jeffrey Scott and Beth Warren, "Campbell's Defense Still in Wings," *Atlanta Journal-Constitution*, 12 February 2006.

77. Stacy Shelton, "Eye to Privatize? Don't Copy Us," *Atlanta Journal-Constitution*, 25 January 2003.

78. Stacy Shelton, "Eye to Privatize? Don't Copy Us," *Atlanta Journal-Constitution*, 25 January 2003.

79. Jim Wooten, "Atlanta Should Keep Water Deal," *Atlanta Journal-Constitution*, 24 September 2002.

80. Jim Wooten, "Atlanta Should Keep Water Deal," *Atlanta Journal-Constitution*, 24 September 2002.

81. Jim Wooten, "Atlanta Should Keep Water Deal," *Atlanta Journal-Constitution*, 24 September 2002.

82. Jim Wooten, "Atlanta Should Keep Water Deal," *Atlanta Journal-Constitution*, 24 September 2002.

83. Carlos Campos and Julie B. Hairston, "Wading into Private Waters, *Atlanta Journal-Constitution*, 27 March 1998.

84. Carlos Campos and Julie B. Hairston, "Wading into Private Waters, *Atlanta Journal-Constitution*, 27 March 1998.

85. Carlos Campos and Julie B. Hairston, "Wading into Private Waters, *Atlanta Journal-Constitution*, 27 March 1998.

86. Carlos Campos, "Water Firm Vows Solid Job but Details Won't Be Aired until Contract OK'd," *Atlanta Journal-Constitution*, 20 September 1998; Carlos Campos and Julie B. Hairston, "Wading into Private Waters, *Atlanta Journal-Constitution*, 27 March 1998.

87. Ann Hardie, "Getting Quick Action on Leak Just a Pipe Dream in Highland Park," *Atlanta Journal-Constitution*, 16 August 1999.

88. Ann Hardie, "Getting Quick Action on Leak Just a Pipe Dream in Highland Park," *Atlanta Journal-Constitution*, 16 August 1999.

89. Doug Payne, "Pump Station Glitch Causes N. Atlanta Tap Water Alert," *Atlanta Journal-Constitution*, 29 June 2000.

90. Stacy Shelton, "Tap Water Alarm Passes with Little Northside Notice," *Atlanta Journal-Constitution*, 30 June 2000.

91. Stacy Shelton, "Tap Water Alarm Passes with Little Northside Notice," *Atlanta Journal-Constitution*, 30 June 2000.

92. Doug Payne, "Pump Station Glitch Causes N. Atlanta Tap Water Alert," *Atlanta Journal-Constitution*, 29 June 2000.

93. Milo Ippolito, "Dirty Tap Water Stirs Flood of Complaints," *Atlanta Journal-Constitution*, June 8, 2002.

94. Milo Ippolito, "Dirty Tap Water Stirs Flood of Complaints," *Atlanta Journal-Constitution*, June 8, 2002.

95. Milo Ippolito, "Dirty Tap Water Stirs Flood of Complaints," *Atlanta Journal-Constitution*, June 8, 2002.

96. Milo Ippolito, "Dirty Tap Water Stirs Flood of Complaints," *Atlanta Journal-Constitution*, June 8, 2002.

97. Charles Yoo, "Families Battle Water Cutoff," *Atlanta Journal-Constitution*, 4 July 2002.

98. D. L. Bennett, "Water Problems Balloon When United Turns It Off," *Atlanta Journal-Constitution*, 22 August 2002.

99. D. L. Bennett, "United Water Offers Money," *Atlanta Journal-Constitution*, 18 September 2002.

100. D. L. Bennett, "United Water Offers Money," *Atlanta Journal-Constitution*, 18 September 2002.

101. D. L. Bennett, "United Water Has Leaky Finances," *Atlanta Journal-Constitution*, 14 December 2002.

102. D. L. Bennett, "Campbell Water Deal Rebuffed," *Atlanta Journal-Constitution*, 4 October 2002.

103. D. L. Bennett, "Campbell Water Deal Rebuffed," *Atlanta Journal-Constitution*, 4 October 2002.

104. D. L. Bennett, "Campbell Water Deal Rebuffed," *Atlanta Journal-Constitution*, 4 October 2002.

105. D. L. Bennett, "Alleged Campbell Letters to Go to Feds," *Atlanta Journal-Constitution*, 12 October 2002.

106. D. L. Bennett, "Water Bills Go Unpaid," *Atlanta Journal-Constitution*, 3 January 2003.

107. D. L. Bennett, "Water Funds Audit Shows Goals Unmet," *Atlanta Journal-Constitution*, 22 January 2003.

108. D. L. Bennett, "Water Funds Audit Shows Goals Unmet," *Atlanta Journal-Constitution*, 22 January 2003.

109. D. L. Bennett, "Water Funds Audit Shows Goals Unmet," *Atlanta Journal-Constitution*, 22 January 2003.

110. D. L. Bennett, "United Water Offers Cost Freeze to Keep Contract," *Atlanta Journal-Constitution*, 17 January 2003.

111. Stacy Shelton, "Eye to the Prize? Don't Copy Us," *Atlanta Journal-Constitution*, 25 January 2003.

112. Eirk Sofge, "The 10 Pieces of U.S. Infrastructure We Must Fix Now," *Popular Mechanics*, May 2008.

## CHAPTER 8. WATER WAR, PART I

1. "Tapped Out," *Upper Chattahoochee Riverkeeper*, n.p., 2009, Web, 30 January 2013.

2. "Tapped Out."

3. "Tapped Out."

4. "Tapped Out."

5. "Priority Use of Allatoona Water Debated at Hearing," *Rome News Tribune*, 15 February 1974: 3.

6. "Priority Use of Allatoona Water Debated at Hearing," *Rome News Tribune*, 15 February 1974: 3.

7. Flood Control Act of 1944, 58 Stat. 887 (1944).

8. Id. at §6.

9. 43 U.S.C. §390b(b).

10. Id.: see also U.S. General Accountability Office, *Water Resources: Corps Lacks Authority for Water Supply Contracts* (Washington, DC: Government Accountability Office, 1991).

11. U.S. General Accountability Office.

12. 43 U.S.C. §390b(d).

13. *State of Florida First Amended Complaint, Alabama v. Army Corps of Engineers*, 382 F. Supp. 2d, 2003 WL 24859220.

14. *Opening Brief of Federal Defendants-Appellants, Alabama v. Army Corps of Engineers*, 424 F.3d 117, 2004 WL 4886093.

15. Id.

16. *State of Florida First Amended Complaint, Alabama v. Army Corps of Engineers*, 382 F. Supp. 2d, 2003 WL 24859220.

17. Id.

18. Id.

19. "Apalachicola Fishermen Fret over Drought to the North," *St. Petersburg Times*, 5 August 1986: 3A.

20. Alan Judd, "Bay Study May Have Far-Reaching Effect," *Gainesville Sun*, 11 August 1991: A4.

21. "Apalachicola Fishermen Fret over Drought to the North," *St. Petersburg Times*, 5 August 1986: 3A. .

22. "Apalachicola Fishermen Fret over Drought to the North," *St. Petersburg Times*, 5 August 1986: 3A.

23. "Apalachicola Fishermen Fret over Drought to the North," *St. Petersburg Times*, 5 August 1986: 3A.

24. Jim Auchumutey, "The Year in Review: '88," *Atlanta Journal-Constitution*, 1 January 1989: N01.

25. David Corvette, "Growth Not Helping Metro Area to Weather Drought," *Atlanta Constitution*, 1 May 1986: A1.

26. David Corvette, "Growth Not Helping Metro Area to Weather Drought," *Atlanta Constitution*, 1 May 1986: A1.

27. David Corvette, "Growth Not Helping Metro Area to Weather Drought," *Atlanta Constitution*, 1 May 1986: A1.

28. William E. Schmidt, "The South: In a Wet Year, Memories of the Dry," *New York Times*, 16 August 1987: 45.

29. David Corvette, "Growth Not Helping Metro Area to Weather Drought," *Atlanta Constitution*, 1 May 1986: A1.

30. David Corvette, "Growth Not Helping Metro Area to Weather Drought," *Atlanta Constitution*, 1 May 1986: A1.

31. Gail Epstein, "The Drought of 1986," *Atlanta Journal-Constitution*, 20 July 1986: A8; David Corvette, "Growth Not Helping Metro Area to Weather Drought," *Atlanta Constitution*, 1 May 1986: A1

32. David Corvette, "Growth Not Helping Metro Area to Weather Drought," *Atlanta Constitution*, 1 May 1986: A1.

33. William E. Schmidt, "The South: In a Wet Year, Memories of the Dry," *New York Times*, 16 August 1987: 45.

34. William E. Schmidt, "The South: In a Wet Year, Memories of the Dry," *New York Times*, 16 August 1987: 45.

35. Bill Shipp, "The Coming Crisis of Quenching Atlanta's Thirst," *Atlanta Journal-Constitution*, 25 May 1986: E1.

36. "New Chattahoochee Dam Recommended," *Rome News-Tribune*, 19 Nov. 1980: 12A.

37. Coughlin.

38. Coughlin.

39. Bill Shipp, "The Coming Crisis of Quenching Atlanta's Thirst," *Atlanta Journal-Constitution*, 25 May 1986: E1.

40. Bill Shipp, "The Coming Crisis of Quenching Atlanta's Thirst," *Atlanta Journal-Constitution*, 25 May 1986: E1.

41. Bill Shipp, "The Coming Crisis of Quenching Atlanta's Thirst," *Atlanta Journal-Constitution*, 25 May 1986: E1.

42. Gail Epstein and Ron Taylor, "New Dam Debated: Future Water Supply Might Take Precedent Over Fine Trout Fishing," *Atlanta Journal-Constitution*, 23 Jun. 1985: D1. Of course, strangely, the only reason why trout could survive the Chattahoochee in the first place was that the Buford Dam had lowered temperatures and quickened the river's current. The dam releases cold, clear water from the bottom of the lake. Before, the Chattahoochee was slow, warm, and very muddy; trout could never have survived in its natural state.

43. Epstein D1.

44. Bill Shipp, "The Coming Crisis of Quenching Atlanta's Thirst," *Atlanta Journal-Constitution*, 25 May 1986: E1.

45. "Water-Project Bill a Mix of Good, Bad," *Atlanta Journal-Constitution*, 31 Mar. 1986: A8. Bill Shipp, "The Coming Crisis of Quenching Atlanta's Thirst," *Atlanta Journal-Constitution*, 25 May 1986: E1.

46. Bill Shipp, "The Coming Crisis of Quenching Atlanta's Thirst," *Atlanta Journal-Constitution*, 25 May 1986: E1.

47. Bert Roughton Jr., "Reagan OKs Dam, Now Metro Area Must Find Funds," *Atlanta Journal*, 18 November 1986: D1.

48. Scott Vaughn, "Gwinnett Favors Equal Split on Cost of Dam," *Atlanta Journal-Constitution*, 3 July 1987: B4.

49. Scott Vaughn, "Gwinnett Favors Equal Split on Cost of Dam," *Atlanta Journal-Constitution*, 3 July 1987: B4.

50. Scott Vaughn, "Gwinnett Favors Equal Split on Cost of Dam," *Atlanta Journal-Constitution*, 3 July 1987: B4.

51. Jim Newton, "Gwinnett Restricts Water Use," *Atlanta Journal*, 4 November 1987: B2.

52. Energy Bar Association, "Report of the Committee on Power Marketing Agencies," *Energy Law Journal* 12 (1991): 195.

53. Charles Seabrook, "Corps, Metro Officials Disagree on Water Needs," *Atlanta Journal-Constitution*, 4 November 1989: C01.

54. Editorial, "Lesson to Learn from 'Water War,'" *Atlanta Journal-Constitution*, 30 November 1989: A22.

55. "Corps Proposes to Kill an Authorized Project," *Engineering News-Record*,

10 November 1988: 15.

56. See Travis M. Trimble, "Environmental Law," *Mercer Law Review* 61 (2010): 1104.

57. Charles Seabrook, "Corps, Metro Officials Disagree on Water Needs," *Atlanta Journal-Constitution*, 4 November 1989: C01.

58. Charles Seabrook, "Ala. Sues to Halt Diversion of Water from Two Rivers," *Atlanta Journal-Constitution*, 29 June 1990: A10.

59. *Motion for Temporary Restraining Order, Preliminary Injunction, and to Have Settlement Agreements Entered into by Defendant Declared Null and Void, Alabama v. Army Corps of Engineers*, 382 F. Supp.2d, 2003 WL 24859221.

60. *Alabama v. Army Corps of Engineers*, 382 F. Supp. 2d 1301.

61. *Opening Brief of Federal Defendants-Appellants, Alabama v. Army Corps of Engineers*, 424 F. 3d 117, 2004 WL 4886093.

62. 42 U.S.C. §§4332 (2) (c).

63. *State of Florida's First Amended Complaint, Alabama v. Army Corps of Engineers*, 382 F. Supp. 2d 1301 (2003) (No. CV-90-BE-1331-E), 2003 WL 24859220 (N.D.Ala.).

64. 16 U.S.C. §1536; *State of Florida's First Amended Complaint, Alabama v. Army Corps of Engineers*, 382 F. Supp. 2d 1301 (2003) (No. CV-90-BE-1331-E), 2003 WL 24859220 (N.D.Ala.).

65. *State of Florida's First Amended Complaint, Alabama v. Army Corps of Engineers*, 382 F. Supp. 2d 1301 (2003) (No. CV-90-BE-1331-E), 2003 WL 24859220 (N.D.Ala.).

66. *State of Florida's First Amended Complaint, Alabama v. Army Corps of Engineers*, 382 F. Supp. 2d 1301 (2003) (No. CV-90-BE-1331-E), 2003 WL 24859220 (N.D.Ala.).

67. 33 U.S.C. §708.

68. *State of Florida's First Amended Complaint, Alabama v. Army Corps of Engineers*, 382 F. Supp. 2d 1301 (2003) (No. CV-90-BE-1331-E), 2003 WL 24859220 (N.D.Ala.).

69. Id.

70. Water Supply Act, 43 U.S.C. §390b(d).

71. *State of Florida's First Amended Complaint, Alabama v. Army Corps of Engineers*, 382 F. Supp. 2d 1301 (2003) (No. CV-90-BE-1331-E), 2003 WL 24859220 (N.D.Ala.).

72. Water Supply Act, 43 U.S.C. §390(a) and (d).

73. USACE ER 1105-2-100, ¶ 3-8(b)(5) (Apr. 22, 2000); *see also* USACE ER 1105-2-100, ¶ 4-32(d)(1) (December 28, 1990).

74. *State of Florida's First Amended Complaint, Alabama v. Army Corps of*

*Engineers*, 382 F. Supp. 2d 1301 (2003) (No. CV-90-BE-1331-E), 2003 WL 24859220 (N.D.Ala.).

75. Many speculated that, if Atlanta successfully won congressional reauthorization, it would open the door for hundreds of other municipalities to pursue reauthorization of other Army Corps projects. Many congressmen, especially those whose districts were on the receiving end of a favorable Army Corps arrangement, were staunchly opposed to reallocation.

76. Carrie Teegardin, "In-Fighting Heats Up," *Atlanta Journal-Constitution*, 2 August 1990: A17.

77. Carrie Teegardin, "Board May Dip into Coffers to Fund Water Fight," *Atlanta Journal-Constitution*, 3 September 1990: J01.

78. Charles Seabrook, "Georgia, Alabama Feud over Water Grows Hotter," *Atlanta Journal-Constitution*, 30 June 1990: A01.

79. Carrie Teegardin, "County Thirsting for Water Sources: Experts Tapping Options from Toilet to Aquifers," *Atlanta Journal-Constitution*, 21 March 1990: J01.

80. Carrie Teegardin, "In-Fighting Heats Up," *Atlanta Journal-Constitution*, 2 August 1990: A17.

81. Douglas L. Grant, "Interstate Allocation of River before the United States Supreme Court: The Apalachicola-Chattahoochee-Flint River System," *Georgia State University Law Review* 21 (2004): 404.

82. Barton H. Thompson Jr., John D. Leshy, and Robert H. Abrams, *Legal Control of Water Resources: Cases and Materials*, ed. Joseph Sax (Eagan, MN: Thomson-West, 2000), 871.

83. Grant 404. Requests were denied for the Arkansas River, the Colorado River, the Connecticut River, the Vermejo River, and the Walla Walla River. Apportionment requests were granted for the Laramie River, the Delaware River, and the North Platte River.

84. Thompson et al. 859; *Texas v. New Mexico*, 352 U.S. 991 (1957); *Arizona v. California*, 298 U.S. 558 (1936).

85. Grant 406.

86. Thompson et al. 835.

87. Thompson et al. 835.

88. Thompson et al. 843.

89. Thompson et al. 843.

90. Thompson et al. 843.

91. "Metro Meeting on Water Reaches No Accord," *Atlanta Journal Constitution*, 31 August 1990: E02.

92. *Motion for Temporary Restraining Order, Preliminary Injunction, and to Have Settlement Agreements Entered into by Defendant Declared Null and Void, Alabama v. Army Corps of Engineers,* 382 F. Supp. 2d, 2003 WL 24859221.

93. Carrie Teegardin, "Tri-State Water War Talks at Standstill," *Atlanta Journal-Constitution,* 5 October 1990: D01.

94. Carrie Teegardin, "Tri-State Water War Talks at Standstill," *Atlanta Journal-Constitution,* 5 October 1990: D01.

95. Editorial, "Alabama Should Rethink 'Water War' Talk," *Atlanta Journal-Constitution,* 5 December 1990: A12.

96. Carrie Teegardin, "Water War Holds Up Feds' Bill," *Atlanta Journal-Constitution,* 13 October 1990: C01.

97. Carrie Teegardin, "Water War Holds Up Feds' Bill," *Atlanta Journal-Constitution,* 13 October 1990: C01.

98. Carrie Teegardin, "Ala. Trying to Dry Up Ga.," *Atlanta Journal-Constitution,* 13 December 1990: A01.

99. Carrie Teegardin, "Ala. Trying to Dry Up Ga.," *Atlanta Journal-Constitution,* 13 December 1990: A01.

100. Carrie Teegardin, "Ala. Trying to Dry Up Ga.," *Atlanta Journal-Constitution,* 13 December 1990: A01.

101. Carrie Teegardin, "Ala. Trying to Dry Up Ga.," *Atlanta Journal-Constitution,* 13 December 1990: A01.

102. Carrie Teegardin, "Ala. Trying to Dry Up Ga.," *Atlanta Journal-Constitution,* 13 December 1990: A01.

103. "South in Brief: Ala. Offers Water to 2 Georgia Towns if Reservoir Held Up," *Atlanta Journal-Constitution,* 21 Mar.ch 1991: A3.

104. "Three-State Water Agreement Hailed as Model for Nation," *Lakeland Ledger,* 4 January 1992: 1B.

105. Jeffrey L. Jordan and Aaron T. Wolf, *Interstate Water Allocation in Alabama, Florida, and Georgia: New Issues, New Methods, New Models* (Gainesville: UP of Florida, 2006), 22.

106. Jordan and Wolf 23.

107. Barlow Burke, "Association of American Law Schools Conference: Transcript of the Section on Natural Resources in Atlanta, Georgia, January 5, 2004," *Georgia State University Law Review* 21 (2004–2005): 264.

108. Jordan and Wolf 23.

109. Kathryn J. Hacker, ed. *Plenary Session: Comprehensive Study of the ACF and ACT River Basins,* Proc. of the 1993 Georgia Water Resources Conference, April 1993, U of Georgia. Athens: U of Georgia P.

110. Hacker.

111. Hacker.

112. Hacker.

113. Hacker.

114. Jordan and Wolf 23; Burke 265.

115. Burke 265.

116. Burke 265.

117. H.J.Res.91.ENR (1997).

118. Burke 266.

119. Burke 266.

120. Charles Seabrook, "Water War May Take Critical Turn," *Atlanta Journal-Constitution*, 20 September 1998: C01.

121. Charles Seabrook, "Water War May Take Critical Turn," *Atlanta Journal-Constitution*, 20 September 1998: C01.

122. Burke 266.

123. Burke 267.

124. Burke 266.

125. Charles Seabrook, "Georgia's Growth Muddies Water Sharing Pact," *Atlanta Journal-Constitution*, 25 April 1998: D05.

126. Charles Seabrook, "Georgia's Growth Muddies Water Sharing Pact," *Atlanta Journal-Constitution*, 25 April 1998: D05.

127. Stacy Shelton, "States Far from Water Pact, Negotiator Says," *Atlanta Journal-Constitution*, 21 April 1999: JJ3.

128. Stacy Shelton, "States Far from Water Pact, Negotiator Says," *Atlanta Journal-Constitution*, 21 April 1999: JJ3.

129. Burke 246.

130. Burke 246.

131. Charles Seabrook, "Fighting Words on Water: Atlanta Could Die of Thirst," *Atlanta Journal-Constitution*, 18 February 2000: A1.

132. Charles Seabrook, "Time, Hope Running Out in Water War," *Atlanta Journal-Constitution*, 22 February 2000: C1.

133. Charles Seabrook, "States' Water Talk at Do-Or-Die Stage," *Atlanta Journal-Constitution*, 1 March 2000: A1.

134. Charles Seabrook, "Dry2k: State Failed to Plan for Drought," *Atlanta Constitution*, 19 June 2000: A1.

135. See Charles Seabrook, "Drought, Drought, Go Away," *Atlanta Journal-Constitution*, 22 February 2001: A1 (Atlanta imposed water restrictions); Burke 246–47 (regulations cut water use from 442 in 2000 to 429 million gallons per day in 2001).

136. Nancy L. Barber and Timothy C. Stamey, U.S. Geological Survey, *Droughts in Georgia* (Washington, DC: Government Accountability Office, 2000), 2.

137. Barber and Stamey 2.
138. Charles Seabrook, "Corps May Drop Lanier Even Lower," *Atlanta Constitution*, 10 August 2000: A1.
139. Charles Seabrook, "Corps May Drop Lanier Even Lower," *Atlanta Constitution*, 10 August 2000: A1.
140. Charles Seabrook, "Florida Opposes Lake Lanier Flow Plan: Wildlife at Risk, Officials Say," *Atlanta Constitution*, 16 August 2000: C1.

## CHAPTER 9. WATER WAR, PART II

1. Opening Brief of Federal Defendants-Appellants, *Alabama v. Army Corps of Engineers*, 424 F. 3d 117, 2004 WL 4886093.
2. Brief of Appellee the State of Georgia in Response to Brief of Appellant Southeastern Federal Power Customers, Inc., *Georgia v. Southeastern Federal Power Customers*, 302 F.3d 1242 (2002) (No. 02-10135D), 2002 WL 32100020.
3. Opening Brief of Federal Defendants-Appellants, *Alabama v. Army Corps of Engineers*, 424 F.3d 117, 2004 WL 4886093.
4. Brief of Appellee the State of Georgia in Response to Brief of Appellant Southeastern Federal Power Customers, Inc., *Georgia v. Southeastern Federal Power Customers*, 302 F. 3d 1242 (2002) (No. 02-10135D), 2002 WL 32100020.
5. See *Georgia v. U.S. Army Corps of Engineers*, Civ. No. 2:01-CV-0026-RWS (N.D. GA).
6. Georgia's complaint alleged that the Army Corps violated certain provisions of the APA when it failed to respond to the formal request within a certain period of time. See Brief of Appellee the State of Georgia in Response to Brief of Appellant Southeastern Federal Power Customers, Inc., *Georgia v. Southeastern Federal Power Customers*, 302 F.3d 1242 (2002) (No. 02-10135D), 2002 WL 32100020.
7. Letter from R. L. Brownlee, to Hon. Roy E. Barnes, Governor of Georgia, Apr. 15, 2002, citing Memorandum of Earl Stockdale, Deputy Gen. Counsel, Dep't. of the Army, regarding Georgia Request for Water Supply from Lake Lanier, Apr. 15, 2002.
8. See Brief of Appellant the State of Georgia, *Alabama v. Army Corps of Engineers*, 424 F. 3d 117, 2004 WL 4886080, *3.
9. Brief of Appellant the State of Georgia, *Alabama v. Army Corps of Engineers*, 424 F.3d 117, 2004 WL 4886080, *3.

10. Id.
11. Id.
12. Id.
13. Id. at *4.
14. Burke 282.
15. Burke 282.
16. Burke 282.
17. Brief of Appellant the State of Georgia, *Alabama v. Army Corps of Engineers*, 424 F. 3d 117, 2004 WL 4886080, *4.
18. Id.
19. Opening Brief of Federal Defendants-Appellants, *Alabama v. Army Corps of Engineers*, 424 F. 3d 117, 2004 WL 4886093.
20. Id.
21. Burke 269.
22. Motion for Temporary Restraining Order, Preliminary Injunction, and to Have Settlement Agreements Entered into by Defendant Declared Null and Void, *Alabama v. Army Corps of Engineers*, 382 F. Supp.2d, 2003 WL 24859221.
23. Brief of Appellant the State of Georgia, *Alabama v. Army Corps of Engineers*, 424 F.3d 117, 2004 WL 4886080, *3.
24. Motion for Temporary Restraining Order, Preliminary Injunction, and to Have Settlement Agreements Entered into by Defendant Declared Null and Void, *Alabama v. Army Corps of Engineers*, 382 F. Supp.2d, 2003 WL 24859221.
25. Brief of Appellant the State of Georgia, *Alabama v. Army Corps of Engineers*, 424 F.3d 117, 2004 WL 4886080, *4.
26. Brief for Appellant Gwinnett County, 2005 WL 4637987 (C.A.11).
27. In Re Tri-State Water Rights Litigation, 639 F.Supp.2d 1308, 1355 (M.D.Fla., 2009).
28. Id.
29. Id.
30. Dan Chapman and Bob Keefe, "Purdue Vows 'Fight to Death' on Lanier," *Atlanta Journal-Constitution*, 22 July 2009: B1.
31. Dan Chapman, "Will Water Ruling Dry Up Growth," *Atlanta Journal-Constitution*, 24 July 2009: A1.
32. Kristi E. Swartz, "Purdue Appoints Water Warriors," *Atlanta Journal-Constitution*, 24 July 2009: B1.
33. Patrick Fox, "Lanier Ruling One Year Later," *Atlanta Journal-Constitution*, 17 July 2010: B1.

34. "Our Water, Our Future," Atlanta Regional Commission (2006).

35. "Our Water, Our Future."

36. "Our Water, Our Future."

37. O.C.G.A. Sec. 12-5-572 (2001).

38. Metropolitan North Georgia Water Planning District, *Water Metrics Report* (2011), 1.

39. Opinion. Sally Bethea, "Regulate Water Transfers Carefully," *Atlanta Journal-Constitution*, 4 January 2011: A13.

40. Opinion. Sally Bethea, "Regulate Water Transfers Carefully," *Atlanta Journal-Constitution*, 4 January 2011: A13.

41. O.C.G.A. 12-5-552(a) (2001).

42. Metropolitan North Georgia Water Planning District, *2008 Activities and Progress Report* (2008), 4.

43. Eric Sirgus, "Atlanta's Sewer Woes Frustrate Georgians," *Atlanta Journal-Constitution*, 13 May 2010: A1.

44. Eric Sirgus, "Atlanta's Sewer Woes Frustrate Georgians," *Atlanta Journal-Constitution*, 13 May 2010: A1.

45. D. L. Bennett, "Sewer Fight Likely in Atlanta," *Atlanta Journal-Constitution*, 12 September 2003: C1.

46. Avital Louria Hahn, "Water Wars: How Do You Finance a Broken-Down System," *Investment Dealer's Digest*, 25 November 2002: 232600.

47. Hahn 232600.

48. Hahn 232600.

49. Ernie Scruggs, "Sewer Hearing Rowdy: Atlanta Residents Voice Fears about Rising Bills," *Atlanta Journal-Constitution*, 30 October 2003: C1.

50. Ty Tagami, "Penny Tax May Help Fix Sewers," *Atlanta Journal-Constitution*, 28 December 2003: F1.

51. Georgia Dept. of Natural Resources, *Revised Total Maximum Daily Load Evaluation for Seventy-Nine Stream Segments in the Chattahoochee Basin for Fecal Coliform* (2008): 6.

52. Charles B. Stockdale et al., "The Ten Biggest American Cities That Are Running Out of Water," *Wall Street Journal*, 1 November 2010.

## CONCLUSION

1. Charles B. Stockdale et al., "The Ten Biggest American Cities That Are Running Out of Water," *Wall Street Journal*, 1 November 2010.

2. "Tapped Out," *Upper Chattahoochee Riverkeeper*, n.p., 2009, Web, 30 January 2013.

3. "Tapped Out."

4. Peter H. Gleick and Heather Cooley, *The World's Water, 2008–2009: The Biennial Report on Freshwater Resources* (Washington, DC: Island Press, 2009), 109.

5. Gleick and Cooley 109.

6. Gleick and Cooley 109.

7. Supreme Court Orders, June 25, 2012.

8. U.S. Army Corps of Engineers, *News Release USACE Issues Legal Opinion to 11th Circuit Court of Appeals*, 26 June 2012.

9. Bill Torpy and Greg Bluestein, "Water Wars: Georgia Not in the Clear on Lanier," *Atlanta Journal-Constitution*, 1 July 2012: A1.

10. Metropolitan North Georgia Water Planning District, *Water Supply and Water Conservation Management Plan* (2009), 3-14.

11. Metropolitan North Georgia Water Planning District, 3-12.

12. Chris Joyner, "Down Payment on Water Strategy," *Atlanta Journal-Constitution*, 21 January 2011: A1.

13. Executive Order, Regarding the Governor's Water Supply Program, January 25, 2011.

14. American Rivers, *Money Pit: The High Cost and High Risk of Water Supply Reservoirs in the Southeast* (2012), 4.

15. American Rivers 4.

16. Hall County Government Board of Commissioners, letter to Mr. Richard Morgan, Re: Hall County's 404 Permit Application and EIS, 10 August 2012.

17. "Bear Creek Reservoir," *South Fulton Municipal Regional Water and Sewer Authority*, n.p., 2009, Web, 30 January 2013.

18. American Rivers 4.

19. "Water Wars: Tennessee, Georgia Locked in Battle over Waterway Access," *CBS This Morning*, 5 April 2013.

# WORKS CITED

Andrews, Sidney. *The South since the War.* Boston: Ticknor & Fields, 1866. Print.

Bartley, Numan V. *The New South: 1945–1980.* Baton Rouge: Louisiana State UP, 1995. Print.

Bayer, Ronald H. *Race and the Shaping of Twentieth-Century Atlanta.* Chapel Hill: U of North Carolina P, 1996. Print.

Benedickson, Jamie. *Culture of Flushing: A Social and Legal History of Sewage.* Vancouver: U of British Columbia P, 2007.

Billington, David P., Donald C. Jackson, and Martin V. Melosi. *The History of Large Federal Dams: Planning, Design, and Construction in the Era of Big Dams.* Denver: Bureau of Reclamation, 2005. Web.

Coughlin, Robert David. *Lake Sidney Lanier: A Storybook Site.* Atlanta: RDC Productions, 1998. Print.

Foner, Eric. *Reconstruction: America's Unfinished Revolution, 1863–1877.* New York: Harper & Row, 1988. Print.

Garrett, Franklin M. *Atlanta and Environs: A Chronicle of Its People and Events.* Vol. 1. Athens: U of Georgia P, 1969. Print.

Garrett, Franklin M. *Atlanta and Environs: A Chronicle of Its People and Events.* Vol. 2. Athens: U Georgia P, 1969. Print.

Gleick, Peter H., and Heather Cooley. *The World's Water, 2008–2009: The Biennial Report on Freshwater Resources.* Washington: Island Press, 2009. Web.

Henderson, Harold Paul. *Ernest Vandiver: Governor of Georgia.* Athens: U of Georgia P, 2000. Print.

Holland, Ann-Christin Sjölander. *The Water Business: Corporations versus People.* London: Zed Books, 2005. Web.

Hoy, Suellen. *Chasing Dirt: The American Pursuit of Cleanliness.* New York: Oxford UP, 1995. Print.

Jordan, Jeffrey L., and Aaron T. Wolf. *Interstate Water Allocation in Alabama, Florida, and Georgia: New Issues, New Methods, New Models.* Gainesville: UP of Florida, 2006. Print.

Keating, Larry. *Atlanta: Race, Class, and Urban Expansion.* Philadelphia: Temple UP, 2001. Print.

Kuhn, Cliff, et al. *Living Atlanta: An Oral History of the City, 1914–1948.* Athens: U of Georgia P, 1990. Print.

Lands, LeeAnn. *The Culture of Property: Race, Class and Housing Landscapes in Atlanta.* Athens: U of Georgia P, 2009. Print.

Larson, Lawrence Harold. *The Urban South: A History.* Lexington: UP of Kentucky, 1990. Print.

Maass, Arthur. *Muddy Waters: The Army Engineers and the Nation's Rivers.* Cambridge: Harvard UP, 1974. Print.

Martin, Thomas. *Atlanta and Its Builders.* Atlanta: Century Memorial, 1902. Print.

Mazmanian, Daniel A., and Jeanne Nienaber. *Can Organizations Change?* Washington: Brookings Institution, 1979. Print.

McMahan, C. A. *The People of Atlanta: A Demographic Study of Georgia's Capital City.* Athens: U of Georgia P, 1950. Print.

Milazzo, Paul Charles. *Unlikely Environmentalists: Congress and Clean Water.* Lawrence: UP of Kansas, 2006. Print.

Morgan, Arthur E. *Dams and Other Disasters.* Boston: P. Sargent, 1971. Print.

Muskie, Edmund S. *Journeys.* Garden City, NY: Doubleday, 1972. Web.

Organisation of Economic Co-Operation and Development. *Energy: The Next Fifty Years.* Paris: OECD, 1999. Web.

Pioneer Citizens' Society of Atlanta. *Pioneer Citizens' History of Atlanta, 1833–1902.* Atlanta: Byrd Printing, 1902. Print.

Pomerantz, Gary M. *Where Peachtree Meets Sweet Auburn: The Saga of Two Families and the Making of Atlanta.* New York: Scribner, 1996. Print.

Reed, Wallace Putnam. *History of Atlanta, Georgia: With Illustrations and Biographical Sketches of Some of Its Prominent Men and Pioneers.* Syracuse: D. Mason & Co., 1889. Print.

Richards, Sam. *Sam Richards' Civil War Diary: A Chronicle of the Atlanta Home Front.* Baton Rouge: Louisiana UP, 1988. Print.

Rome, Adam Ward. *Bulldozer in the Countryside: Suburban Sprawl and the Rise of American Environmentalism.* Cambridge: Cambridge UP, 2004. Print.

Russell, James M. *Atlanta 1847–1890: City Building in the Old South and the New.* Baton Rouge: Louisiana State UP, 1988. Print.

Rutheiser, Charles. *Imagineering Atlanta: The Politics of Place in the City of Dreams.* Brooklyn: Verso, 1996. Print.

Sherman, William T. *Memoirs of General W. T. Sherman.* Ed. Charles Roster. New York: Penguin Books, 1885. Print.

Shiva, Vandana. *Water Wars: Privatization, Pollution, and Profit.* Cambridge, MA: South End Press, 2002. Print.

Smith, Douglas L. *The New Deal in the Urban South.* Baton Rouge: Louisiana State UP, 1988. Print.

Tarr, Joel. *The Search for the Ultimate Sink: Urban Pollution in Historical Perspective.* Akron: U of Akron P, 1996. Web.

Thompson, Barton H., Jr., John D. Leshy, and Robert H. Abrams. *Legal Control of Water Resources: Cases and Materials.* Ed. Joseph Sax. Eagan, MN: Thomson-West, 2000. Print.

Thompson, Clara Mildred. *Reconstruction in Georgia: Economic, Social, Political, 1865–1874.* New York: Columbia UP, 1915. Print.

United States Geological Survey. *How Much Water Is in the Apalachicola, Chattahoochee, and Flint Rivers, and How Much Is Used?* Washington: Government Printing Office, 2007. Web.

Urban Institute. *Urban Sprawl: Causes, Consequences, and Policy Responses.* Ed. Gregory Squires. Washington: Urban Institute Press, 2002. Print.

Wood, Richard G. *Stephen Harriman Long, 1784–1864: Army Engineer, Explorer, Inventor.* Glendale, CA: A. H. Clark, 1966. Print.

# INDEX

Made in the USA
Columbia, SC
31 August 2019